OUR
UNDEMOCRATIC
CONSTITUTION

OUR UNDEMOCRATIC CONSTITUTION

WHERE THE CONSTITUTION GOES WRONG
(AND HOW WE THE PEOPLE CAN CORRECT IT)

SANFORD LEVINSON

Sept 18, 2006
With thanks for your
interest in these important
questions.

[signature]

OXFORD
UNIVERSITY PRESS

2006

OXFORD

UNIVERSITY PRESS

Oxford University Press, Inc., publishes works that further
Oxford University's objective of excellence
in research, scholarship, and education.

Oxford   New York
Auckland   Cape Town   Dar es Salaam   Hong Kong   Karachi
Kuala Lumpur   Madrid   Melbourne   Mexico City   Nairobi
New Delhi   Shanghai   Taipei   Toronto

With offices in
Argentina   Austria   Brazil   Chile   Czech Republic   France   Greece
Guatemala   Hungary   Italy   Japan   Poland   Portugal   Singapore
South Korea   Switzerland   Thailand   Turkey   Ukraine   Vietnam

Published by Oxford University Press, Inc.
198 Madison Avenue, New York, New York 10016

www.oup.com

Oxford is a registered trademark of Oxford University Press

Library of Congress Cataloging-in-Publication Data
Levinson, Sanford, 1941–
Our undemocratic constitution : where the constitution goes wrong
(and how we the people can correct it) by Sanford Levinson.
p. cm.
ISBN-13 978-0-19-530751-1
ISBN 0-19-530751-8
1. Constitutional law—United States. 2. Law reform—United States. I. Title.
KF4552.L484 2006
342.7302—dc22   2006011704

1 3 5 7 9 8 6 4 2

Printed in the United States of America
on acid-free paper

FOR MORTON HORWITZ, FRANK MICHELMAN,
SCOT POWE, AND MARK TUSHNET, OLD FRIENDS
AND MODELS OF SCHOLARLY ENGAGEMENT

CONTENTS

PRELUDE

THE WISDOM OF THOMAS JEFFERSON

Some men look at constitutions with sanctimonious reverence, and deem them like the arc [*sic*] of the covenant, too sacred to be touched. They ascribe to the men of the preceding age a wisdom more than human, and suppose what they did to be beyond amendment. I knew that age well; I belonged to it, and labored with it. It deserved well of its country. It was very like the present, but without the experience of the present; and forty years of experience in government is worth a century of book-reading; and this they would say themselves, were they to rise from the dead. I am certainly not an advocate for frequent and untried changes in laws and constitutions. I think moderate imperfections had better be borne with; because, when once known, we accommodate ourselves to them, and find practical means of correcting their ill effects. But I know also, that laws and institutions must go hand in hand with the progress of the human mind. As that becomes more developed, more enlightened, as new discoveries are made, new truths disclosed, and manners and opinions change with the change of circumstances, institutions must advance also, and keep pace with the times. We might as well require a man to wear still the coat which fitted him when a boy, as civilized society to remain ever under the regimen of their barbarous ancestors. . . . Let us, as our sister States have done, avail ourselves of our reason and experience, to correct the crude essays of our first and unexperienced, although wise, virtuous, and well-meaning councils. And lastly, let us provide in our constitution for its revision at stated periods. . . . Each generation is as independent as the one preceding, as that was of all which had gone before. It has then, like them, a right to choose for itself the form of government it believes most promotive of its own happiness.[1]

OUR
UNDEMOCRATIC
CONSTITUTION

INTRODUCTION

A TALE OF TWO SIGNINGS

In 1987, I went to a marvelous exhibit in Philadelphia commemorating the bicentennial of the drafting there of the U.S. Constitution. The visitor's journey through the exhibit concluded with two scrolls, each with the same two questions: First, "Will You Sign This Constitution?" And then, "If you had been in Independence Hall on September 17, 1787, would you have endorsed the Constitution?" The second question clarifies the antecedent for "this" in the first: It emphasizes that we are being asked to assess the 1787 Constitution. This is no small matter inasmuch, for example, it did not include *any* of the subsequent amendments, including the Bill of Rights. Moreover, the viewer had been made aware in the course of the exhibit that the 1787 Constitution included several terrible compromises with slavery.

Even in 1987, I tended to regard the original Constitution as what William Lloyd Garrison so memorably called "A Covenant with Death and an Agreement With Hell"[1] because of those compromises. So why did I choose to sign the scroll? As I explained in the final chapter of a 1988 book, *Constitutional Faith*,[2] I was impressed that

Frederick Douglass, the great black abolitionist, after an initial flirtation with Garrison's rejectionism, endorsed even the antebellum Constitution. He argued that the Constitution, correctly understood, was deeply antislavery at its core.[3] The language of the Constitution—including, most important, its magnificent Preamble—allows us to mount a critique of slavery, and much else, from within. I was convinced by Douglass—and many other later writers—that the Constitution offers us a language by which we can protect those rights that we deem to be important. We need not reject the Constitution in order to carry on such a conversation. If the Constitution at the present time is viewed as insufficiently protective of such rights, that is because of the limited imagination of those interpreters with the most political power, including members of the Supreme Court. So I was willing in effect to honor the memory of Douglass and the potential that was—and is—available in our Constitution, and I added my signature to the scroll endorsing the 1787 Constitution.

On July 3, 2004, I was back in Philadelphia, this time to participate in the grand opening of the National Constitution Center. The exhibit culminates in "Signers' Hall," which features life-sized (and life-like) statues of each of the delegates to the convention. Many of the delegates appear to be holding animated conversations or, as in the case of Alexander Hamilton, striding forcefully toward George Washington—who quite literally, because of his height, towers over the room. As one walks through the hall and brushes against James Madison, Hamilton, and other giants of our history, one can almost feel the remarkable energy that must have impressed itself on those actually in Independence Hall.

As was true in 1987, the visitor is invited to join the signers by adding his or her own signature to the Constitution. Indeed, the center organized a major project during September 2004, cosponsored with the Annenberg Center for Education and Outreach, called "I Signed the Constitution." Fifty sites in all of the states were available for such a signing. Both the temporary 1987 exhibit and the permanent one at the National Constitution Center leave little doubt about the proper stance that a citizen should take toward our founding document.

This time, however, I rejected the invitation to re-sign the Constitution. I have not changed my mind that the Constitution in many ways offers a rich, even inspiring, language by which to envision and defend a desirable political order. Nor does my decision not to sign the scroll at the National Constitution Center necessarily mean that I would have preferred that the Constitution go down to defeat in the ratification votes of 1787–1788. Rather, I treated the center as asking me about my level of support for the Constitution *today* and, just as important, whether I wish to encourage my fellow citizens to reaffirm it in a relatively thoughtless manner. As to the first, I realized that I had, between 1987 and 2004, become far more concerned about the inadequacies of the Constitution. As to the second, I think that it is vitally important to engage in a national conversation about its adequacy rather than automatically to assume its fitness for our own times. Why I believe this is in a real sense the topic of this book.

My concern is only minimally related to the formal rights protected by the Constitution. Even if, as a practical matter, the Supreme Court reads the Constitution less protectively, with regard to certain rights, than I do, the proper response is not to reject the Constitution but to work within it by trying to persuade fellow Americans to share our views of constitutional possibility and by supporting presidential candidates who will appoint (and get through the Senate) judges who will be more open to better interpretations. Given that much constitutional interpretation occurs outside the courts, one also wants public officials at all levels to share one's own visions of constitutional possibility—as well, of course, as of constitutional constraints. And this is true even for readers who disagree with me on what specific rights are most important. It is always the case that courts are perpetually open to new arguments about rights—whether those of gays and lesbians or of property owners—that reflect the dominant public opinion of the day. Indeed, liberals should acknowledge that even a Supreme Court composed of a majority of political conservatives—a total of seven justices were appointed by Republican presidents—nonetheless broke new ground in protecting gays and lesbians by overturning Texas's prohibition of "homosexual sodomy."[4] I applauded that decision; more important is the fact that the public at large, by 2003, also seemed more than willing to accept the Court's views. The country may be clearly divided about gay and lesbian marriage, but relatively few people any longer seem to endorse a constitutional vision that allows the criminalization of such sexual practices.

So, what accounts for my change of views since 1987? The brief answer—to be spelled out in the remainder of the book—is that I have become ever more despondent about many structural provisions of the Constitution that place almost insurmountable barriers in the way of any acceptable notion of democracy. I put it this way to acknowledge that "democracy" is most certainly what political theorists call an "essentially contested concept." It would be tendentious to claim that there is only one understanding—such as "numerical majorities always prevail"—that is consistent with "democracy." Liberal constitutionalists, for example, would correctly place certain constraints on what majorities can do to vulnerable minorities.

That being said, I believe that it is increasingly difficult to construct a theory of democratic constitutionalism, *applying our own twenty-first-century norms*, that vindicates the Constitution under which we are governed today. Our eighteenth-century ancestors had little trouble integrating slavery and the rank subordination of women into their conception of a "republican" political order. *That* vision of politics is blessedly long behind us, but the Constitution is not. It does not deserve rote support from Americans who properly believe that majority rule, even if tempered by the recognition of minority rights, is integral to "consent of the governed."

I invite you to ask the following questions by way of preparing yourself to scrutinize the adequacy of today's Constitution:

1. Even if you support having a Senate in addition to the House of Representatives, do you support as well giving Wyoming the same number of votes as California, which has roughly seventy times the population?

2. Are you comfortable with an Electoral College that, among other things, has regularly placed in the White House candidates who did not get a majority of the popular vote and, in at least two cases over the past fifty years, who did not even come in first in that vote?

3. Are you concerned that the president might have too much power, whether to spy on Americans without any congressional or judicial authorization or to frustrate the will of a majority of both houses of Congress by vetoing legislation with which he disagrees on political grounds?

4. Do you really want justices on the Supreme Court to serve up to four decades and, among other things, to be able to time their resignations to mesh with their own political preferences as to their successors?

5. Do you support the ability of thirteen legislative houses in as many states to block constitutional amendments desired by the overwhelming majority of Americans as well as, possibly, eighty-six out of the ninety-nine legislative houses in the American states?

One might regard these questions as raising only theoretical, perhaps even "aesthetic," objections to our basic institutional structures *if* we felt truly satisfied by the outcomes generated by our national political institutions. But this is patently not the case. Consider the results when samples of Americans are asked whether they believe the country is headed in the right or the wrong direction. In April 2005, a full 62 percent of the respondents to a CBS poll indicated that they believed that the country was headed in "the wrong direction."[5] A year later, a similar CBS poll found that 71 percent of the respondents said that the country was "on the wrong track."[6] One might feel that the country is headed in the wrong direction even if our major political institutions were perceived to be fully competent in addressing major issues, if one thought that we were in fact at the mercy of events—like an oncoming asteroid—simply beyond any human intervention. But surely the sense of dissatisfaction is related for most Americans to a belief that our political institutions are *not* adequately responding to the issues at hand. Any reader can certainly construct her own list of issues that are not seriously confronted at all—or, if confronted, resolved in totally inadequate ways—by the national government. Serious liberals and conservatives would likely disagree on the particular failings, but both, increasingly, would share an attitude of profound disquiet about the capacity of our institutions to meet the problems confronting us as a society.

To be sure, most Americans seem to approve of their particular members of Congress. The reason for such approval, alas, may be the representatives' success in bringing home federally funded pork, which scarcely relates to the great national and international issues that we might hope that Congress could confront effectively. In any event, we should resist the temptation simply to criticize specific inhabitants of national offices, however easy that is for most of us to do, regardless of political party. An emphasis on the deficiencies of particular office-holders suggests that the cure for what ails us is simply to win some elections and replace those officeholders with presumptively more virtuous officials. But we are deluding ourselves if we believe that winning elections is enough to overcome the deficiencies of the American political system.

Polling data relating to the specific institutions offers further insights, even as we must recognize both that they measure support for particular officials and that support levels go up as well as down. That being said, consider that, as I write these lines in May 2006, a *New York Times*/CBS poll taken between May 4–8, 2006, finds that only 31 percent of the respondents approve of George W. Bush's conduct as president, which ties him with his father, George H. W. Bush, at the low point of his presidency, though he remains ahead of Presidents Nixon and Carter at the low point of their tenures in office.[7] Yet President Bush has a *higher* approval rating than Congress. The same poll found that only 23 percent of those responding "said they approve of the job Congress is doing, down from 29 percent in January."[8] And another poll, taken earlier, found that Republican congressional leaders were approved by only 33 percent of the respondents, one point less than their Democratic counterparts (34 percent).[9]

Compared to the president and Congress, members of the Supreme Court might feel considerably better. Yet even there, the data are mixed. For example, a May 2005 poll conducted by Quinnipiac University found that only 44 percent of voters approved of the decisions of the Supreme Court, down from 56 percent approval in a March 5, 2003, poll.[10] An analysis of public opinion and the Court during the period of William Rehnquist's chief justiceship—1986–2005—found a general diminution of support for the Court over those years, though several polls continue to show that the majority of the public retains "confidence" in the Court. Still, according to Wisconsin political science professor Herbert Kritzer, a June 2005 poll by the Pew Research Center for the People and the Press finding that 57 percent of its respondents are favorable to the Court "is at the lowest level since it began, falling under 60 percent for the first time."[11] As John Roberts took the helm of the Supreme Court in September 2005, almost a third of the population (31 percent) expressed "not very much" confidence (25 percent) or "none at all" (6 percent) in the judiciary, even if this was offset by the 55 percent who expressed a "fair amount" of confidence. Only 13 percent had a "great deal" of confidence.[12] Interestingly, Kritzer relates the general drop in support for the Court to "the general demonization of government, particularly the federal government, that took place over the past 25 years."[13]

We must recognize that a substantial responsibility for the defects of our polity lies in the Constitution itself. A number of wrong turns were taken at the time of the initial drafting of the Constitution, even if for the best of reasons given the political realities of 1787. Even the most skilled and admirable leaders may not be able to overcome the barriers to effective government constructed by the Constitution. No less a founder than Alexander Hamilton emphasized that "[a]ll observations" critical of certain tendencies in the Constitution "ought to be referred to the composition and structure of the government, not to the nature or extent of its powers."[14] He is correct. In many ways, we are like the police officer in Poe's classic *The Purloined Letter*, unable to comprehend the true importance of what is clearly in front of us.

If I am correct that the Constitution is both insufficiently democratic, in a country that professes to believe in democracy, *and* significantly dysfunctional, in terms of the quality of government that we receive, then it follows that we should no longer express our blind devotion to it. It is not, as Jefferson properly suggested, the equivalent of the Ark of the Covenant. It is a human creation open to criticism and even to rejection. To convince you that you should join me in supporting the call for a new constitutional convention is what this book is about.

ONE

THE RATIFICATION REFERENDUM

SENDING THE CONSTITUTION TO A NEW CONVENTION FOR REPAIR

The U.S. Constitution is radically defective in a number of important ways. Unfortunately, changing the Constitution is extremely difficult, for both political and constitutional reasons. But the difficulty of the task does not make it any less important that we first become aware of the magnitude of the deficiencies in the current Constitution and then turn our minds, as a community of concerned citizens, to figuring out potential solutions. This book is organized around the conceit that Americans in 2008 will have the opportunity to vote on the following proposal: "Shall Congress call a constitutional convention empowered to consider the adequacy of the Constitution and, if thought necessary, to draft a new constitution that, upon completion, will be submitted to the electorate for its approval or disapproval by majority vote? Unless and until a new constitution gains popular approval, the current Constitution will continue in place."

Although such a referendum would be unprecedented with regard to the U.S. Constitution, there is certainly nothing "un-American" about such a procedure. As Professor John J. Dinan has noted in his recent comprehensive study of what he terms "the American state constitutional tradition," fourteen American states in their own constitutions explicitly give the people an opportunity "to periodically vote on whether a convention should be called."[1] Article XIX of the New York Constitution, for example, provides that the state electorate be given the opportunity every twenty years to vote on the following question: "Shall there be a convention to revise the constitution and amend the same?" Should the majority answer in the affirmative, then the voters in each senate district will elect three delegates "at the next ensuing general election," while the state-wide electorate "shall elect fifteen delegates-at-large."[2] It should occasion no surprise that one author has described such a "mandatory referendum" as a means of "enforcing the people's right to reform their government."[3]

It is no small matter to give people a choice with regard to the mechanisms—as well as the abstract principles—by which they are to be governed. The imagined referendum would allow "We the People of the United States of America," in whose name the document is ostensibly "ordain[ed]," to examine the fit between our national aspirations, set out in the Preamble to the Constitution, and the particular means chosen to realize those goals.

I am assuming that those reading this book are fellow Americans united by a deep and common concern about the future of our country. In the next six chapters, I hope to convince you that, as patriotic Americans truly committed to the deepest principles of the Constitution, we should vote yes and thus trigger a new convention. My task is to persuade you that the Constitution we currently live under is grievously flawed, even in some ways a "clear and present danger" to achieving the laudable and inspiring goals to which this country professes to be committed, including republican self-government.

I believe that the best way to grasp the goals of our common enterprise is to ponder the inspiring words of the Preamble to the Constitution:

We the People of the United States, in Order to form a more perfect Union, establish Justice, insure domestic tranquility, provide for the common defence, promote the general Welfare, and secure the Blessings of Liberty to ourselves and our Posterity, do ordain and establish this Constitution for the United States of America.

It is regrettable that law professors rarely teach and that courts rarely cite the Preamble, for it is *the single most important part* of the Constitution. The reason is simple: It announces the *point* of the entire enterprise. The 4,500 or so words that followed the Preamble in the original, unamended Constitution were all in effect merely means that were thought to be useful to achieving the great aims set out above. It is indeed the ends articulated in the Preamble that justify the means of our political institutions. And to the extent that the means turn out to be counterproductive, then we should revise them.

It takes no great effort to find elements in the original Constitution that run counter to the Preamble. It is impossible for us today to imagine how its authors squared a commitment to the "Blessings of Liberty" with the toleration and support of chattel slavery that is present in various articles of the Constitution. The most obvious example is the bar placed on Congress's ability to forbid the participation by Americans in the international slave trade until 1808.[4] The most charitable interpretation of the framers, articulated by Frederick Douglass, is that they viewed these compromises with the acknowledged evil of slavery as temporary; the future would see its eradication through peaceful constitutional processes.[5]

One might believe that the Preamble is incomplete because, for example, it lacks a commitment to the notion of equality. Political scientist Mark Graber has suggested that the reference to "*our* Posterity" suggests a potentially unattractive limitation of our concerns *only* to members of the American political community, with no notice taken of the posterity of other societies, whatever their plight. Even if one would prefer a more explicitly cosmopolitan Preamble, I find it hard to imagine rejecting any of the overarching values enunciated there. In any event, I am happy to endorse the Preamble as the equivalent of our creedal summary of America's civil religion.

There are two basic responses to the discovery that ongoing institutional practices are counterproductive with regard to achieving one's announced goals. One is to adjust the practices in ways that would make achievement of the aims more likely. This is, often, what we mean by the very notion of rationality: One does not persist in behaviors that are acknowledged to make more difficult the realization of one's professed hopes. Still, a second response, which has its own rationality, is to adjust the goals to the practices. Sometimes, this makes very good sense if one comes to the justified conclusion that the goals may be utopian. In such cases, it is a sign of maturity to recognize that we will inevitably fall short in our aims and that "the best may be enemy of the good" if we are tempted to throw over quite adequate, albeit imperfect, institutions in an attempt to attain the ideal.

Perhaps one might even wish to defend the framers' compromises with slavery on the ground that they were absolutely necessary to the achievement of the political union of the thirteen states. One must believe that such a union, in turn, was preferable to the likely alternative, which would have been the creation of two or three separate countries along the Atlantic coast. Political scientist David Hendrickson has demonstrated that many of the framers—and many other theorists as well—viewed history as suggesting a high probability that such separate countries would have gone to war with one another and made impossible any significant measure of "domestic tranquility."[6] Hendrickson well describes the Constitution as a "peace pact" designed to prevent the possibility of war. If there is one thing we know, it is that unhappy compromises must often be made when negotiating such pacts. Of course, American slaves—and their descendants—could scarcely be expected to be so complacently accepting of these compromises, nor, of course, should *any* American who takes seriously the proclamation of the Pledge of Allegiance that ours is a system that takes seriously the duty to provide "liberty and justice for all."

Not only must we restrain ourselves from expecting too much of any government; we must also recognize that the Preamble sets out potentially conflicting goals. It is impossible to maximize the achievement of all of the great ends of the Constitution. To take an obvious example, providing for the "common defence" may require on occasion certain incursions into the "Blessings of Liberty." One need only refer to the military draft, which was upheld in 1918 by the Supreme

Court against an attack claiming that it constituted the "involuntary servitude"—that is, slavery—prohibited by the Thirteenth Amendment.[7] We also properly accept certain limitations on the freedom of the press with regard, say, to publishing certain information—the standard example is troop movements within a battle zone—deemed to be vital to American defense interests. The year 2005 ended with the beginning of a great national debate about the propriety of warrantless interceptions of telephone calls and other incursions on traditional civil liberties in order, ostensibly, to protect ourselves against potential terrorists.

Even if one concedes the necessity of adjusting aims in light of practical realities, it should also be readily obvious that one can easily go overboard. At the very least, one should always be vigilant in assessing such adjustments lest one find, at the end of the day, that the aims have been reduced to hollow shells. It is also necessary to ask if a rationale supporting a given adjustment that might well have been convincing at time A necessarily continues to be present at time B. Practical exigencies that required certain political compromises in 1787 no longer obtain today. We have long since realized this about slavery. It is time that we apply the same critical eye to the compromise of 1787 that granted all states an equal vote in the Senate.

To criticize that particular compromise—or any of the other features of the Constitution that I shall examine below—is not necessarily to criticize the founders themselves. My project—and, therefore, your own vote for a new convention, should you be persuaded by what follows—requires no denigration of the founders. They were, with some inevitable exceptions, an extraordinary group of men who performed extraordinary deeds, including drafting a Constitution that started a brand-new governmental system. By and large, they deserve the monuments that have been erected in their honor. But they themselves emphasized the importance—indeed, necessity—of learning from experience.

They were, after all, a generation that charted new paths by overturning a centuries-long notion of the British constitutional order because it no longer conformed to their own sense of possibility (and fairness). They also, as it happened, proved ruthlessly willing to ignore the limitations of America's "first constitution," the Articles of Confederation. Although Article XIII of that founding document required unanimous approval by the thirteen state legislatures before any amendment could take affect, Article VII of the Constitution drafted in Philadelphia required the approval of only nine of the thirteen states, and the approval was to be given by state conventions rather than by the legislatures.

The most important legacies handed down by the founding generation were, first, a remarkable willingness to act in bold and daring ways when they believed that the situation demanded it, coupled with the noble visions first of the Declaration of Independence and then of the Preamble. Both are as inspiring—and potentially disruptive— today as when they were written more than two centuries ago. But we should also be inspired by the copious study that Madison and others made of every available history and analysis of political systems ranging from ancient Greece to the Dutch republic and the British constitutional order. We best honor the framers by taking the task of creating a republican political order as seriously as they did and being equally willing to learn from what the history of the past 225 years, both at home and abroad, can teach us about how best to achieve and maintain such an order. At the time of its creation, we could legitimately believe that we were the only country committed to democratic self-governance. That is surely no longer the case, and we might well have lessons to learn from our co-venturers in that enterprise. To the extent that experience teaches us that the Constitution in significant aspects demeans "the consent of the governed" and has become an impediment to achieving the goals of the Preamble, we honor rather than betray the founders by correcting their handiwork.

OVERCOMING VENERATION

The rest of this book will try to persuade you to vote yes in the forthcoming referendum. I may fail in this aim, but if I do so, I hope that it is because of considered reflection (even if followed by rejection) of my arguments. I suspect, though, that at least some readers might find it difficult to accept even the possibility that our Constitution is seriously deficient because they venerate the Constitution and find the notion of seriously criticizing it almost sacrilegious.

In an earlier book, *Constitutional Faith*,[8] I noted the tension between the desire of James Madison that Americans "venerate" their Constitution and the distinctly contrasting views of his good friend Thomas Jefferson that, instead, the citizenry regularly subject it to relentless examination. Thus, whatever may have been Jefferson's insistence on respecting what he called the "chains" of the Constitution, he also emphasized that the "Creator has made the earth for the living, not the dead."[9] It should not be surprising, then, that he wrote to Madison in 1789, "No society can make a perpetual constitution, or even a perpetual law."[10]

Jefferson and Madison might have been good friends and political associates, but they disagreed fundamentally with regard to the wisdom of subjecting the Constitution to critical analysis. Jefferson was fully capable of writing that "[w]e may consider each generation as a distinct nation, with a right, by the will of its majority, to bind themselves, but none to bind the succeeding generation, more than the inhabitants of another country."[11] His ultimate optimism about the Constitution lay precisely in its potential for change: "Happily for us, that when we find our constitutions defective and insufficient to secure the happiness of our people, we can assemble with all the coolness of philosophers, and set it to rights, while every other nation on earth must have recourse to arms to amend or restore their constitutions."[12] I should concede—if that is the proper word—at the outset that this book is written in a Jeffersonian vein.

Madison, however, would have none of this. He treated 1787 almost as a miraculous and singular event. Had he been a devotee of astrology, he might have said that the stars were peculiarly and uniquely aligned to allow the drafting of the Constitution and then its ratification. Though Madison was surely too tactful to mention this, part of the alignment was the absence of the famously contentious Jefferson and John Adams. Both were 3,000 miles across the sea, where they were serving as the first ambassadors from the new United States to Paris and London, respectively. Moreover, it certainly did not hurt that Rhode Island had refused to send any delegates at all and therefore had no opportunity to make almost inevitable mischief, not to mention being unable to vote in an institutional structure where the vote of one state could make a big difference. And, if pressed, Madison would presumably have agreed that the Constitutional Convention—and the ratifying conventions thereafter—would never have succeeded had the delegates included American slaves, Native Americans, or women in the spirit of Abigail Adams. She had famously—and altogether unsuccessfully—told her husband that leaders of the new nation should "remember the ladies."[13] One need not see the framers in Philadelphia as an entirely homogeneous group—they were not—in order to realize that the room was devoid of those groups in America that were viewed as merely the *objects*, and not the active *subjects*, of governance.

Madison sets out his views most clearly in the *Federalist*, No. 49, where he explicitly takes issue with Jefferson's proposal for rather frequent constitutional conventions that would consider whether "alter[ation]" of the constitution might be desirable. Madison acknowledges the apparent appeal, in a system where "the people are the only legitimate fountain of power," of "appeal[ing] to the people themselves." However, "there appear to be insuperable objections against the proposed recurrence to the people." Perhaps the key objection is that "*frequent appeal to the people would carry an implication of some defect in the government [and] deprive the government of that veneration which time bestows on every thing, and without which perhaps the wisest and freest governments would not possess the requisite stability.*" Only "a nation of philosophers" can forgo this emotion of veneration—and, therefore, feel free of guilt-ridden anxiety about the idea of constitutional change. However, "a nation of philosophers is as little to be expected as the philosophical race of kings wished for by Plato."[14]

Madison is thus fearful of "disturbing the public tranquillity by interesting too strongly the public passions." The success of Americans in replacing a defective Articles of Confederation with a better Constitution does not constitute a precedent for future action. We should "recollect," he says, "that all the existing constitutions were formed in the midst of a danger which repressed the passions most unfriendly to order and concord." Moreover, the people at large possessed "an enthusiastic confidence . . . in their patriotic leaders," which, he says, fortunately "stifled the ordinary diversity of opinions on great national questions." He is extremely skeptical that the "future situations in which we must expect to be usually placed" will "present any equivalent security against the danger" of an excess of public passion, disrespect for leaders, and the full play of diverse opinions.[15] In case there is any doubt, he writes of his fear that the "*passions,* therefore, not the *reasons,* of the public would sit in judgment."[16]

Madison's view of his fellow Americans was far closer to that of Alexander Hamilton, with whom he had coauthored the *Federalist.* One can doubt that Madison expressed any reservations when hearing Hamilton, addressing his fellow delegates to the Philadelphia convention on June 18, 1787, denounce the conceit that "the voice of the people" is "the voice of God." On the contrary, said Hamilton: "The people are turbulent and changing; they seldom judge or determine right."[17] Although Madison was not opposed to constitutional amendment as such, he clearly saw almost no role for a public that would engage in probing questions suggesting that there might be serious "defects" in the Constitution. Only philosophers (like himself?) or, perhaps, "patriotic leaders" could be trusted to engage in dispassionate political dialogue and reasoning. In contrast, the general public should be educated to feel only "veneration" for their Constitution rather than be encouraged to use their critical faculties and actually assess the relationship between the great ends set out in the Preamble and the instruments devised for their realization.

Prior to World War II, the spirits of both Jefferson and Madison can be said to have been represented in American thought; a tradition of constitutional critique contended with veneration.[18] Among the most famous examples of the former is Woodrow Wilson's *Congressional Government,* written while he was a graduate student at Johns Hopkins and initially published in 1885,[19] which called for a more parliamentary mode of government. He had, in 1879, written of the "fear that grave, perhaps radical, defects in our mode of government are militating against our liberty and prosperity."[20] Wilson's critical spirit lived on in the work of many others, though none achieved the presidency. Rexford Guy Tugwell, a leading New Dealer and close associate of

Franklin Roosevelt, devoted the last thirty years of his life to drafting a new constitution adequate to the new times.[21] He was, I suspect, widely regarded as a crank or, at best, a relic of an earlier era, when there was a genuine audience for those who were willing to question traditional verities, such as J. Allen Smith[22] or the better-known Charles Beard[23] or Vernon Parrington.[24]

Pre–World War II American "legal realists" were happy to accept Oliver Wendell Holmes's invitation to pour "cynical acid" and therefore assay the validity of conventional wisdom.[25] For too many Americans, however, the meaning of World War II was the almost "self-evident truth" that our Constitution was basically perfect inasmuch as it seemingly operated to allow our victory over fascist tyranny.[26] And what few doubts remained were for many stilled by the Warren Court's 1954 declaration, in *Brown v. Board of Education*, that the segregationist legacy of slavery was constitutionally intolerable. Because the Supreme Court spoke in the name of the Constitution, support for the work of the Court easily translated, for most Americans, into equal support of the Constitution in all respects.

This is a mistake. To the extent that we continue thoughtlessly to venerate, and therefore not subject to truly critical examination, our Constitution, we are in the position of the battered wife who continues to profess the "essential goodness" of her abusive husband. To stick with the analogy for a moment, it may well be the case that the husband, when sober or not gambling, is a decent, even loving, partner. The problem is that such moments are more than counterbalanced by abusive ones, even if they are relatively rare. And he becomes especially abusive when she suggests the possibility of marital counseling and attendant change. Similarly, that there are good features of our Constitution should not be denied. But there are also significantly abusive ones, and it is time for us to face them rather than remain in a state of denial.

TRAPPED INSIDE THE ARTICLE V CAGE

The framers of the Constitution were under no illusion that they had created a perfect document. The best possible proof for this proposition comes from George Washington himself. As he wrote to his nephew Bushrod two months after the conclusion of the Philadelphia convention over which he had presided, "*The warmest friends and the best supporters the Constitution has do not contend that it is free from imperfections*; but they found them unavoidable and are sensible if evil is likely to arise there from, the remedy must come hereafter." Sounding a remarkably Jeffersonian note, Washington noted that the "People (for it is with them to Judge) can, as they will have the advantage of experience on their Side, decide with as much propriety on the alteration[s] and amendment[s] which are necessary." Indeed, wrote the man described as the Father of Our Country, "I do not think we are more inspired, have more wisdom, or possess more virtue, than those who will come after us."[27]

Article V itself is evidence of the recognition of the possibility—and inevitable reality—of imperfection, else they would have adopted John Locke's suggestion in a constitution that he drafted for the Carolina colonies that would have made the document unamendable.[28] It is an unfortunate reality, though, that Article V, practically speaking, brings us all too close to the Lockean dream (or nightmare) of changeless stasis.

As University of Houston political scientist Donald Lutz has conclusively demonstrated, the U.S. Constitution is the most difficult to amend of any constitution currently existing in the world today.[29] Formal amendment of the U.S. Constitution generally requires the approval of two-thirds of each of the two houses of our national Congress, followed by the approval of three-quarters of the states (which today means thirty-eight of the fifty states). Article V does allow the abstract possibility that amendments could be proposed through the aegis of a constitutional convention called by Congress upon the petition of two-thirds of the states; such proposals, though, would still presumably have to be ratified by the state legislatures or, in the alternative, as was done with regard to the Twenty-first Amendment repealing the prohibition of alcohol required by the Eighteenth Amendment, by conventions in each of the states. As a practical matter, though, Article V makes it next to impossible to amend the Constitution with regard to genuinely controversial issues, even if substantial—and intense—majorities advocate amendment.

As I have written elsewhere,[30] some significant change functionally similar to "amendment" has occurred informally, outside of the procedures set out by Article V. One scholar has aptly described this as a process of "constitutional change off-the-books."[31] Yale law professor Bruce Ackerman has written several brilliant books detailing the process of "non–Article V" amendment,[32] and I warmly commend them to the reader. Yet it is difficult to argue that such informal amendment has occurred, or is likely to occur, with regard to the basic *structural* aspects of the American political system with which this book is primarily concerned.

It is one thing to argue, as Ackerman has done, that the New Deal worked as a functional amendment of the Constitution by giving Congress significant new powers to regulate the national economy. Similarly, one could easily argue that the president, for good and for ill, now possesses powers over the use of armed forces that would have been inconceivable to the generation of the framers. Whatever the text of the Constitution may say about the power of Congress to "declare war" or whatever the original understanding of this clause, it is hard to deny that many presidents throughout our history have successfully chosen to take the country to war without seeking a declaration of war (or, in some cases, even prior congressional approval of any kind).[33] Ackerman and David Golove have also persuasively argued that the Treaty Clause, which requires that two-thirds of the Senate assent to any treaty, has been transformed through the use of "executive agreements." Although such agreements are unmentioned in the text of the Constitution, presidents have frequently avoided the strictures of the Treaty Clause by labeling an "agreement" what earlier would have been viewed as a "treaty." Thus, the North American Free Trade Agreement did not have to leap the hurdles erected by the Treaty Clause; instead, it was validated by majority votes of both the House of Representatives and the Senate.[34]

These developments are undoubtedly important, and any complete analysis of our constitutional system should take account of such flexibility. But we should not overemphasize our system's capacity to change, and it is *constitutional stasis* rather than the potential for adaptation that is my focus.

This book has almost nothing in common with a whole spate of contemporary books, most of them by colleagues who teach within the legal academy, that focus on issues of constitutional *interpretation* or even on historical developments that have brought in their wake significant changes in what might be termed our "operative" Constitution. Not a single sentence in this book will discuss, for example, whether the Constitution guarantees a right to privacy; whether "affirmative action" is allowed by the Fourteenth Amendment; whether the First Amendment, correctly interpreted, allows the criminalization of "hate speech"; or whether it violates the Establishment Clause of the First Amendment to provide state or federal funds to church-related schools.

These issues are interesting and important. But any issue that is agreed to be subject to interpretation can be (relatively) successfully managed. Whatever your own answers to these just-mentioned questions, you are well advised to use your political energies to elect compatible federal legislators and presidents, who will in turn nominate and confirm judges with palatable views of what the Constitution allows (or disallows). Successful resolution of most interpretive dilemmas, from the perspective of any given person, requires only compatible decision makers and not genuine transformation of the Constitution's text.

This is, however, not the case with regard to the structural issues that are the topic of the book. One cannot, as a practical matter, litigate the obvious inequality attached to Wyoming's having the same voting power in the Senate as California. Nor can we imagine even President George W. Bush, who has certainly not been a shrinking violet with regard to claims of presidential power, announcing that Justice John Paul Stevens—appointed in 1976 and embarking on his fourth decade of service on the Supreme Court at the age of eighty-six—is simply "too old" or has served "long enough," and that he is therefore nominating, and asking the Senate to confirm, a successor to Justice Stevens in spite of the awkward fact that the justice has not submitted his resignation.

In any event, it is time to move to the main thrust of this book, which is why the Constitution makes it unacceptably difficult to achieve the inspiring goals of the Preamble and, therefore, warrants our disapproval. Most of the book is "destructive," devoted to critique. I will not offer the text of a brand-new Constitution, though some of my suggestions for a new text should be obvious enough on the basis of the critique. But a complete draft, which will necessarily involve much delicate negotiation and tradeoffs, should come after, and not before, a vital national conversation. I shall, however, conclude with some reflections on how, if you agree with me as to the serious deficiencies of the present Constitution, We the People might attempt to do something about it.

Although I am asking you to take part in a hypothetical referendum and to vote no with regard to the present Constitution, I am *not* asking you to imagine simply tearing it up and leaping into the unknown of a fanciful "state of nature." All you must commit yourself to is the proposition that the Constitution is sufficiently flawed to justify calling a new convention authorized to scrutinize all aspects of the Constitution and to suggest such changes as are felt to be desirable. The new convention would be no more able to bring its handiwork into being by fiat than were the framers in Philadelphia. All proposals would require popular approval in a further national referendum. This leaves open the possibility that, even after voting to trigger the convention, you could ultimately decide that the "devil you know" (the present Constitution) is preferable to the "devil you don't" (the proposed replacement). But the important thing, from my perspective, is to recognize that there are indeed "devilish" aspects of our present Constitution that should be confronted and, if at all possible, exorcised. To complete this metaphor, one might also remember that "the devil is in the details." This helps to explain the fact that this book offers a detailed look at the existing Constitution in order to substantiate my overall argument.

TWO

OUR UNDEMOCRATIC
LEGISLATIVE PROCESS

One of the relatively few pieces of legislation passed by Congress in 2005 was a $24 billion highway spending bill, which included $453 million in funds for two Alaska bridges. One of them, to cost $223 million, was quickly labeled the "Bridge to Nowhere" inasmuch as it would, according to the *Washington Post*, simply "replace a 7-minute ferry ride in a sparsely populated area of Alaska."[1] The remaining funds would have gone to what the *Post* terms "the magnificently named 'Don Young's Way'—hint: Mr. Young, Alaska's sole House member, conveniently happens to chair the transportation committee—[and will serve as] a down payment on a billion-dollar bridge across an inlet in Anchorage to a nearly deserted port."[2] One might doubt that Mr. Young, for all his clout, could have done this all by himself. Surely it helps that Alaska's senior senator, Ted Stevens, the longest-serving Republican in the Senate, is himself the chair of the Senate Commerce, Science, and Transportation Committee, which controls matters of vital interest to Alaskans. He is also a member of the Senate Appropriations Committee, whose decisions vitally affect every senator.

According to the *Post*, "Of the $24 billion in earmarked projects in the most recent transportation bill, nearly $1 billion went to Alaska, putting the nation's 47th most populous state just behind California and Illinois" in absolute dollar amounts. In per capita spending, though, Alaska won in a walk: "The measure provided $1,597 in earmarked funding for every man, woman and child in the state."

Perhaps needless to say, neither of these worthy servants of the (Alaskan) people saw any merit in post-Katrina suggestions by Oklahoma Republican senator Tom Coburn that the funds for such indecent pork be returned to the national government for distribution to more needful, though less well represented, parts of the country. Indeed, the *Post* described Senator Stevens as throwing a "hissy fit," including a highly implausible threat to resign from the Senate should the Senate endorse Senator Coburn's proposal. An amendment by Coburn was rejected by a vote of 82–15. In context, the *Post* described the fifteen votes as a "landslide," given the usual deference given to such senatorial titans as Stevens.[3] Ultimately, national outrage led Congress to eliminate the designated funding for the two bridges, but Alaska still got the $453 million to spend as it wished. Alaskans will be laughing all the way to the bank.

The Bridge to Nowhere incident provides a capsule illustration of what is wrong with the contemporary Congress. What is essential is the realization that the Bridge to Nowhere is directly linked to deep constitutional structures that make such legislation close to inevitable. In a trillion-dollar budget, $453 million may not sound like much. But, as the late Everett McKinley Dirksen, the Republican Senate leader during the 1960s, once said, "A billion here, a billion there, and pretty soon you're talking about real money."[4]

The Bridge to Nowhere involves legislation that *did* get through Congress and receive presidential assent. But I could also have begun this chapter with a reference to Congress's inability to pass significant legislation regarding issues about which the public is legitimately worried. Significant distortions and outright failures of American politics are produced because of—and not merely in spite of—the structure of the government imposed by the Constitution, whatever the contribution of other factors like the mode of campaign financing. Such failures of both omission and commission are the central topic of this chapter.

I begin with Article I of the Constitution, concerning the powers of Congress, not only because it immediately follows the Preamble. More important, it most directly involves the heart of our political system, which relies on *representative government*. Two major considerations help to explain a person's commitment to a given political order, including our own. One is the degree to which we believe that we have a genuine say in choosing those who will represent us in institutions ranging from a local city council to the national Congress. And, at least in the modern world, one is also concerned that one has an *equal say*. It is surely better to have *some* say than *no* say (as by being deprived of the right to vote at all), but it denies the formal premise of a democratic political system to say that some people get a systematically larger say than do others. This commitment is most concisely captured in the slogan "one person, one vote," which has been the mantra of the Supreme Court since 1963.[5] To the degree that Congress is in significant ways *unrepresentative*, we have less reason to respect it in terms of what has, since 1787, become our operative understanding of republican government.

We are also justifiably concerned with more practical aspects of our system as well. Thus, the second consideration involves *outcomes*— including allocations of taxpayer dollars to build bridges to nowhere. To the extent that we are satisfied with the output of a given institution, we may feel a commitment to it even if it is less representative than we might ideally like. After all, we even have the historical notion of "benevolent despotism," which refers to monarchical regimes that nonetheless had wide political support because the king, such as Frederick the Great in Prussia, was perceived to govern broadly "in the public interest." Still, such regimes were few and far between, not least because we are rightly skeptical that such altruism is often found in those with the powerful personalities linked with leadership of any kind, especially "despotic."

Whatever the institutions' imperfections, one way to test the commitment of Americans to their specific political institutions is simply to ask them if they "approve" or "disapprove" of those currently inhabiting them. To be sure, disapproval of a particular president or Congress does not necessarily translate into disapproval of the institution in the abstract, but it should certainly awaken people to the fact that the institution does not guarantee attractive leadership. Consider, then, that not since February 1997 has the national Gallup poll found more than 38 percent of the American public approving how members of Congress are handling their jobs. To be sure, the gross number conceals greater complexities. Thus, 57 percent of "self-described Republicans" thought well of Congress, "compared to 29 percent of independents and 22 percent of Democrats."[6]

What might account for this pattern of approval and disapproval? One explanation might surely be ruthless partisan gerrymandering in the House of Representatives, where electoral districts are self-consciously drawn to maximize the probability that the party doing the line drawing will be able to elect its candidates. As Alex Aleinikoff and Sam Issacharoff elegantly—and depressingly—put it more than a decade ago:

> In a democratic society, the purpose of voting is to allow the electors to select their governors. *Once a decade, however, that process is inverted, and the governors and their political agents are permitted to select their electors.* Through the process of redistricting, incumbent office holders and their political agents choose what configuration of voters best suits their political agenda.[7]

This fundamental corruption of the democratic process serves, among other things, to elect ever more representatives who need to appeal only to "the base" of their own parties rather than to more "centrist" voters in the middle. It means, among other things, that members of minority parties in gerrymandered districts are, as a practical matter, absolutely irrelevant to the choice of their purported representative. It also means that the House majority is more likely to disdain the very idea of working with the opposition, which is perceived simply as "the enemy." In the case of the current House of Representatives, Democrats could just as well stay at home as show up at the Capitol, given that they are utterly frozen out of participation in the affairs of the House.

As it happens, the Constitution certainly does not require—and some lawyers even think it should be interpreted as preventing—the kind of gerrymandering that has destroyed the House of Representatives as a forum of genuine deliberation and turned it into a venue for ever more poisonous partisan warfare. I believe that such gerrymandering—which is engaged in by both parties alike, though Republicans have recently had more opportunity to take advantage of it—is a true disease, threatening the very notion of representative democracy. It is not, however, a major focus of this book inasmuch as I am interested almost exclusively in what I am terming the "hardwired" parts of the Constitution. These include *bicameralism* and, most important, the *indefensibly apportioned Senate*, which gives equal voting power to Wyoming and California alike. These basic structures help to explain why it is so difficult to pass legislation in the national interest even if the House were more fairly apportioned.

However divided we are as a country these days, what paradoxically may unite far more than a majority of Americans are deep feelings of inefficacy with regard to being able to participate in what are ostensibly institutions promoting self-governance, as well as feelings of dismay at the actual legislation that is passed (or not passed). Indeed, more than one representative and senator has accompanied retirement from Congress with comments about their own frustration at the difficulty of actually getting anything done with regard to the issues that motivated them to run for public office in the first place. No doubt, many factors contribute to the poisonous atmosphere that many analysts detect in contemporary American politics.[8] These include the increasing importance of highly intense single-issue groups, from all ends of the political spectrum, to the corrosion of democratic values generated by the increasing role of lobbyists, who get much of their clout from the way we finance political campaigns. But we should also be aware that the Constitution itself deserves some of the blame.

BICAMERALISM AND THE GENERAL PROBLEM OF "VETO POINTS"

The most important thing to know about Article I is that it divides Congress into two separate and basically equal branches, the House of Representatives and the Senate, and that the Senate, unlike the

House, is organized on a principle of the equal voting power of each state. Bicameralism as such may not be so unusual, though more than two-thirds of the countries around the world have only one-house legislatures.[9] "The larger countries of the world," however, "tend to have bicameral parliaments," though China is a spectacular exception: Almost 3,000 members are elected to five-year terms in the single National People's Assembly.[10] One can, of course, doubt that the assembly actually governs in any serious way. Surely, it is hard to imagine an assemblage of 3,000 representatives functioning effectively to make controversial decisions.

The United States is unusual among even bicameral countries in having such a strongly bicameral legislature. Thus, of the eight European countries that have two legislative houses, six are described as only "weakly" bicameral, because, in effect, one house can almost certainly prevail against the opposition of the other. In France, for example, the government of the day can, if there appears to be irresolvable conflict between the National Assembly and the Senate, simply stipulate that the popularly elected National Assembly have the last word.[11] Democrats can only shudder when imagining a similar power by President Bush in effect to eliminate the power of the Senate by declaring that, in cases of conflict, the House of Representatives will automatically prevail. Only two European countries, Germany and Switzerland, merit the designation of "strongly" bicameral, though even Germany has a procedure for breaking deadlocks that effectively gives the last word to the popularly elected Bundestag.[12]

It is no coincidence that Germany and Switzerland are also strongly *federal*, as, of course, are the United States and other such bicameral countries as Canada and Australia. Bicameralism to some extent may be a proxy for the degree that one is committed to preferring the dispersion of loyalties and identities attached to federalism as against focusing more strongly on a single *national* identity.

In any event, it is exceptional to see two legislative houses that are equal in power. The British may have their House of Lords to complement the House of Commons. Not since 1911, though, has the House of Lords enjoyed any real parity of power with the House of Commons, and it has become ever weaker in the almost full century since. As every

American knows, however, the parity between the House and Senate is very real, save only for those matters assigned exclusively to the Senate, such as the confirmation of federal officials (most notably, perhaps, judges) and the ratification of treaties. The particular prerogative of the House to initiate tax legislation is, as an empirical matter, far less significant than the prerogatives of the Senate.

Bicameralism is probably thought by most Americans to be the natural mode of organizing a government. After all, unless you live in Nebraska, which is the sole unicameral state, you live in a state with both upper and lower houses. Perhaps this is explainable by the desire to emulate the national Constitution. Perhaps it is because Americans were simply unable, save in Nebraska, to imagine alternatives. It should be obvious, though, that the federalism explanation for bicameral national legislatures makes no sense with regard to states unless one seriously believes that each given county in a state is the equivalent of each state in the union. Other arguments, almost invariably involving a basic fear of what is thought to be unchecked majority power, are necessary.

The maverick former governor of Minnesota, Jesse Ventura, strongly urged that Minnesota emulate Nebraska by abolishing its Senate. Not surprisingly, his suggestion went nowhere, not least because it was met with predictable hostility from the senators being asked to give up their jobs. As political scientist John Roche once suggested, paraphrasing the well-known comment of Lord Acton, it is not so much power that corrupts as the prospect of losing power. What I shall call "Roche's dictum" explains much about why we may be destined—or should the word be "doomed"—to remain behind the bars of constitutional iron cages, whether national or state.

Is bicameralism *necessary* to achieve the purposes set out in the Preamble? Surely the answer is no. The United States, after all, is not the only democratic polity in the world that takes seriously the values captured in the Preamble. If one looks only at the polities closest to us in political heritage, the countries in Western Europe, a majority, as noted above, have unicameral legislatures and no strongly counterbalancing executive (as in France).

This is not to say that bicameralism might not have its strengths, but one should be careful to specify what they are thought to be. At the time of the founding, for example, one of the strongest arguments made for the Senate was the importance of offering guaranteed representation to America's financial elites as a way of protecting private property. As Akhil Reed Amar notes, at the Philadelphia convention, "Gouverneur Morris openly advocated a Senate limited to men of 'great personal property' and animated by 'the aristocratic spirit.'"[13] Morris lost. There are no property qualifications for membership in the Senate, though the contemporary Senate is often described as a "millionaires' club" wildly unrepresentative of the actual distribution of income in the United States.[14]

Putting the "aristocratic" defense of bicameralism to one side, contemporary supporters of a second house cite as its main advantage its subordination of strictly "majoritarian democracy"—assuming that the single house in a parliamentary system is elected on a democratic basis—to the considerable virtues of trying to achieve a broader consensus. And, of course, one should be aware that even those strongly committed to democracy as an overriding value should take notice of vagaries in any electoral process that might well allow majorities of representatives to be chosen by a minority of the voting population (especially if we include the population that is eligible to vote but does not do so). In any event, "the presence of two legislative houses requires a broader constituency base to support any legislation."[15]

Political scientist Arend Lijphart is probably the best-known proponent of what he terms a "consensus model" of political choice. This model "does not differ from the majoritarian model in accepting that majority rule is better than minority rule." However, "it accepts majority rule only as a *minimum* requirement: instead of being satisfied with narrow decision-making majorities, it seeks to maximize the size of those majorities" by aiming "at broad participation in government and broad agreement on the policies that the government should pursue."[16] As Mark Graber, who generally finds "consensualism" more attractive than unalloyed "majoritarianism," puts it, "judging a system of highly separated powers, including a bicameral legislature, on majoritarian criteria is a bit like evaluating a Marx brothers film for plot."[17]

The greatest champion of consensualism rather than majoritarianism in our history, ironically or not, was John C. Calhoun, whose theory of "concurrent majoritarianism" was a justification in effect for giving the South an absolute veto over policies regarding slavery, including proposals to ban the movement of slaves into the territories of the United States. However, as Graber well argues in his monumental study of pre–Civil War American politics,[18] almost all major American political figures adopted some form of consensualism, even if none took it to the extremes of Calhoun. The most significant illustration of the point is the attempt by both the Whig and Democratic parties to be truly national parties, which involved, for better and for worse, the attempt to soften party views on such regional issues as slavery. The very structure of American politics, by which *all* members of Congress are elected locally, defeated consensualism, and the prewar party system collapsed during the 1850s. The Republican party was a decidedly regional party, and its first president, Abraham Lincoln, is described by Graber as almost Jacobin in his view of the right of a legislative majority to do as it pleased. Still, the American system, for better and for worse, continues to subordinate any simple notion of majority rule to the difficult political tasks of achieving primacy in two quite different legislative houses plus the presidency, not to mention the need for assuring as well the acquiescence of yet a third branch, the judiciary.

It is clear, then, that the tension between majoritarianism and more consensual methods of governance is central to anyone who would design a new constitution or evaluate an old one. A Christmas Day 2005 story on political developments in Iraq quoted the Iraqi president, Jalal Talabani, who was referring to the contention between Sunnis and Shi'ites in that country: "Without the Sunni parties there will be no consensus government[,] . . . without consensus government there will be no unity, there will be no peace."[19] It is hard to disagree with Talabani, and one might apply his comment to polities well beyond the borders of Iraq. One must be clear, though, what one means by "consensus government." With regard to the contemporary United States, for example, one would be hard put to say that it operates under anything close to a consensus government, given the almost unprecedented unity of the Republican party in recent years as it has enjoyed control of all branches of the government. This is not to say that the Republican party is a monolith; there are certainly tensions within its coalition of sometimes opposed forces. Even so, it is hard to view the present Republican leadership as very interested in reaching out to its political opponents.

As already noted, almost all American states are bicameral. Many used to organize their upper houses on the basis of such entities as counties rather than population. My home state of North Carolina, for example, used to emulate the U.S. Senate by having each of its hundred counties elect one senator, regardless of population. Such "little federalism" systems were swept aside in the 1964 *Reynolds v. Sims* decision by the Supreme Court,[20] which stated that the Equal Protection Clause of the Fourteenth Amendment required the application of a "one-person, one-vote" metric to both houses of a state legislature, and all states now comply with that decision. Today, almost all upper houses differ from the lower houses either by length of term or by the number of people represented. In California, for example, each of the 40 senators serves for four years, 20 beginning their terms every two years, while the 80 members of the California Assembly must face the voters every two years. Or one might prefer the New York pattern, where senators must confront their constituents at the same two-year intervals as representatives, but there are only 50 senators, as against the significantly larger assembly, composed of 150 members. Each senator, then, necessarily represents roughly three times the population—and a larger geographical territory—than any member of the lower house. The fact that New York is functionally governed by a three-man troika consisting of the governor, the speaker of the assembly, and the majority leader of the Senate raises questions beyond the scope of this book, though it also points to the limits of what one can learn from looking only at constitutional design.

There may obviously be much to be said for bicameralism. If one focuses on different lengths of terms, one usually defends the upper house by suggesting that the longer terms allow a valuable corrective to the responsiveness of members of the lower house to the passions of the moment because of their fear of losing votes in what is perceived as an imminent election. James Madison, for example, defended the Senate in *Federalist*, No. 63, by asserting that it would "be sometimes necessary as a defense to the people against their own temporary error and delusions,"[21] and longer terms may help provide such a defense. If one focuses instead on the greater population or area represented by senators as against representatives, then one usually defends the former as being less parochial than the latter, even as one immediately turns around and defends the representatives as being more sensitive to local concerns than are the senators.

As one looks abroad, other models (and justifications) of bicameralism present themselves. Germany, for example, uses the upper house of the Bundesrat to reinforce its commitment to federalism by making the officials of the various *lander* governments the members of the Bundesrat.[22] Although the original U.S. Constitution was also federalism-reinforcing by giving state legislatures the appointment power, this was a far more limited protection of explicitly state governmental interests than that developed in Germany. Another federal country, Australia, uses its Senate as a means of generating a wider array of political perspectives.[23] This is done by adopting *proportional representation* in the election of the six senators from each of the six Australian states. This means, as a practical matter, that a mobilized party representing approximately 15 percent of the electorate can gain at least one seat in the Senate.

Whatever the undoubted attractions of bicameralism, it always makes it harder to pass legislation. Two bodies rather than one must agree on any given legislation. One might well believe that most Americans would regard this hurdle as a price worth paying inasmuch as they share Madison's expressed fear of legislation based on "error and delusions." The "sober second thoughts" provided by the Senate—interestingly enough, one rarely sees a defense of the House of Representatives based on such sobriety—is thus a safeguard against foolish legislation. To be sure, this illustrates an important feature of the Constitution that underscores many of its features: Those who framed the document, and those who venerate it today, are fundamentally fearful of change and are willing to pay a high price to prevent what they would deem to be unfortunate changes.[24]

Anyone called upon either to design a constitution directly or, as with participants in the upcoming referendum, to assess a design, must inevitably try to assess the relationship between any given institutional structure and what might be termed a "propensity to pass bad legisla-tion." Bad and, even more to the point, "awful" legislation is an evil against which we are trying to guard. But we also desire the passage of good—and especially "wonderful"—legislation, which means that we always have to be attentive to the extent to which guarding against the risk of bad legislation ends up being counterproductive insofar as it prevents as well the passage of good legislation. If one is especially fearful of bad legislation—and especially if one believes that most bad legislation is worse, on some relevant measure, than offsetting good legislation that might otherwise be passed—then one will obviously want to make it quite difficult to pass any legislation at all. The fact that some good legislation will inevitably fail to pass as well may be thought to be a cheap price to pay. But others may be less fearful of change and more confident as well that bad legislation, after being identified as such, can be defeated or, even if passed and implemented, can relatively easily be repealed. In this case, one would obviously support a more permissive legislative process even at the cost of the passage of additional bad legislation.

One may also be concerned about the *volatility* of change. It is reasonable to believe that a political system, overall, is better off with a minimum of disruptive changes. Such kinds of changes are far more likely in a unicameral system within a political system featuring at least two strong political parties that alternate power. Thus, in Great Brit-ain, the socialist nationalization of industry, in what now seem to be the "old days" after World War II, was followed by the privatization of such industries when more conservative parties came to power. Among other things, this obviously makes the overall economic situation less predict-able, with attendant costs. Thus, Roger D. Congleton has pointed to data from Europe suggesting that "bicameralism may improve public policy by making it more predictable and more consensual—especially in settings where policy deliberations are partisan."[25]

I believe there is much in the status quo to bemoan. Therefore, I am inclined to believe that it is much too hard to pass legislation in the United States, but this is obviously a value judgment. I will confess to some pleasure in the ability of the Democratic minority, especially in the Senate, to block certain programs pushed by the Republican party, but I was far less pleased when Republican minorities during the Clinton administration were able to exercise similar blocking power with regard to some of that administration's programs. This simply recognizes the fact that it is basically impossible to discuss the *procedures* of government without paying some attention to one's own political views about the *substance* of politics. In any event, all participants in the forthcoming referendum must analyze the extent to which bicameralism—or, in effect, the "tricameralism" generated by the presidential veto, to which I will presently turn—can be blamed for what they regard as serious deficiencies in the operation of the American polity.

I believe that the bicameral structure of Congress goes a long way in explaining the peculiar impeachment drama of President Bill Clinton in 1998–1999: Republicans in the House of Representatives knew from day one that there was no genuine possibility of gaining in the Senate the constitutionally required two-thirds majority necessary to convict Clinton and remove him from office. This reality licensed the House Republicans to "play to their base" in a way that I am convinced they would have chosen not to do had the House had the final decision on removing the president from office. This would, among other things, have given the White House to Vice President Al Gore and made him a much more formidable candidate for the presidency in 2000. If I am correct, then this is a model illustration of how bicameralism encourages irresponsible posturing by legislators who count on other players in the American institutional game—including presidents with their vetoes or judges with their powers of judicial review—to save the country from what they might well believe, at least in private, would be folly.

Perhaps one believes, not without justice, that some of my preferred examples of the costs of bicameralism—the inability seriously to confront our medical care dilemma and the Clinton impeachment—are just what one would expect from someone with my own basically left-of-center political beliefs. But surely someone who supported President Bush's program of radically revising, if not eliminating entirely, the Social Security system created during the New Deal could also agree that bicameralism, in this instance, united the Democratic opposition in the Senate plus a few Republican holdouts and doomed that presumptively worthy enterprise. In the old days, one might have been forgiven a presumption that a critique of the status quo bias attached to bicameralism (and the presidential veto) would generally reflect a leftist, or "progressive," sensibility. But today, when the political status quo includes the congealed policies attached to the New Deal of Franklin Roosevelt and the Great Society of Lyndon Johnson—and, for that matter, the quite remarkable expansions of federal entitlement programs that took place during the Nixon administration—one can find just as much frustrated desire for change on the right.

Even if no two persons can necessarily be expected to agree on what kind of change is desirable, it should be relatively easy these days to find a wide range of agreement that the American system is impervious to needed changes. So then the question becomes: Is it worth it, in order to deprive your opponents of the opportunity to work their political will, to make it more difficult to pass your own favorite programs? Or, on the contrary, would you rather have a greater likelihood of achieving your own goals even if this means that your opponents would be more likely to succeed if and when they are in power? Our Constitution should appeal far more to persons with the first set of preferences, especially if they basically have no positive legislative agenda of their own, than to those who actually desire significant change from the status quo.

There is much to be said on both sides of the bicameralism debate, and it would be folly to predicate my call for a new convention simply on bicameralism itself. Indeed, even if one is convinced by this book to support such a convention, I can well imagine urging its members to retain the general structure of bicameralism even as they engage in the necessary reform of some of the specifics of our particular version of bicameralism.

BICAMERALISM OR TRICAMERALISM: WHY SHOULD THE PRESIDENT HAVE THE VETO POWER?

The previous section considered some implications for the legislative process of the fact that there are two separate houses of Congress and, therefore, by definition, at least two "veto points"—that is, the ability to say no to legislative proposals—that any proposal must elude. As a matter of fact, though, we might as easily be described as living in a *tricameral* system inasmuch as the president quite literally has a constitutionally assigned veto power. And, interestingly, that power appears in Article I instead of in Article II, which generally concerns the powers of the president. This should underscore the extent to which it may be misleading to refer to any rigid "separation of powers." The American president plays a crucial—and, I would argue, inordinate—role in the legislative process itself.

Article I, section 7, clause 2, states in suitably turgid prose:

> Every Bill which shall have passed the House of Representatives and the Senate, shall, before it become a Law, be presented to the President of the United States; If he approve he shall sign it, but if not he shall return it, with his Objections to that House in which it shall have originated, who shall enter the Objections at large on their Journal, and proceed to reconsider it. If after such Reconsideration two thirds of that House shall agree to pass the Bill, it shall be sent, together with the Objections, to the other House, by which it shall likewise be reconsidered, and if approved by two thirds of that House, it shall become a Law.

This is no small power. A report prepared by the Congressional Research Service of the Library of Congress describes it as "among [the president's] most significant tools in legislative dealings with Congress. It is effective not only in preventing the passage of legislation undesirable to the President, but also, as a threat sometimes forcing Congress to modify legislation before it is presented to the President."[26] A presidential veto in one instant transforms Congress from an internally majoritarian institution, at least with regard to the votes needed to pass legislation, into a *supermajoritarian* one. Each house of Congress now needs to summon up a full two-thirds of the members present and voting in order to exercise its will. Consider the congressional attempt to override President Clinton's veto of the Partial-Birth Abortion Ban Act of 1995. Although the House voted 285–137 to override it, it was sustained because 41 of the 98 voting senators voted against the override (which means, by definition, that 57 senators supported it). For some readers, this will no doubt be a happy example of the use of the presidential veto power; for others, not. In any event, it certainly exemplifies the power that a dedicated president can exercise to thwart what, on the surface, is the desire of strong political majorities.

Although most presidents and other state leaders throughout the world have some form of a veto over legislation, there is nothing inevitable about such a choice. Switzerland, for example, does not give its president a veto power at all.[27] The Constitution of South Africa that went into force in 1996 gives the president a limited veto.[28] The president can, should he or she have "reservations about the constitutionality" of a particular bill, "refer it back to the National Assembly for reconsideration." Should the parliament "fully accommodate . . . the President's reservations, the President must assent to and sign the Bill." Should the assembly not prove so accommodating, the president can refer the bill "to the Constitutional Court for a decision on its constitutionality." If "the Constitutional Court decides that the Bill is constitutional, the President must assent to and sign it." The South African president, therefore, cannot veto a bill simply because he or she believes it to be unwise. The decision as to the wisdom or unwisdom of legislation is left exclusively to the parliament.

Over the course of American history, presidents have vetoed 2,550 bills, and Congress has overridden only 106 of them.[29] More than 95 percent of all presidential vetoes are successful—at least from the president's perspective. As a practical matter, the power of the U.S. president is far closer to that of the president of Cyprus, who has an absolute power to veto legislation, which the legislature has no opportunity to override, than that of the South African or Swiss presidents.

Perhaps some of the 2,550 bills were passed with the expectation—and perhaps even the hope—of a veto. As we have already seen, one function that multiple veto points serve is to allow a certain amount of posturing—what social scientists call "strategic misrepresentation" and what others might even define as "lying to their constituents"—by public officials who depend on other institutions to take the heat for blocking legislation supported by a local constituency. This may even help to explain some of the votes for the Partial-Birth Abortion Ban Act of 1995. It is completely implausible, however, to believe that such posturing on the part of purported supporters of legislation explains more than a fraction of the vetoed bills. Surely, most readers of this book, whatever their political views, can think of at least one exercise of the veto power by either President George H. W. Bush or by President Bill Clinton that infuriated them and the party with which they identify. And, just as much to the point, each reader can think of unfortunate compromises that were forced on the legislative majority in order to escape threatened vetoes. The veto—including simply the threat to do so—is one of the most powerful tools of modern presidents.

Many years ago, the president was described by the late political scientist Clinton Rossiter as the "chief legislator" within our system as well as the "chief executive."[30] Rossiter was emphasizing the modern role of the president in *initiating* legislation, which is then introduced to Congress by friendly legislators. There may be much to be said for this role of the modern president as a mode of overcoming the almost inevitable fragmentation of the Congress. But the highly desirable ability of a president to initiate a conversation, as it were, by proposing legislation in no way entails endorsing the president's ability to structure the ensuing conversation by threatening to veto legislation, let alone actually to bring the conversation to an often abrupt halt by exercising the veto power.

Early presidents were very restrained in their use of the veto. George Washington vetoed two bills (neither of which was overridden), while Adams and Jefferson had veto-less presidencies. James Madison vetoed five bills and his successor, James Monroe, one, before John Quincy Adams emulated his father and vetoed none. Andrew Jackson vetoed five bills, including his historic veto of the bill renewing the charter of the Bank of the United States, but his successor, Martin Van Buren, vetoed none. This pattern may be explained simply by reference to the fact that Congress at the time passed relatively little legislation; it was nowhere near the permanent legislature that it has become in our own time.

It may also be explained at least in part by a tension in the very notion of the veto as part of the constitutional system. Was the veto a way by which the president exercised his oath to "preserve, protect, and defend the Constitution of the United States"? If so, this would suggest that a president could properly veto a bill only if he believed that it raised constitutional questions. Otherwise, the basic notion of separation of powers, by which the Congress makes laws and the president merely takes care to enforce them, would not authorize presidential intervention into the ordinary political process of deciding whether something should become law in the first place. Thus, one of Washington's vetoes was indeed constitutionally based as was, at least in part, the famous veto of the Bank Renewal Bill by Andrew Jackson, which argued that Congress simply did not have the power it claimed. But Washington's second veto made no reference to the Constitution, and no clear pattern emerged in the early years that would restrict the veto to constitutional issues.

A recent study of the evolution of the presidency has suggested that Jackson "set in train a series of events that would alter the constitutional foundations of the presidential office," including his more aggressive use of the veto power:

> Settled practice [prior to Jackson] authorized vetoes where Congress's authority to legislate in a given area was constitutionally murky or where hasty consideration produced legislation with remediable technical deficiencies. The overriding constitutional function of the veto was to aid Congress in the performance of its deliberative functions.

It did *not* operate "to substitute the president's judgment for the Congress's on national policy matters."[31] Even Jackson, who was scarcely modest in his view of his own power, couched his opposition to the bank in constitutional terms rather than say only that he believed the bank to be unsound public policy.[32]

Slowly but surely, though, presidents stopped thinking of themselves as merely the enforcer of laws passed by an autonomous Congress so long as they were thought to be constitutional. Instead, the president was a key political—and not only formal—participant in the process by which laws were made (or were prevented from being made) in the first place. University of Minnesota professor Michael Stokes Paulsen states what is probably current conventional wisdom when he writes, "The President may [veto a bill] on any grounds he sees fit."[33]

Early presidents, including Jackson himself, would almost undoubt-edly be surprised—and some might well be shocked—by the extent to which vetoes, or even the threats of vetoes, have become a standard operating procedure of American politics.

Whereas only thirty-six bills had been vetoed through the presi-dency of Abraham Lincoln (who vetoed only two bills), Andrew Johnson, Lincoln's successor, vetoed twenty-one bills, of which a full fifteen were overridden by Congress. No veto had ever been overrid-den prior to the presidency of John Tyler, the first vice president to enter the White House as the result of a presidential death, in 1841; his nickname, especially among his political opponents, was "His Accidency." Yet five of Tyler's vetoes were sustained. Franklin Pierce, a candidate for the title of our most obscure full-term president (1853–1857), saw five of his nine vetoes overridden.

Pierce and Andrew Johnson, who not at all coincidentally almost always emerge near the bottom in the rankings of American presidents, stand together in the percentage of their vetoes overridden. Richard Nixon and Gerald Ford are the only other presidents who even come close. Nixon saw seven of his twenty-six vetoes overridden, while his successor suffered that indignity with regard to twelve of his forty-eight vetoes. Both, of course, were Republican presidents faced with Demo-cratic Congresses. But even Ford, our only unelected president—putting disputes about the 2000 election of George W. Bush to one side—was able to prevail a full 75 percent of the time in what were often quite bitter policy disputes having nothing to do with constitutional understandings. Bill Clinton was even more successful in staving off what he deemed to be undesirable legislation passed by the post-1994 Republican Congress. Of his thirty-six vetoes, only two were overridden.

But some vetoes are not even subject to legislative override, as difficult as that process is. Thus, the last sentence of the Veto Clause states that, although a statute will automatically take effect "within ten Days (Sundays excepted) after it shall have been presented to [the president]," in the absence of a formal veto, this is not the case if "the Congress by their Adjournment prevent its Return, in which Case it shall not be a Law." This establishes the so-called pocket veto power of the president, who may simply place a bill passed by Congress in the days immediately prior to its adjournment in his pocket, secure in the knowledge that it will not become law without his signature. During the regular session, the president is forced either to accept legislation, even without his formal signature, or to veto it. Now the president, by doing nothing at all, can prevail in any policy struggle with Congress. There have been 1,066 bills that have died through the pocket veto process. But the pocket veto has become less significant inasmuch as Congress is increasingly in almost year-round session. "Adjournments," in contrast to "recesses," now usually take place in December, and Congress reconvenes at the beginning of January. Circumstances may have taken care of the potential for gross abuse of this particular presidential power.

Is the presidential veto a desirable part of our political system? It does, after all, exemplify just one more antimajoritarian feature of our Constitution that serves to make it ever harder to pass legislation departing from the status quo.

A common feature of newspaper columns on the game of contract bridge is to ask readers, who have full knowledge of the cards in the four hands, whether they would rather play offense (that is, try to make the contract) or defense (that is, try to defeat it). Similarly, with regard to the game of American politics, one can always ask the player which side she would rather play if the only thing she cared about was winning—as against, say, the "justice" of the outcome, which is irrelevant in most games. From this Olympian perspective, in which one basically disdains the mere mortals whose lives may be at stake, it is almost self-evident that one should always choose to play defense, given the number of veto points facing any legislation.

This book concerns only the formal points generated by the Constitution itself. I do not concern myself in this chapter, for example, with the internal operations of the committee systems of the House or Senate, which themselves set up even more gates through which supporters of any given bill must move. It is very hard to believe that we are well served by all of these gates, both constitutionally constructed and institutionally created. To believe this requires as well the belief that deviations from the status quo present the greatest danger to the United States. Only this would explain why one would find it for the best that the offense undergo such far greater trials than the defense in any playing of the legislation game.

The question is not whether a Constitution-based veto power is justified. Presidents do, after all, take a solemn oath to "preserve, protect, and defend the Constitution," and, as a formal matter, it is hard to square the oath with a duty to sign what they believe to be unconstitutional legislation. And it might therefore make sense to put an extra burden of decision making on Congress—even to suspend ordinary majority rule in favor of supermajoritarianism—upon the receipt of such a veto, especially when accompanied, as it should be, by a well-reasoned opinion explaining the president's interpretation of the Constitution. As noted earlier, the South African Constitution does give the president this limited kind of veto power (though a veto does not transform the parliament into a supermajoritarian institution). But the South African president cannot necessarily win a struggle over constitutional interpretation, as the U.S. president, as a matter of practice, is extremely likely to. Instead, the final decision as to constitutionality is given to the South African Constitutional Court.

As it happens, I strongly believe that the president *should* view herself as accountable to constitutional norms, which means that I have no objection to a Constitution-based veto, even if it is unclear whether the president in such circumstances should be allowed the last word. There is at least one interesting implication that follows from ascribing such accountability to the president. If, for example, one accepts the notion that the president has a duty to veto ostensibly unconstitutional legislation, then it becomes hard to justify the view that the Take Care Clause forces a president to enforce legislation on the books (including, perhaps, legislative overrides of the veto) that the president deems to be unconstitutional.[34] Indeed, I believe quite strongly (and have testified before Congress) that the president *does* have a duty to engage in serious constitutional interpretation and can legitimately refuse to enforce such ostensibly unconstitutional laws. This may be especially true when the offensive legislation is attached as one part of what is now termed "omnibus legislation," when Congress passes thousand-page bills containing literally hundreds of different provisions. If the principal provisions are important enough, presidents feel absolutely hamstrung in vetoing the bill in its entirety. Rightly or wrongly, we usually do not accord the president the power to exercise a *line-item veto* that allows her to pick and choose among the provisions of omnibus bills.[35]

None of the arguments that view the president as defender of the Constitution, with whatever powers may be attached to that, work to justify a president's policy-based vetoes. At that point, the president in effect becomes a one-person third legislative chamber, able with the stroke of a pen to negate the views of at least 218 members of the House of Representatives (the bare majority of all 435 representatives) and 51 senators (the bare majority of the 100 senators). Of course, it could even be the case that the president is rendering irrelevant the views of 350 members of the House and 66 members of the Senate inasmuch as the 34 "loyalists" in the Senate would be enough to uphold the veto. Critics of the Supreme Court often accuse it of acting in a "counter-majoritarian" manner when it holds unconstitutional legislation that has the approval of Congress (and usually the president as well). But the Supreme Court in our entire history has declared only approximately 160 national laws to be unconstitutional.[36] This pales into insignificance before the 2,550 instances of the presidential veto, very few of which make reference to the duty to preserve constitutional norms. At least equally important, no doubt, are the number of changes, or simply failures to initiate legislation in the first place, produced by the threats of countless additional vetoes.

A common defense of the veto is that the president represents the entire American people in a way that is not true of the Congress. A member of Congress may be said to represent the people of District 10 of Massachusetts or even the entire state of Illinois, but there is nothing in the institutional structure of Congress to encourage even a single member of either the House or the Senate to take a national perspective. Interestingly, what I will call the "tribune of the people" defense of the presidential veto depends for its cogency on agreeing with the proposition that the essentially parochial members of Congress cannot necessarily, or even often, be trusted to come together in a way that serves the national interest, but that the president can. I will address this argument in the next chapter, when I consider the Electoral College that formally elects presidents.

More optimistically, one might assert that 2,550 vetoes are not that many, when compared with the overall number of laws passed. This suggests that we might actually take heart in the relative paucity of vetoes. From this perspective, the fact that George W. Bush has yet to veto a bill (as of June 2006) is evidence of how well Congress served the national interest between 2001 and 2006. I strongly suspect that at least some readers will agree with me in rejecting such a comforting view.[37] Moreover, it has increasingly become clear that President Bush far prefers what might be called "surreptitious vetoes," which are manifested in his delivering "signing statements" when ostensibly consenting to legislation, which argue that he has no duty to enforce any law that he views as making an incursion on presidential prerogatives.[38] I have already indicated that I have no objection in principle to a president's using the Constitution as a shield against enforcing presumptively unconstitutional laws. The use of such signing statements goes back at least to the Wilson Administration. To this extent I agree with Michael Kinsley that it is a mistake to criticize the president for viewing himself as an independent constitutional interpreter who takes his commitment to the Constitution seriously, even if this means an unwillingness to enforce certain legislation passed by Congress.[39]

But this acceptance of an important theoretical point does not excuse the profligacy with which the Administration has chosen the stealth route rather than to confront what it views as congressional overreaching directly by vetoing the legislation. Although signing statements go back at least to the Wilson administration, Professor Christopher Kelley notes that their use really expanded during the Reagan administration, which elaborated a theory of the "unitary executive" that greatly enhanced presidential power.[40] Presidents George H. W. Bush and Bill Clinton also made use of signing statements, but no president has used them so frequently—or made such sweeping claims of power—as George W. Bush. The Bush administration has become almost fanatically concerned to protect what it controversially believes to be its own prerogatives of office. It has proved completely unwilling to engage in the kind of direct challenge to—and conversation with—Congress that is captured in an actual veto message. Such messages not only give Congress, and the engaged American public, an opportunity to consider carefully the president's arguments; they also provide an occasion for the Congress, which may well reflect public opinion, to express its disagreement by overriding the veto. There will be further discussion of the Bush administration and its views of presidential prerogative in chapter 3.

In any event, it is far more likely that the number of vetoes by particular presidents is correlated with the capture of the Congress by the political opposition. Presidents are obviously more likely to be presented with unpalatable bills if the Congress is controlled by the opposition party than by their own. To be sure, Franklin Roosevelt vetoed an almost staggering 372 bills, far more than all of his twentieth-century predecessors combined, even though Congress was controlled by the Democrats throughout his presidency. Interestingly enough, in his twelve years in office, he vetoed only 68 more bills than did Grover Cleveland during his first term of office (1885–1889), even though Democrats controlled the House of Representatives throughout his term. Harry Truman, faced with a Republican Congress between 1947 and 1949, vetoed 180 bills in his seven years in office. It should not be surprising, then, that Truman's successor, Dwight D. Eisenhower, vetoed 73 bills, although only 28 bills were vetoed in the following eight years of the Kennedy and Lyndon Johnson presidencies (12 and 16, respectively). Both Kennedy and Johnson, of course, had Democratic Congresses. Richard Nixon, in only six years, vetoed the same total number of bills, while his successor, Gerald Ford, vetoed 48 bills in his truncated two-year term of office. In turn, President Jimmy Carter found only 13 bills to be veto-worthy.

This pattern raises more general questions about "divided government" and whether our Constitution should be praised or condemned for the tolerance, as it were, that it displays toward such divisions. And, most to the point, should it be enough for a political party to capture only the presidency in order to be able to forestall presumptively popular congressional legislation?

Many readers might answer this last question with a resounding yes, because of the unique degree of popular approval enjoyed by the president; he (and, in the future, she) is often described as the "people's choice." Unfortunately, this claim is demonstrably false. And this is true even if one does not dwell on the facts that Al Gore in 2000, like Richard Nixon forty years before,[41] received more votes than his opponent, and that four of our eleven post–World War II presidents— Harry Truman (1948), John F. Kennedy (1960), Richard Nixon (1968), and Bill Clinton (both 1996 and 2000)—received less than 50 percent of the popular vote, while yet another, Gerald Ford, received nary a single popular vote endorsing his occupancy of the White House. Whatever explains the legitimacy of the exercise of the veto power by these presidents, it is not that they were necessarily more representative of the collective American people than was the Congress.

One might well reply, altogether accurately, that it is just as bogus to declare that the modern Congress is necessarily any more representative of the collective majority than is the president. There is certainly some truth to this, especially when one considers the Senate, to which I will now turn. It is impossible to describe the Senate as a remotely majoritarian institution. The dreadful fact is that none of the great institutions of American politics can plausibly claim to speak for the majority of Americans, even though all assert such claims. And the deviation from democratic legitimacy has significant consequences for the actual output of our political system and, therefore, the likelihood that it will effectively confront the problems facing the majority of Americans.

OUR ILLEGITIMATE SENATE

It is clause 1 of section 3 that should appall most Americans and lead them to support a new convention: "The Senate of the United States shall be composed of two senators from each State, *chosen by the Legislature thereof*, for six Years, and each Senator shall have one Vote." The italicized section is no longer an operative part of our constitutional order; it was repealed in 1913 by the Seventeenth Amendment, requiring the popular election of senators. This was no small change inasmuch as it significantly diluted the power of state-level politicians to control who got to the Senate. Two respected scholars have even described it as "the most direct alteration in the system of federalism since the Civil War Amendments."[42] There are, to be sure, some persons who lament the passage of the Seventeenth Amendment precisely because it lessened the degree to which the interests of state political officials are represented in the Senate.[43] Most of us, I strongly suspect, view this particular emendation of the original Constitution as desirable and would presumably object instead to the unamended Constitution. I will have more to say about the Seventeenth Amendment in chapter 6.

Although there was much discussion at the Constitutional Convention about the length of the senatorial term—there were even proposals for life tenure—I suspect that the country has probably been reasonably well served by the six-year term. It encourages taking a more long-term view than do members of the House, who are constantly aware that they will face a new election literally within twenty-two months of taking their oaths of office. (A new term of Congress begins in early January, and the next election for the House will be in early November of the following year.) The only serious criticism that has really been offered of six-year terms is by James Sundquist, who sees "off-year" elections for senators as simply one more force contributing to the inability to form a truly effective government after elections and to pass legislative programs.[44] I shall discuss Sundquist's general argument presently.

The central problem is in the requirement that there shall be "two Senators from each State," with "each Senator" having "one Vote." Alaska, Delaware, Montana, North Dakota, South Dakota, Vermont, and Wyoming each have twice the number of senators as they do representatives in the House. Of these states, Wyoming is the smallest, with approximately 500,000 residents counted in the 2000 census; the largest is Montana, with about 905,000 residents. Together, these seven states have approximately 4.8 million residents. They elect among themselves fourteen senators, as distinguished from, say, Minnesota, whose approximately 4.9 million residents are represented by a grand total of two senators. Another five states—Hawaii, Idaho,

Maine, New Hampshire, and Rhode Island—have the same number of senators as they do representatives. Of these, the largest is Idaho, with just short of 2 million people. So, almost a full quarter of the Senate is elected by twelve states whose total population, approximately 14 million, is less than 5 percent of the total U.S. population.

Although it is unrealistic to think that the fourteen senators from the seven smallest states would be united on any given controversial issue—they come from different regions of the country and have senators representing different political parties—should that ever occur, they would offset a similarly hypothetical united group of senators from California, Florida, Illinois, New York, Ohio, Pennsylvania, and Texas, whose collective population in 2000 was approximately 124 million. To put it mildly, there is simply no defense for this other than the fact that equal representation of the states was thought necessary in 1787 to create a Constitution that would be ratified by the small states. Though this may explain the distorted representation given to Delaware, it scarcely justifies the excess of power enjoyed by the other six smallest states, which were admitted to the union later. The explanation for *their* representation is the so-called equal footing doctrine, which holds that all new states will be admitted on the same terms as the original states.

It surely should occasion no surprise that most contemporary authors who have preceded me in writing about perceived deficiencies of the Constitution have concentrated particular fire on equal voting power in the Senate.[45] The eminent Yale political scientist Robert Dahl recently asked, "How democratic is the American Constitution?" His answer is, in effect, "not nearly enough," and his exhibit A is the Senate. Although he notes that "[s]ome degree of unequal representation also exists in the other federal systems" throughout the world, "the degree of unequal representation in the U.S. Senate is by far the most extreme." Consider that California has just short of seventy times the population of Wyoming.[46] Dahl suggests that we imagine two friends who live close to one another, one on the California side of Lake Tahoe, the other in Nevada. As they talk about upcoming elections, it turns out that the Nevada neighbor has seventeen times the voting power of his California friend[47] with regard to electing a senator and, as we shall see in chapter 3, relatively more voting power as well with regard to choosing the president.[48]

Perhaps the most dramatic way of illustrating the disparity among the states is by looking at the vote totals of two incumbent senators returned to office in the 2004 election. Barbara Boxer of California won approximately 6,453,000 votes to retain her seat. Alaska's Lisa Murkowski retained her seat by winning approximately 148,000 votes. South Dakota's John Thune, incidentally, upset Senate minority leader Tom Daschle by receiving just over 50 percent (197,814) of the total 391,093 votes cast. Lest one think that Republicans are automatically advantaged by the Senate's malapportionment, note that North Dakota is represented by two Democratic senators, as is (functionally) Vermont, given that the nominally independent (and formerly Republican) Senator Jim Jeffords most often votes with the Democrats. Moreover, South Dakota continues to have one Democratic senator even after Senator Daschle's defeat, as does Montana.

It is not a cogent response, incidentally, to say that any such inequalities are vitiated by the fact that the House of Representatives is organized on the basis of population, putting to one side issues raised by partisan gerrymandering. The very nature of bicameralism, after all, requires that both houses assent to any legislation. By definition, this means that *the Senate can exercise a veto power* on majoritarian legislation passed by the House that is deemed too costly to the interests of small states, which are overrepresented in the Senate. A similar point can be made with regard to the presidential veto, especially when the president is of a different party than the majority of Congress, as was the case, for example, with Richard Nixon, Ronald Reagan (during part of his term), George H. W. Bush, and Bill Clinton (for the bulk of his term). Indeed, one central reality of the American Constitution is that it generates so many different veto points with regard to blocking the wishes of even an energized majority.

Moreover, the Senate has created its own internal rules, such as the filibuster, that allow a forty-one-senator minority to block legislation that has been passed by the House of Representatives and is supported by a majority of the Senate (and, for that matter, by the president). Should the participants in the filibuster be disproportionately from small states,

then the filibuster only reinforces the already entrenched disproportionate power of the small states. As a matter of fact, though, the politics (and political morality) of the filibuster may be more complex, not
least because of the disproportionality of the allocation of votes in the
Senate.

As of 2006, the ostensible Democratic "minority" of the Senate in
fact represents a majority of the country overall. That is, if one adds up
the populations of the states, using either official 2000 census data or
unofficial 2004 estimates of population, one discovers that Democrats
represent states with a total population of roughly 3 million more persons than do Republicans (splitting the population evenly in the cases
of states represented by both one Democrat and one Republican). The
imbalance was even greater before the 2004 election, when Florida and
South Dakota were represented by two Democrats and Georgia, North
Carolina, and South Carolina by one Democrat (though Illinois had a
Republican senator then). Or consider the fact that the ninety-six Democratic candidates who ran for the Senate between 2000 and 2004 received a total of 99,670,071 votes while the ninety-nine Republican
candidates in the same period received only 97,300,545 votes.[49] (Apparently, the Democrats did not bother to contest four elections of the
total hundred, while the Republicans sat out one race.) Given the close-
ness of the voting totals, one might, therefore, expect a closely divided
Senate such as occurred in 2000, when the initial allocation was 50–50
until Vermont's Jim Jeffords left the Republican party to become an
independent and thereby transferred control to the Democrats. Instead,
Republicans hold fifty-five seats, the Democrats forty-four, and the independent Jeffords one. The current division of power in the Senate is
a complete artifact of the particular states electing particular senators.
It has literally nothing to do with measuring national majority sentiment.
"Majority rule" within the Senate may have only a random relationship
to majority rule within the country as a whole.

Should this matter to other than political junkies? Much of Dahl's
argument is devoted to the offense to democratic values, expressed in
the mantra of one-person, one vote, when there is such a patent inequality of voting power. But to pitch the argument at this level of
abstraction may not be enough to persuade the ordinary voter who is

not a devotee of political theory. One might share an aesthetic distaste for such manifest inequalities, but feel that this doesn't count as a breakage sufficient to require fixing. So the real question is whether these abstract inequalities translate into actual differences in political outcomes. How are the great bulk of American citizens, who live in large states, genuinely victimized by the inequalities of power instantiated in the organization of the Senate? Why should they find this a sufficient reason to refuse to assent to the Constitution in the forthcoming referendum?

Lynn Baker and Samuel Dinkin offer a terse summary of the practical consequences of the inequality of voting power in the Senate:

> First, the Senate ensures that the federal government will systematically redistribute income from the large states to small states. Second, it provides racial minorities a voice in the federal lawmaking process that is disproportionately small relative to their numbers. Third, it protects diversity among the states by making federal homogenizing legislation more difficult to pass.[50]

Their analysis was based largely on formal models of political economy.

A seminal recent book by two political scientists drew together a great deal of empirical data to go along with more formal analysis. The aptly titled *Sizing Up the Senate: The Unequal Consequences of Equal Representation*[51] demonstrates at length the subtle and not-so-subtle consequences of equal representation, which should indeed generate concern, if not outright anger, among residents of large states. A subtle consequence: Small-state senators have greater incentives to concentrate on a few issues central to the bulk of their constituents, such as, for example, subsidies for growing wheat or corn or, as viewers of *West Wing* were reminded in a notable episode, transforming corn into ethanol.

A large-state senator cannot concentrate on such issues in the same way because it is likely, in a large state, that significant numbers of voters have conflicting interests. New York's Senator Hillary Rodham Clinton, for example, may have upstate farmers to worry about, but she also must take into account the potential costs of certain agricultural policies to her urban constituents who must buy groceries. Concomitantly, if she focuses only on the urban voters, she becomes vulnerable to a challenger who promises to give the rural interests more attention. Lee and Oppenheimer suggest that small-state senators "tend to seek assignment to committees that help them obtain particularized benefits for their [more or less homogeneous] constituents."[52] They quote one small-state senator as noting that "you can run for the U.S. Congress saying you are going to represent the _____ industry totally and not do anything else," as distinguished from "the diversity you'd have to represent in a large state."[53] Thus, assignments to the committees dealing with agriculture or energy are more likely to be prized by small-state senators than placement on more general committees like the Judiciary Committee or the Foreign Relations Committee.[54]

Senators from small states need generally to spend less time on constituency contact. Paradoxically, though, it is far easier for a resident of a small state to gain actual access to his or her senator, which simply compounds the advantage of small-state residents vis-à-vis their large-state counterparts.[55] (A North Dakota acquaintance reports that there is nothing special about the opportunity to meet and talk with one of the state's two senators. Politics there continues to be a "retail" enterprise, as distinguished from the distinctly impersonal and "wholesale" politics practiced in large states.) Furthermore, and not unrelated to the difference between retail and wholesale campaigning, small-state senators usually spend less time raising campaign funds. For all of these reasons, Lee and Oppenheimer demonstrate, small-state senators are more likely to become party leaders. Indeed, these political scientists go so far as to suggest that it is "unlikely, if not impossible, for senators from the most populous states to become party leaders."[56] Consider in this context that Senator Harry Reid of Nevada (2000 population of approximately 2 million) succeeded South Dakota senator Tom Daschle (757,000) as the Democratic leader in the Senate following Daschle's defeat in the 2004 election. Similarly, Bill Frist of Tennessee (5,700,000) was the Republican choice to succeed Trent Lott of Mississippi (2,850,000) following the latter's resignation from the leadership following a controversy over remarks he had made in praise of Strom Thurmond. Lott, of course, had succeeded Robert Dole of Kansas (2,670,000). Republicans seem to draw their leadership more from midsized than from small-sized cases, but neither party seems interested in looking to the most populous states for their leaders. The House of Representatives offers a more complex picture, not least because all congresspersons represent districts of close to the same size. Still, the Speaker of the House is Dennis Hastert of Illinois, and the House majority leader prior to his own forced resignation was Tom DeLay of Texas. DeLay was immediately succeeded by Ray Blount from Missouri (another midsized state), who was then displaced by John Boehner of Ohio, a significantly larger state. And the current Democratic leader in the House is Nancy Pelosi from California.

Again, one might regard this as simply "inside the beltway" (or political science) gossip unless one can point to tangible differences in political outcomes connected to the distorted voting power possessed by the small states, the greater constituent access by small-state residents, and the increased access by small-state senators to positions of institutional leadership. Consider, then, that small-state senators have significant advantages beyond their simple vote when bargaining with their colleagues on what is to be included in—or dropped from—legislative proposals. "Senate apportionment produces a dynamic whereby coalition leaders (regardless of the size of the state they represent) have incentives to seek out senators from less populous states to build winning coalitions at a relatively low cost to the program budget." Small-state senators are thus well positioned to receive windfalls that are less likely to be available to large-state senators, who, as noted above, cannot be so single-minded in pursuit of given legislative ends and whose demands may also be far more expensive than those made by small-state senators.[57]

It now becomes readily understandable that "the smallest states are remarkably advantaged over all other states in per capita terms" with regard to enjoying benefits from federally financed programs.[58] Sometimes, this is the result of direct programs, as with the now-infamous Bridge to Nowhere discussed at the beginning of this chapter. Other times, it is the result of complex funding formulas that, by guaranteeing all states a given minimum of funds, regardless of population, end up inordinately benefiting small states. If one wishes confirmation from the daily headlines, one need only read of the almost lunatic formula by which Congress has been allocating funds ostensibly for "homeland security." Each resident of Wyoming receives exactly seven times the per capita funding received by residents of New York, $37.94 as against $5.42.[50] And, given what we have learned about bridge funding, it surely occasions no surprise to discover that each Alaskan is the beneficiary of $30.42 of Homeland Security funds. Surely, this is not the way a serious country would confront what its leaders call the "global war against terrorism," unless our leaders seriously believe that al Qaeda is a greater threat to Wyoming, Alaska, North Dakota ($30.81/person), and Montana ($22.86) than to New York, California ($5.05), or the important port state of Maryland ($7.60). Interestingly, the District of Columbia, which doesn't even have a vote in Congress, was supported in 2004 at a level of $33.72 per capita, but one presumes that this was because members of Congress felt themselves to be at risk and therefore were willing to spend accordingly. All of this amply endorses Lee and Oppenheimer's less anecdotal and more scientific "model predict[ing] that the smallest states will receive about $120 per capita [in overall federal expenditures] while the largest states receive only $82."[60]

Citizens of the District of Columbia might feel well protected with regard to their security—at least if they live near members of Congress. They otherwise have a special reason to vote yes in the forthcoming referendum: They lack any vote at all in Congress. They do have a nonvoting delegate to the House of Representatives, but not even this kind of symbolic representation in the Senate. Several years ago, citizens of the District drafted a "state constitution," and Congress in 1978 proposed an amendment reading that "[f]or purposes of representation in the Congress, election of the President and Vice President, and article V of this Constitution, the District constituting the seat of government of the United States shall be treated as though it were a State."[61] This would have given the District a voting representative in the House and two members in the Senate. The proposed amendment basically went nowhere and expired in 1985. One contributing reason for the paucity of ratifications, one suspects, is that Republican states had no incentive at all—other than abstract fairness—to give the Democrats almost guaranteed additional seats in the House and Senate. I must confess to my own ambivalence about the proposed amendment inasmuch as I see no good reason at all to add what would in effect be yet one more small state with grossly disproportionate voting power. As a Democrat, I would applaud the additional votes; as an American, I believe that it would be far better to eliminate the small-state advantage than to accept a notion of state equality that leads to such manifest inequality in the actual level by which the American citizenry is represented. Friends of mine from Washington correctly protest against "taxation without representation." It does not follow, though, that they are entitled to taxation with overrepresentation.

Two legal scholars, Yale law professor William Eskridge and Vanderbilt law professor Suzanna Sherry, have each proclaimed the Senate to be the least defensible and most harmful aspect of the modern Constitution.[62] Each used the same example of the impact of the malapportioned voting power of the senators: the 52–48 confirmation of Clarence Thomas to become a lifelong justice of the U.S. Supreme Court. Sherry notes that the senators voting against Thomas came from states containing 52 percent of the population, whereas his supporters represented only 48 percent. Eskridge argues that if the House had had the power to vote yea or nay on Thomas, then, assuming the individual senators' votes would have been reflected in their state delegations to the House (with such delegations being split in those states, as in California or New York, where one senator voted to confirm and the other to reject the nomination), Thomas would have failed by a close but nonetheless decisive vote of 224–211. Sherry notes that if the Republican senators from New York (Alfonse D'Amato) and California (John Seymour) had opposed Thomas, which would have meant his opposition by senators representing 62 percent of the country, he would still have been confirmed because Vice President Dan Quayle would have been able to cast the decisive vote as president of the Senate.

The equal-vote rule in the Senate makes an absolute shambles of the idea that in the United States the majority of the people rule. At least seven times in the sixty-eight years between the 65th and 99th Congresses, the notional "majority party" in control of the Senate was elected from states with less than a majority of the population.[63] On many other occasions, the minority party benefited from the apportionment bias inasmuch as it gained more seats in the Senate than would have been the case had population alone determined the allocation of votes. Interestingly, in only two of the forty-one Senate sessions analyzed by Lee and Oppenheimer was the consequence of the apportionment neutral in the sense that the allocation of seats matched national voting totals.

I noted earlier the shift in party control of the Senate in 2001 because of the "defection" of Vermont senator Jim Jeffords from the Republican party. Though in some sense this might have been just from the perspective of majoritarianism, given the voting totals noted earlier, it also underlines the arbitrary degree of power enjoyed by a small-state senator. Jeffords had been reelected to the Senate in 2000 with 189,133 votes.[64] Had the Republican senators in fact won a majority of the national vote, they could be more legitimately excused for the animosity they felt toward Jeffords after he left their party. As it was, however, his "betrayal" of the Republican party simply made it possible for the national majority to rule, at least until the elections of 2002 and then, even more so, 2004 operated, courtesy of the small-state advantage, to give the Republicans fifty-five votes as against the Democrats' forty-four (with Jeffords remaining, notionally, an independent). At the present time, a bill could pass the Senate "with the votes of 51 Republicans whose share of the total [national] vote was less than 20%."[65]

One might also note that the small states tend to be far less urban and to have far fewer nonwhite residents, both absolutely and as a percentage of overall population. At least the District of Columbia, were it treated as a state, would increase the urbanity of the Senate, and it might well send two African Americans to the Senate, which is the same number of African Americans elected to the Senate in the entire twentieth century. Poverty statistics are more complex, since many small states suffer from rural poverty that is certainly no less wrenching than its urban counterpart. But no one could seriously describe the small states as "representative" of the overall American mosaic.[66]

It should now be clear that the equal representation of stunningly unequal numbers of voters has consequences that go beyond giving offense to devotees of democratic theory. There is a steady redistribution of resources from large states to small states.[67] This could easily be justified—at least if one is a political liberal—if there were reason to believe that largeness was correlated with richness and smallness with poverty. There is not. As the late Senator Daniel Patrick Moynihan noted, in 1999 only New Mexico had a greater percentage of its citizens living in poverty than New York. Yet, because New York ranked forty-first in per capita levels of payments and services received from the federal government, this meant, practically speaking, that New Yorkers were exporting significant amounts of money to other states with less poverty. Over the period of 1963–1999, New York taxpayers paid out $252 billion more in taxes than were received back in federal payments or services.[68] Other major outpayers were California, Illinois, and New Jersey, each with a significant level of poverty and other needs among its own citizens.[69] For Moynihan, one implication was a need to rethink some of the assumptions behind the New Deal, with its emphasis on federal programs financed through ever-greater federal revenues. As one journalist wrote, "New Deal–type government has become a bad deal for New York" and other large states.[70] At the very least, it should be clear that these consequences of our legislative system and the incentives it creates with regard to patterns of federal spending may have unanticipated political valence.

The Senate represents a travesty of the democratic ideal, with consequences that are harmful to most members of the American political community. It alone provides ample reason for anyone who lives in a large state to reject the current Constitution and to refer it to a new constitutional convention for redrafting.

Lee and Oppenheimer make the profound point that the advantages accruing to small states cannot possibly be defended on the basis of the "original intent of the framers," even if one emphasizes that it was the framers themselves who decided to capitulate to the demands of small states for voting equality in the Senate. But they inhabited a country whose total population at the time was approximately 3 million, near to but less than the population in 2000 of Connecticut or Oregon. Even those framers who looked forward to an ever-expanding United States had literally no conception of how much the country would grow in population. Thomas Jefferson, for example, "estimated that it would take one hundred generations to populate the new territory" of the Louisiana Purchase, which more than doubled the size of the country in 1803.[71] Indeed, three of our five largest states—California, Texas, and Florida—were not even part of the territory of the United States in 1787. The framers were designing a political system for a quite tiny country (in population) that reached westward only to the Mississippi River (and, of course, it hardly controlled the entire Mississippi, the delta of which was then held by Spain). It has expanded almost a hundred times in population—the 2000 census counted approximately 281 million residents, with another 10 million or so living abroad—and now extends to the mid-Pacific and, if one includes Puerto Rico, to the mid-Caribbean.

Moreover, the framers envisioned senators as quasi emissaries from their state legislatures, even if they also enjoyed the valuable independence that comes from receiving their salary from the national government and enjoying a guaranteed six-year term of office. However visionary some of the framers might have been, they could not conceivably "have foreseen the effects of apportionment on Senate elections,"[72] since the very notion of popular elections for the Senate was unavailable to them. One can go so far as to say that almost the entire development of American politics and society since 1787 "has caused Senate apportionment to have other effects that the framers could not have anticipated."[73] Indeed, it is worth quoting Lee and Oppenheimer at some length with regard to the utter irrelevance of looking to the generation of 1787 for guidance as to how we today should assess the allocation of voting power in the Senate:

> They drafted the Constitution before the invention of the modern political party and thus could not have foreseen the effects of apportionment on partisan control of the Senate. The same obviously applies to the ways Senate apportionment shapes the strategic behavior of senators. The framers could hardly have expected that it would influence senators' choice of committee assignments, their level of national media coverage,[74] or their ability to pursue party leadership. None of these institutions—the congressional committee system, national news media, or institutionalized party leadership—existed in 1787.[75]

Relying on the wisdom of the framers with regard to the Senate today is the equivalent of relying on the wisdom of George Washington as a general to decide how to fight the war in Iraq or, even more to the point perhaps, to respond to threats of nuclear war. He was an able, perhaps a great, general and leader. But this does not mean that he had the slightest comprehension of how one should conduct warfare even after the development of the more-or-less modern rifle in 1850, let alone tanks, planes, and nuclear weapons.

One can readily understand the forces behind the original Connecticut Compromise of 1787 that gave us our particular Senate in the first place. It was relatively clear that the small states would simply refuse to agree to any constitution that did not include equal voting power in the Senate. Opponents of such equality, like James Madison, were forced to give up rather than run the almost certain risk of failure of the entire enterprise. In the same manner, one can understand why the equal vote in the Senate is protected even against Article V amendment inasmuch as it specifies that "no State, without its Consent, shall be deprived of its equal Suffrage in the Senate." This presumably requires unanimous consent for any constitutional amendment that would change the allocation of voting power. As a practical matter, it is almost impossible to imagine that Wyoming or Alaska would assent to the elimination of its advantage under the current rules. Every Alaskan—all 629,000 of them —has a good reason to vote no in our upcoming referendum and thus support the status quo. For them, the allocation of power in the Senate is a gift that keeps on giving. But every Californian—all 34 million of them, regardless of their political party identification—has an equally good reason to vote yes on this basis alone.

THE SPECIAL PROBLEM OF DIVIDED GOVERNMENT: HOW SEPARATE DO WE WANT OUR INSTITUTIONS TO BE?

The earlier discussion of bicameralism and its role in delaying legislation was quite formal and a bit abstract. It did not, for example, take into account the extraordinarily important role that political parties play in our political system.[76] Most of the framers were appalled by the idea of political parties, which they identified as "factions" committed to gaining what they termed "partial" interests rather than being truly devoted to the general interest. This basically apolitical vision of American politics collapsed by the mid-1790s, and most political scientists today would argue that a strong system of contending political parties is essential to the achievement of democratic ideals. Be that as it may, the intersection of modern political parties and the divided institutional structure of the U.S. government poses its own problems.

Political parties may help to make possible the overcoming of the fragmentation generated by separate branches of government.[77] This, almost by definition, is most likely to be true when one party controls both houses of Congress and the presidency—and, therefore, is likely as well to gain control of the judiciary because of the commonality of party interests between the president who nominates judges and the Senate that confirms them. One problem, ironically, is that one-party dominance of the national political institutions, as has been the case since 2001, also calls into question the presumed virtue of bicameralism in promoting a politics of consensus instead of majoritarianism. But most readers of this book have spent most of their lives under a "divided government," where one party controlled the White House while the other party controlled at least one house, and quite possibly both houses, of the Congress. More has been written about the problems—even dangers—of such divided government than about one-party government.

James L. Sundquist, a political scientist who has given much thought to this issue, believes that the Constitution fundamentally discourages the likelihood of creating an effective government. He views the frequency of elections for the House of Representatives—the entire membership runs for reelection every two years—as impairing the achievement of a strong consensus among president, House, and Senate as to what the country needs.[78]

One should realize that many of the ostensible problems attached to divided government are derived from the presidential veto power, discussed earlier.[79] If the president has no veto power, then, as a practical matter, any deadlock that occurs will be between the House and

Senate. Should Congress be able to unite behind particular legislation, it would simply become law, though it could always be challenged as unconstitutional in the courts. But this is not the constitutional system we have, and therefore there is a far higher probability of divided government inasmuch as a political coalition must capture *three* institutions— House, Senate, and presidency—in order to be assured of escaping both figurative and literal vetoes over its political agenda.

One might argue that divided government is exactly the American way, in a far deeper sense than merely pointing to the phenomenon of different parties controlling Congress or the presidency. The U.S. Constitution is built on the framework of separated institutions, with different powers and different electoral bases. They were meant not only to be separate, in a variety of complicated senses, some of which will be explored below, but also to check and balance each another, presumably in order to preclude the possibility of oppression or even tyranny.

An anecdote from a 1987 trip to China, where I participated in a seminar on the Constitution on the occasion of its bicentennial, offers an especially vivid illustration of the consequences of our institutionally divided structure of government. During the week that I was there, the Congress, by joint resolution, had condemned the oppression by China of the people of Tibet. But the official spokesman for the U.S. Department of State had announced that the United States treats events in Tibet as an internal matter for the People's Republic of China, and therefore the United States had no comment on what was happening there. A Chinese scholar was justifiably confused and asked me, "What *is* the position of your government?" My reply was that the United States did not have *a* government in the sense that his question suggested. Her Majesty, the queen of England, might have "a government" whose policies on any given issue are instantly identifiable. We in the United States, on the other hand, have distinctly separated institutions that on occasion sharply contend with one another to make declarations in the name of the United States. In this instance, Congress had one policy, the president another. The central challenge facing all presidents is to form a government in a sense that goes far beyond simply appointing persons of their own choice to cabinet positions. Sundquist is concerned with *both* aspects of divided government:

those produced by the very institutional structure of our Constitution and those generated by the fact that each of these institutions may on occasion be controlled by members of different political parties.

One-party government has been the exception rather than the rule since the end of World War II (when Democrat Harry Truman was faced almost immediately with a Republican Congress between 1946 and 1948). Although at least one eminent political scientist has suggested that divided government makes no real difference with regard to the prospects for passing important legislation,[80] I suspect that most persons are unconvinced. Or, even if he was correct about the era about which he was writing, when Democratic and Republican leaders and ordinary representatives and senators often enjoyed cooperative relationships and even friendships with one another, the party system as it developed in the 1980s and thereafter is far more polarized, with cooperation between the two parties often nonexistent. I believe, for example, that an event of truly historic importance was the circulation by William Kristol, a leading Republican conservative strategist—he had been chief of staff for Vice President Dan Quayle during the first Bush administration—in December 1993 of a strategy document emphasizing that Republicans should oppose any and all Clinton health care proposals "sight unseen." The reason was simple: Any success on the part of the Clinton administration in alleviating the health care dilemma would constitute a "serious political threat to the Republican party." To a substantial degree, Kristol's advice was well taken; what was widely perceived as Clinton's failure to move forward on health policy contributed to the sea-change congressional elections of 1994.

Sundquist endorses the idea of extending the length of terms in the House of Representatives to four years. Moreover, he would have all of the representatives elected during presidential election years, because he believes that this would lead to fewer divided governments and, therefore, would increase the ease with which a president could achieve the legislation that was, at least in theory, endorsed by the electorate. If that is thought to be too radical (or simply unwise, as I believe is the case), then one could emulate California and elect half the membership every two years, with each member serving a four-year term. Suffice it to say that on balance I do not see the two-year term as a major reason to vote against the Constitution, though anyone persuaded by Sundquist's probing arguments should certainly believe that this is a serious deficiency of the present Constitution.

Sundquist does not address an increasingly obvious cost of "unified" government. The capture of both houses of Congress and the presidency by the same party significantly diminishes the possibility of serious legislative oversight of the executive branch. It turns out that James Madison was simply incorrect in *Federalist*, No. 51, when he suggested that the structure of separated branches would assure that each branch would be eager to check the other inasmuch as the interests of representatives and senators will ostensibly "be connected with the constitutional rights" of their own institutions.[81] As Daryl Levinson (no relation) has demonstrated in a brilliant article, most members of Congress are far less concerned with protecting the constitutional prerogatives of the House and Senate to oversee the executive than in gaining reelection and, perhaps more significant with regard to the present discussion, remaining loyal to their political party.[82] The president automatically is the party leader and can usually count on loyalists in Congress to circle the wagons around what are invariably described as "partisan" attacks on executive actions. Even David Mayhew, who downplays the importance for legislative achievement of the difference between unified and divided government, agrees that unified one-party government brings with it far fewer investigations by Congress of potential presidential misconduct or simple ineptitude.[83]

Sundquist is also critical of the second clause of section 6 of Article I:

> No Senator or Representative shall, during the Time for which he was elected, be appointed to any civil Office under the Authority of the United States, which shall have been created, or the Emoluments whereof shall have been encreased [*sic*] during such time; and no Person holding any Office under the United States, shall be a member of either House during his Continuation in Office.

What this means, in ordinary language, is that no person can serve in the executive and legislative branches at the same time.[84]

The source of this provision, as Sundquist writes, is a concern to create "a safeguard against corruption of the legislature."[85] The fear most often expressed was that legislators would create a myriad of unnecessary offices for themselves to fill: George Mason of Virginia warned that without such a prohibition "we shall have ambassadors to every petty state in Europe—the little republic of St. Marino not excepted," and Massachusetts's Elbridge Gerry equally spoke of the "intrigues of ambitious men for displacing proper offices, in order to create vacancies for themselves."[86] Yet there was also a concern that allowing members of Congress to hold executive positions as well would give too much power to the president, who could dangle such jobs as plums to tempt representatives and senators who might otherwise have opposed the president's policies. To be sure, there were those who thought it important to allow such temptation. Alexander Hamilton rejected the notion that this would constitute "corruption." Instead, he argued, it constituted "an essential part of the weight which maintained the equilibrium of the Constitution."[87] Maryland's John Francis Mercer agreed, warning that to deprive the chief executive of this bargaining chip would turn him into "a mere phantom of authority."[88] Sundquist notes, "Those who . . . preferred, if not a phantom, at most a weak and controlled executive, supported the prohibition."[89]

Sundquist argues that this ban on interbranch service no longer serves its anticorruption purpose inasmuch as "membership in the Congress has become a full-time job with pay and prestige superior to all but the highest posts in the executive branch," not to mention that most members of Congress can expect a significantly longer tenure in office than is true of members of the executive branch.[90] It is, therefore, relatively rare that members of Congress resign their posts to join the executive. Two recent counterexamples—Porter Goss, who became director of the Central Intelligence Agency, and Rob Portman, who became the president's trade representative, were from the House—just as was the case with Norman Minetta, the sole Democrat in President Bush's cabinet (as secretary of transportation). Senators appear far more unwilling to trade their prerogatives of office for jobs in the executive branch even at the cabinet level. One suspects that John Ashcroft would have preferred to have been reelected senator from

Missouri instead of being available, because he had been fired by the Missouri electorate, to accept President Bush's offer to become attorney general. William H. Cohen was the sitting senator from Maine when he accepted an appointment as President Clinton's secretary of defense in December 1996; he had, however, in effect already retired inasmuch as he did not run for reelection in that year.

To be sure, there are occasional exceptions, as when Ohio senator William Saxbe accepted President Nixon's entreaty to become attorney general to succeed the disgraced John Mitchell. And, interestingly, the so-called Emoluments Clause came into play since the Congress had only recently increased the salary of the attorney general. The Senate held several days of interesting hearings on how to interpret the clause, and the ultimate decision was to allow Saxbe to take office so long as he waived any right to claim the salary increase and accepted only the salary offered prior to the legislation.[91]

If one accepts the proposition that the clause, however much it might have made sense in 1787, is no longer very useful today, at least with regard to its original purpose, then the obvious question is the degree of harm it does. Answering this question requires us to decide how much we prefer strongly separated branches of government—especially when different political parties control the separate branches—as against some mixture of the branches. Parliamentary systems, of course, lack any serious separation at all inasmuch as the dominant power (or coalition) within the parliament selects the executive officers, who are members themselves of the existing parliament. Tony Blair was obviously under no duty to resign his membership in Parliament in order to become prime minister of Great Britain; the very notion would strike anyone from the United Kingdom as little short of bizarre. Indeed, Blair's status as a member of Parliament is perhaps most dramatically instantiated when he engages in the weekly "question period," when he is subject to often vigorous and hostile questioning by his fellow parliamentarians. American presidents, on the other hand, need never subject themselves to such interrogation, for which ever more infrequent news conferences serve as an exceedingly pale and inadequate substitute.

In any event, Sundquist sees more costs than benefits to the current operation of the Ineligibility Clause. Allowing the appointment of some members of Congress to executive branch positions, without forcing them to resign (or even to accept a diminished salary should they have had the bad luck to be appointed immediately after a salary increase had been voted by Congress) "would broaden the range of talent available to a president when he assembles his administration."[92] It could make great sense, to take Sundquist's example, to appoint the chair of a small business subcommittee in the House or Senate as the head of the Small Business Administration or the chair of a veterans affairs committee to preside over the Veterans Administration, even if we would certainly expect them to cede their chairs to others in order to control for obvious conflicts of interest with regard to congressional oversight. But, as Sundquist argues, "Authors of laws could be invited to take responsibility for their execution."[93] Just as much to the point is that they could report back to their colleagues about the actual operation of the laws with a credibility (and, not insignificantly, the potential power to do something about it) that ordinary executive branch officials lack when they are subjected to oversight through the ordinary congressional committee process.

As suggested earlier, ultimate assessment of the Ineligibility Clause (and of many other constitutional provisions) requires a basic decision with regard to the degree of parliamentary government one wishes. Suffice it to say for now that few other countries in the world have adopted our degree of separation of powers, and many of these, by any conceivable criteria, are as free, as democratic, and as desirable places in which to live as the United States. At the very least, this proves that our obsession with keeping the branches separate cannot easily be defended on the ground that it is necessary to achieve any of the great ends of the Preamble. I will return to some of the issues posed by the separation of branches in the next chapter, which will concentrate on the presidency.

THE CONSTITUTION AS INADVERTENT PROMOTER OF DISCONTINUITY IN GOVERNMENT (AND PRESIDENTIAL DICTATORSHIP)

The next issue to be treated is almost certainly unfamiliar to most readers of this book, including professional legal academics. Yet, in the aftermath of the terrorist attacks of September 11, 2001, and the justified fears that many have about the possibility of a devastating attack on Washington, D.C., it may be one of the most important issues raised in this book. Full appreciation of the problem requires understanding the interplay of various constitutional provisions regarding the organization of both the House and the Senate. Consider first what happens in the case of a vacancy. With regard to the Senate, "[I]f Vacancies happen by Resignation, or otherwise . . . , the Executive [of the state] thereof may" appoint a replacement to serve until a successor can be elected. This is retained by the Seventeenth Amendment, which in general requires the popular election of senators. The drafters were being rather tactful in their use of the word "otherwise," given that the most common explanation for the occurrence of a vacancy is the death of a senator. The provision regarding members of the House is interestingly different: "When vacancies happen in the Representation from any State, the Executive Authority thereof shall issue Writs of Election to fill such Vacancies."[94] That is, there is no such thing, within the conceptual world of the Constitution, as an appointed member of the House of Representatives. Each and every member of the House comes with the imprimatur of support from his or her constituents. Senators, on the other hand, can in certain circumstances be appointed by their states' governors, even if they must run for election in relatively short order; this has come to mean in most instances the next regularly scheduled statewide election.

So far, so good. It is hard to summon up any deeply felt opposition—or perhaps any feelings at all—concerning what might be called the "replacement rules" for the House and Senate, at least in normal times. But we are increasingly being told that these are not normal times. Instead, we must think of the possibility of terrorist assaults on our basic institutions. The Pentagon was attacked directly by one of the planes on September 11, 2001, and it is widely believed that the Capitol or the White House was the destination of United Airlines flight 93 that went down over Pennsylvania. So we are forced to imagine a future attack on Washington that kills or disables vast numbers of representatives and disables a majority of senators. (The reason for the difference in verbs will become clear in just a moment.)

At this point, it becomes necessary to consider an even more obscure part of the Constitution known only to those interested in the
arcana of congressional procedure: Article I, section 5, provides that
"a Majority of each [of the House and Senate] shall constitute a Quorum
to do Business." That is, a majority of the membership of each house—
normally, at this point in history, 218 representatives and 51 senators—
must be available in order for the house to be legally constituted in
order to conduct business. Return now to the hypothetical attack,
which kills or disables, say, 225 members of the House and disables
51 members of the Senate.

Begin with the House. If the members are killed, as a technical
matter there is no problem with regard to reaching a quorum to do
business, because one could easily read "a Majority of each" to refer
to actual, living members. So, as a theoretical matter, if, say, 215 representatives survived, in whatever condition, then only 108 would have
to be present in order to do business, and legislation could be passed
with the approval of only 55 of these 108. As a theoretical matter, if
only three survive, two of them could constitute a quorum and, should
they agree, pass all the legislation they might desire. It should be obvious that this creates problems of its own with regard both to democratic legitimacy and to the quality of deliberation one would want
following such an attack (or, for that matter, at any other time). One
would, I believe, want a full complement of representatives as soon as
possible. Yet, under the Constitution, *there is no way of filling the vacancies in the House other than by election.* This means that the House
would be deprived of literally hundreds of members for at least the
30–45 days that is the bare minimum in which one could hold an election. It should go without saying that one might find this far too short
a period in a country traumatized by such an attack, which would have
other things on its mind than choosing new representatives.

No such problems are presented if a majority of the Senate is killed,
since the Constitution does indeed provide for the immediate appointment of successors by state governors. At least in theory, were all 100
senators the victims of a terrorist attack, the Senate as an institution
could be replaced the very next day by gubernatorial appointments.

The more serious problem, ironically, is presented not by death, but, rather, by *disability*, and this may even be true for representatives as well. If one reads the Constitution to require the presence of a majority of its *living* members, which is certainly the most plausible reading, then it could well be the case that neither the House nor the Senate could muster a quorum at a time of national trauma, because a majority of its membership would be physically unable to come to the Capitol or wherever the body might wish to convene. Or, should some fluke result in the disability of hundreds of representatives while senators either escaped unscathed or were killed, the Senate could meet, but the House could not. Under bicameralism, this is fatal to the legitimate passage of any laws.

The Constitution is written for what might be termed "retail" vacancies, which occur only occasionally and are easily subject to being handled by the existing rules, which require an election to fill a vacancy in the House and a senator to be dead prior to a gubernatorial appointment of a successor. Should "wholesale" vacancies occur, however, the present Constitution is nothing less than a ticking time bomb. It would itself add to the degree of national catastrophe by instantly rendering inoperative or illegitimate what may be the most basic, because the most clearly tied to the people—as is the case even with the malapportioned Senate—of our governmental institutions. One might well believe that remaining national leaders would properly ignore these constitutional provisions and engage in needed, nationally supported, improvisation. This is to say, though, that almost literally one of the first things our leaders would do is put aside what are in fact significant, albeit arcane, provisions of the Constitution because they were properly regarded as dysfunctional.

I am not the first person to notice this problem. Indeed, a remarkable and genuinely bipartisan commission convened jointly by the liberal Brookings Institution and the conservative American Enterprise Institute—co-chaired by the late Lloyd Cutler and former senator Alan Simpson—has studied this problem and recommended a corrective constitutional amendment that could respond to this exigency.[95] Even if one regards the possibility as unlikely—the equivalent of a Force 5 hurricane or a dangerous tsunami—we have recently learned to our peril that "unlikely" does not mean "impossible." The prudent thing to do is to purchase insurance against the catastrophic damage likely to ensue upon its occurrence. The proposed Twenty-eighth Amendment would provide just such insurance, by allowing states to pass legislation creating alternatives to elections to replace representatives in the case of such wholesale deaths and to allow governors to replace disabled senators, at least temporarily, should they be unable to meet their legislative duties. The proposed amendment has been introduced by Texas senator John Cornyn and has been the subject of hearings before the Senate Judiciary Committee (in which I participated). It is an eminently sensible response to a constitutional glitch that only recently has been diagnosed.

At the time of this writing (May 2006), it has gone nowhere. A large part of the explanation is the recalcitrant opposition of Representative James Sensenbrenner, the chair of the House Judiciary Committee, who is adamantly opposed to any deviation from election as the source of a representative's presence in the House. Alan Simpson, who represented Wyoming for many years in the Senate, has accused Sensenbrenner, a fellow conservative Republican—it should be obvious that this issue is not a partisan one in standard terms—of behaving "rudely" in refusing even to hold hearings on the amendment or otherwise "listen . . . to one shred of what we are saying."[96] And even if two-thirds of the House and Senate could be persuaded to propose a corrective amendment, it would still be at the mercy both of the possibility that thirteen legislative houses in the fifty states would resist ratifying it and of the sheer passage of time that might well be necessary to gain the assent of thirty-eight states.

Interestingly, Congress and the states did act responsibly by proposing and ratifying in 1967 the Twenty-fifth Amendment, which addresses the problem of a disabled president. In a very grim sense, the United States was fortunate that John F. Kennedy was killed instantly in 1963 rather than, as with Woodrow Wilson following a serious stroke in 1919, left significantly impaired. Had a surviving Kennedy been so selfish as Wilson was—he was patently unable to perform his duties, and his wife in a significant sense became acting president—then the country would have faced a political and constitutional nightmare. The Twenty-fifth Amendment, at least in theory, offers a solution to such a dilemma by allowing "the Vice President and a majority of either the principal officers of the executive departments [the cabinet] or of such other body as Congress may by law provide," to transmit to the leaders of the House and the Senate "their written declaration that the President is unable to discharge the powers and duties of his office." In such a case, "the Vice President shall immediately assume the powers and duties of the office as Acting President," presumably until the president regains his capacities to govern. This part of the amendment has never been tested. Such "Acting Presidents" as there have been were explicitly delegated their brief time in office by presidents undergoing operations, and those presidents resumed their office upon rapid recovery. Further historical research will presumably reveal whether Ronald Reagan was already suffering from Alzheimer's disease during his second term of office and whether, therefore, a responsible cabinet should have invoked the procedures of the amendment. In any event, the Constitution does provide, at least formally, for a solution to the problem of the disabled president. It is with regard to Congress that the Constitution is fatally defective.

This may be yet another instance of a constitutional deficiency that in itself probably does not constitute sufficient reason to vote for a new convention. Yet, when added to the many other deficiencies, including some with less theoretical costs to the public weal, it should add to the confidence with which one supports the convention. A revised constitution would surely respond to the problem identified by the commission and try to prevent a circumstance arising that would lead, as night follows day, to a presidential dictatorship (assuming that the president is alive and able to dictate). It is unthinkable, after all, that we would really tolerate the delay before Congress could be "properly" reconstituted. We would instead demand—and no doubt get—strong presidential (or other) actions predicated on the claim that "necessity" licenses a president, or perhaps the head of the joint chiefs of staff, to act independently of any congressional authorization and, in effect, to become both the legislator and the enforcer of the law. There is a deep irony presented by the quorum problem: To a great extent, our existing Constitution can be understood only against a background of an almost paranoid concern for the separation of powers and concomitant checking and balancing of one institution by another. Yet the mixture of a catastrophic attack and the operation of quite esoteric provisions concerning the replacement of vacancies and quorum rules almost guarantees the de facto absence of a functioning Congress and the concomitant centralization of basically dictatorial power in the president, if we are lucky.

THE QUESTIONABLE LEGITIMACY OF LAME-DUCK CONGRESSES

I conclude this chapter with a look at another obscure provision that, nonetheless, has deep practical importance. The final clause of Article I, Section 4, provides: "The Congress shall assemble at least once in every Year, and such Meeting shall be on the first Monday in December, unless they shall by Law appoint a different day." Although it is possible to believe that it made sense when drafted in 1787, it turned out to be a bizarre, almost surely pernicious feature of the Constitution in practice. What this means in practice is that new members of Congress elected in, say, 1800 or 1860—I do not choose these dates at random—were not to convene and start exercising legislative power until December 1801 or 1861, unless called into earlier special session by the president, who would not take office until March 4 of 1801 or 1861. So, in the famous deadlocked election of 1800, when the Democratic-Republicans Thomas Jefferson and Aaron Burr were tied in the electoral vote, the deadlock was broken not by the new spate of Jeffersonians elected in the 1800 elections but, rather, by the lame-duck House of Representatives still controlled by the repudiated Federalists. Similarly, the Republican representatives elected in 1860 were not scheduled to meet until December 1861. The existing Congresses expired on March 4, the date of the new president's inauguration.

This meant, among other things, that Congress was not in session[97] when Abraham Lincoln took his oath of office on that date, and he chose not to convene a special session of Congress until July 4. The late Clinton Rossiter, in a book tellingly titled *Constitutional Dictatorship*, wrote:

The eleven weeks between the fall of Sumter and July 4, 1861 constitute the most interesting single episode in the history of constitutional dictatorship. The simple fact that one man was the government of the United States in the most critical period in all its 165 years and that he acted on no precedent and under no restraint, makes this the paragon of all democratic, constitutional dictatorships.[98]

The Italian political theorist Georgio Agamben is even stronger in his language: "In the ten weeks that passed between [the outbreak of war on] April 15 and [the return of Congress on] July 4, Lincoln in fact acted as an absolute dictator."[99] One might well believe that Agamben goes overboard in his description of Lincoln as "an absolute dictator" while accepting his (and Rossiter's) general point. And the major point for the purposes of this book is that Lincoln's actions were enabled by what one might otherwise think was only a technical provision of the Constitution dealing with the mundane issue of the time of meeting.

The Twentieth Amendment provides a partial corrective to this patent deficiency of the original Constitution by providing that the terms of new members of Congress shall begin at noon on January 3 following the year of their election. As we shall see in chapter 3, this amendment also moved up the Inauguration Day of the newly elected president. And, just as much to the point, "The Congress shall assemble . . . at noon on the 3rd day of January, unless they shall by law appoint a different day [if, for example, January 3 is a Saturday or Sunday]." This is surely better than the original Constitution, but one might still wonder why newly elected members of Congress do not take their oaths of office (and displace their predecessors, in cases of electoral defeats) immediately upon their certification by election. A lame-duck Congress, almost by definition, includes some number of defeated—or, perhaps less problematically, retiring—representatives and senators. It is surely questionable that repudiated legislators can take part in major congressional decisions, whether the passage of important legislation or the impeachment of a sitting president.[100]

John Copeland Nagle has suggested that one of the major purposes of the Twentieth Amendment "was to abolish lame duck sessions of

Congress," save for emergencies (such as the outbreak of war) in which decisions simply *had* to be made rather than wait for the new, more democratically legitimate Congress.[101] Consider in this context the ratification of the revised General Agreement on Trade and Tariffs by the lame-duck Congress in December 1994, just before the new Republican Congress elected in the sea-change election of that year took office. It is hard to understand why such a momentous decision should be made by a Congress many of whose members had been repudiated by an aroused electorate (whatever I may personally think of the choices made by that electorate). Similarly, Bruce Ackerman has cogently argued that there was something profoundly questionable about the decision of the post-1998–election House of Representatives to barrel ahead with voting to impeach President Clinton, given that the most plausible reading of the results of those midterm elections is that the public in general had little desire to see that happen. I shall have more to say later in this volume about the most serious problem linked to the Twentieth Amendment, which is the president's inauguration date.

CONCLUSION

It is the Congress that makes most plausible the proud claim that in the United States "the people rule." But it should now be clear that the Constitution makes that claim less tenable inasmuch as majority rule is significantly stymied by the operation of the Constitution itself. That would be far more acceptable if we could be confident that it contributed to the kind of "consensual democracy" of which Lijphart and Graber speak and, as well, to the passage of legislation designed to speak to great national needs rather than to serve local or politically partial interests. But, alas, that is hardly the case either. There is good reason that almost two-thirds of the American public express a lack of confidence in Congress. The next step is to realize that the Constitution itself contributes to the kinds of behavior that seem increasingly dysfunctional in meeting the real problems that confront the United States both at home and abroad.

THREE

THE LEGACY OF ARTICLE II

TOO-POWERFUL PRESIDENTS, CHOSEN IN AN INDEFENSIBLE PROCESS, WHO CANNOT BE DISPLACED EVEN WHEN THEY ARE MANIFESTLY INCOMPETENT

The year 2006 began with the country roiled in debate about the extent of presidential power. The president in question, of course, is George W. Bush, who was named president in 2000 even though he notably came in second to Al Gore in the overall national presidential vote. Returned to office in the 2004 election, he will, barring personal catastrophe or impeachment, enjoy the full powers of the presidency, whatever they may be, until the inauguration of his successor on January 20, 2009. None of these facts is without relevance to debating the powers enjoyed by the president.

The Bush administration has identified itself as a "war presidency," the war in question being the "global war against terror," including, at least according to the administration, the invasion of Iraq in 2003 and its aftermath. The debate about Iraq certainly precedes 2006. The particular topic of the 2005–2006 debate involved disclosures that the National Security Agency (NSA) for the previous four years had been conducting so-called data mining—the interception of telephone calls, e-mails, and other forms of electronic communication—in likely violation of a law passed by Congress in 1978, the Foreign Intelligence Surveillance Act (FISA). Although the Bush administration implausibly claims that the congressional Authorization for the Use of Military Force, passed following the events of September 11, makes FISA irrelevant, the far more important argument is that the president possesses the "inherent power" to order such surveillance, regardless of any attempts by Congress to limit that power. A similar argument was made in a 2002 memorandum prepared at the direction of the White House with regard to whether the president—or, perhaps more to the point, any subordinate officials responding to presidential directives— was bound by both domestic and international prohibitions of the use of torture as a means of interrogation. The answer was no.

The issue of torture was also at the heart of a law passed by Congress at the end of 2005 barring the use of torture or other "cruel, inhuman, or degrading" methods of interrogation by any American official, military or civilian, anywhere in the world. The administration had vehemently opposed the legislation, authored by Arizona senator John McCain, himself a victim of torture during the Vietnam War, and threatened to veto it. When it became clear that there were enough votes to override a veto, President Bush ostentatiously appeared to embrace the bill. However, when signing it, he issued a written statement emphasizing:

> The executive branch shall construe [the McCain amendment] in a manner consistent with the constitutional authority of the President to supervise the unitary executive branch and as Commander in Chief and consistent with the constitutional limitations on the judicial power, which will assist in achieving the shared objective of the Congress and the President . . . of protecting the American people from further terrorist attacks.[1]

As a conservative political scientist, Matthew Franck, put it, "the signing statement . . . conveys the good news that the president is not taking the McCain amendment lying down."[2] What this means, in effect, is that the president believes that he has wide-ranging discretion to decide *which* laws he shall, as the Constitution puts it, "take care" to execute. Any law that he believes invades his own powers he will feel free to ignore. If he believes that torture is necessary, he has the power to order it, whatever Congress may attempt to prohibit. A recent story by *Boston Globe* reporter Charlie Savage begins, "Bush has quietly claimed the authority to disobey more than 750 laws enacted since he took office, asserting that he has the power to set aside any statute passed by Congress when it conflicts with his interpretation of the Constitution."[3] As indicated in my earlier discussion of this issue in chapter 2, I believe that the issue of presidential authority to interpret the Constitution is in fact quite complicated and that it is therefore a mistake to condemn a president for claiming such authority. Still, as I also argued there, I think there is no doubt that President Bush is making claims substantially more far-reaching than any of his predecessors in office. There is more than a touch of *"L'etat c'est moi"* in Bush's conception of his role.

Stuart Taylor, Jr., a moderate, even conservative, legal journalist, has recently referred to "claims by the Bush administration that the commander-in-chief has near dictatorial powers to wage war against terrorists, at home as well as abroad—often in secret and certainly without public consent." There is, he writes, a threat of "creeping presidential autocracy" and the "eviscerat[ion of] our system of checks and balances."[4] As with criticisms of congressional structure, such concerns are not of interest to lawyers or political theorists alone. Presidential decisions involve not only our privacy, but also quite literally issues of life and death.

It is hard to imagine any questions of more practical importance to our constitutional system than those surrounding the selection, retention, and powers of the president. Alas, the current Constitution is deficient in almost all relevant respects.

OUR DREADFUL SYSTEM
OF PRESIDENTIAL SELECTION

The Constitution does structure the presidential selection process in a number of important ways, almost none of them for the better. Although I shall spend the bulk of this section on the Electoral College, one should note that the Qualifications Clause for the presidency presents its own problems, which will be considered in chapter 5. Surely the central demand we must make of the Constitution is that it at least tend toward—even if it may be asking too much to *guarantee*—that presidents of the United States demonstrate a sufficient level of integrity and competence to merit the confidence of the people as they exercise the immense powers of their office.

The question of integrity (and much else) is linked to the actuality of who is chosen to be president. At least since James Bryce at the end of the nineteenth century, analysts have bewailed the allegation that what used to be called "the best men" did not aspire to the White House (or perhaps a career in politics at all). One continues to hear such analyses, sometimes focused on the now "permanent campaign" for the office, sometimes on the altogether unseemly time and energy that must be spent raising money in order to be a viable candidate. And these don't even speak to the fact that every successful politician must have a demonstrated capacity to suffer fools gladly. There may be some truth to such arguments, though I suspect they are overblown and often serve as covers for traditional elites who bewail their loss of power to the great unwashed, who no longer defer to the elites' self-styled bestness. In any event, these criticisms have little to do with the Constitution itself and everything to do with broader developments in the society, including the development of mass political parties and the displacement of traditional elites.

It is the Electoral College that supplies the decisive and overriding reason for rejecting the status quo and supporting a convention entitled to propose significant revisions. It is an undemocratic and perverse part of the American system of government that ill serves the United States.

I mentioned earlier the bogus nature of the claim that the president of the United States is necessarily "the people's choice." This is obviously clearest in circumstances like 1960 and 2000, when Richard Nixon and Al Gore, respectively, won pluralities of the vote over their winning opponents, John F. Kennedy and George W. Bush. But it is also important to note that neither Nixon nor Gore could have claimed to be the choice of a majority of the voters. Nixon's 34,108,147 votes might have been more than Kennedy's 34,049,976 votes, but they still constituted only 49.3 percent of the entire vote. Similarly, Gore might have beaten Bush by 539,893 votes, but Gore's overall percentage was even less than Nixon's, 48.3 percent.[5] Ironically, Richard Nixon would ascend to the presidency in 1968 with 43.4 percent of the popular vote, which was otherwise split between the Democrat Hubert H. Humphrey (42.7 percent) and the egregious George C. Wallace, the segregationist governor of Alabama, who received almost 10 million of the roughly 73.5 million total votes.[6] Amazingly, Nixon is not even the winner in the "least popular among successful candidates" sweepstakes. Bill Clinton received only 43 percent of the popular vote in 1992 (he would rise to 49.2 percent in 1996). But even Clinton is well ahead of Woodrow Wilson, who in 1912 became president with only 41.9 percent of the popular vote, and, the all-time winner, Abraham Lincoln, who swept the electoral vote (59.1 percent) while winning only 39.8 percent of the popular vote.[7] Whatever else may be said about these presidents, that they received a popular mandate to govern is most certainly not one of them.

As the United States is launched on a crusade to export "democracy" around the world, it is well worth asking whether any country committed to democracy would emulate the American process of selecting presidents. One need not speculate on the answer. No country has, for the good and sufficient reason that our system has little, if anything, to do with adherence to democratic values. So now, let us make our descent into the belly of the beast, the Electoral College, for a demonstration of why this is so.

It is an embarrassing fact of the American system that American citizens do not cast their ballots directly for their favorite candidates for the presidency. Instead, they vote for electors ostensibly (but not always) committed to a given candidate. The Byzantine procedures by which we elect our presidents are spelled out in clauses 2 and 3 of Article II, section 1, and in the Twelfth Amendment (which modified the original clause 3, which I omit below). These are, I am sad to say, additional examples of constitutional turgidity that are extremely important in understanding what is wrong with our Constitution.

Clause 2. Each State shall appoint, in such Manner as the Legislature thereof may direct, a Number of Electors, equal to the whole Number of Senators and Representatives to which the State may be entitled in the Congress: but no Senator or Representative, or Person holding an Office of Trust or Profit under the United States, shall be appointed an Elector.

Amendment XII.

The Electors shall meet in their respective states, and vote by ballot for President and Vice-President, one of whom, at least, shall not be an inhabitant of the same state with themselves; they shall name in their ballots the person voted for as President, and in distinct ballots the person voted for as Vice-President, and they shall make distinct lists of all persons voted for as President, and of all persons voted for as Vice-President, and of the number of votes for each, which lists they shall sign and certify, and transmit sealed to the seat of the government of the United States, directed to the President of the Senate;—The President of the Senate shall, in the presence of the Senate and House of Representatives, open all the certificates and the votes shall then be counted;—The person having the greatest number of votes for President, shall be the President, if such number be a majority of the whole number of Electors appointed; and if no person have such majority, then from the persons having the highest numbers not exceeding three on the list of those voted for as President, the House of Representatives shall choose immediately, by ballot, the President. But in choosing the President, the votes shall be taken by states, the representation from each state having one vote; a quorum for this purpose shall consist of a member or members from two-thirds of the states, and a majority of all the states shall be necessary to a choice. And if the House of Representatives shall not choose a President whenever the right of choice shall devolve upon them, before *the fourth day of March next following, then the Vice-President shall act as President, as in the case of the death or other constitutional disability of the President.*[8]—The person having the greatest number of votes as Vice-President, shall be the Vice-President, if such number be a majority of the whole number of Electors appointed, and if no person have a majority, then from the two highest numbers on the list, the Senate shall choose the Vice-President; a quorum for the purpose shall consist of two-thirds of the whole number of Senators, and a majority of the whole number shall be necessary to a choice. But no person constitutionally ineligible to the office of President shall be eligible to that of Vice-President of the United States.

Since my fondest hope is that you, the reader, are a member of the general public and not, therefore, a trained constitutional lawyer, let me try to offer a reader-friendly translation of this remarkably murky prose:

1. It is electors, not the public, who cast the decisive votes for president, and the electors are chosen on a state-by-state basis, with each state having electors equal to the total number of its senators (always two) and representatives (which vary by overall population).

2. The electors gather in their respective state capitals to cast their votes; by a congressional statute passed in 1934, the current date is the second Wednesday in December.[9]

3. Thanks to the Twelfth Amendment, each elector casts two separate votes, one for the presidency, the other for the vice presidency. The original Constitution did not separate the voting by office, which resulted, among other things, in the infamous 1800 deadlock between Thomas Jefferson and Aaron Burr, whose resolution threatened the country with civil war.[10] Fortunately, the Twelfth Amendment has made it unnecessary to discuss further this truly lunatic feature of the original Constitution (which depended, among other things, on the nonexistence of political parties), other than to say that it demonstrates almost perfectly the proposition that a decision rule that made sense to obviously bright and well-intentioned individuals could—and within twelve years—turn out to be nothing less than potentially catastrophic.

4. Electors cannot vote for two candidates from their own state. This might have made good sense in 1787 or even a modicum of sense in 1803, when it was retained in the Twelfth Amendment. It makes almost no sense today, though it did provide me an opportunity to suggest in the *New York Times* and then to participate in a lawsuit arguing that Texas electors could not vote for both George W. Bush and Dick Cheney because both were Texans.[11] Incredibly, it turned out that the one and only constitutional law case on which Harriet Miers, President Bush's ill-fated 2005 nominee to the Supreme Court, had ever worked was this very one. Not surprisingly, she won the case.

5. If a majority of electoral votes are cast for given candidates for president and vice president, there is no further problem, though, as already amply demonstrated, there is no necessary reason to believe that these Electoral College winners won a majority or even a plurality of the popular vote.

6. If, however, there is no majority, then the fun begins, with separate tracks being provided for the presidential and vice-presidential candidates.

7. The names of the three presidential candidates with the highest number of electoral votes are sent to the House of Representatives, which chooses among them *on a one state, one vote basis.* This is just another version of the equal allocation of voting power in the Senate.

8. In the meantime, the Senate is sent only the names of the two highest recipients of votes for the vice presidency. Each of the senators casts an individual ballot deciding between them; this obviously means that each state has an equal number of votes, as in the House.

9. A moment's reflection reveals that it is far easier to resolve electoral vote deadlocks for the vice presidency than for the presidency. One reason that this is fortunate is not only that the Senate is relatively easily assured that it will have a president, but also, and perhaps more important, that the vice president–elect is on call to take the presidential reins should the House continue to be dead-

locked, as is not inconceivable, beyond the constitutionally mandated day on which the new administration is to take office.

I hope that every reader now understands what Article II and the
Twelfth Amendment inflict on the United States. And I hope you are
inclined to agree that this is not one of those instances where to understand is to forgive.

Some readers may remember a restaurant placemat given to children, in which they were shown a picture and then asked to identify
all of the errors in it, for example, the fact that a person was clearly
wearing two different socks or that a river was flowing uphill. One might
well treat the Electoral College as that kind of exercise, given the number of problems contained within it. Professor George Edwards has
devoted an entire book to explaining *Why the Electoral College Is Bad
for America.*[12] I have space for only the most glaring problems.

The most important of all has been amply covered: the fact that the
Electoral College does, with some frequency, select as president candidates who did not even win a majority of the popular vote and, on at
least two occasions in the last fifty years, the candidate who came in
second in the popular vote. One response to this latter point is that one
cannot legitimately infer from the popular vote in the election system
we have to a hypothetical vote in a direct-election system where every
person's vote counted equally across the country, which is most certainly
not the case with the Electoral College. The fact is that presidential
candidates and their campaign managers are not trying to win the popular
vote, except as an afterthought. They are dedicated to putting together
a coalition of states that will provide a majority of the electoral votes.

Key to understanding contemporary elections is the fact that, with
the exception of Maine and Nebraska, the winner in a given state gets
all of a state's electoral votes. Thus, in 2000, Bush received all twenty-
five of Florida's votes, which was enough to give him the four-vote
Electoral College victory that propelled him to the White House. Given
that Maine and Nebraska adopted a system whereby one vote is awarded
for each congressional district carried and then two votes for the winner of the statewide vote, it is obvious that the winner-take-all system
is not constitutionally required. Nevertheless, it is the system adopted

by forty-eight of the fifty states and the District of Columbia. It inflicts its own harm on the integrity of the American political system by creating the phenomenon of "battleground" states, defined as those states, small or large, that are viewed as close to evenly split between the two parties. This means that "predictable states" are simply written off, so far as campaigning is concerned. And the battleground is shrinking. A *New York Times* editorial noted that, in 1960, "24 states, with 327 electoral votes, were battleground states." By 2004, "only 13 states, with 159 electoral votes, were."[13]

As a result, the vast majority of states—with a similarly vast majority of the population—become utterly irrelevant in the ostensibly national campaign because their preferences in the national election are completely predictable. As someone who lives in both Massachusetts and Texas, I saw nothing at all of the 2004 presidential campaign, except in the media. During the 2004 presidential campaign, a full 99 percent of all advertising expenditures by the two campaigns occurred in only seventeen of the states;[14] Florida and Ohio alone accounted for more than 45 percent ($111. million) of the $235,416,458 spent in all of those states, and three more states—Iowa, Pennsylvania, and Wisconsin—brought the total to above 70 percent. Similarly, Florida and Ohio received substantially more candidate visits (sixty-one and forty-nine, respectively) than did any other state. Wisconsin received fifteen times as many visits (thirty-one) as did California.[15] New York received a grand total of one visit. "In short, polling, advertising, and campaigning are not merely skewed toward about a dozen and a half states in presidential campaigns, but the remaining two thirds of the states are, for all practical purposes, *excluded* from the campaign. They are mere spectators in the election process."[16]

Given the reality of electoral votes, instead of what might be termed the "real votes" of individual citizens, it is a matter of complete indifference to candidates and their campaign organizations whether the turnout in a given state is 40 percent or 60 percent, so long as they can confidently predict that, whatever the turnout is, a given candidate will still win. The Bush campaign, therefore, had no interest in putting scarce funds into a get-voters-to-the-polls program in Texas or Wyoming, nor did Senator John Kerry have any interest in a similar program in Massachusetts. Both campaigns were, instead, vitally, almost pathologically, interested in Florida and Ohio. It is almost certainly the case that a truly national election, instead of the congeries of state-by-state elections that we now have, courtesy of the Electoral College, would increase turnout inasmuch as there would be more incentive for everyone to vote, in both (and other) parties. And, with increased turnout, we might get different winners than those now holding the gold medal at the end of the election race.

The battleground phenomenon explains not only variations in visitations by candidates. Anyone living in the United States in late October 2000 would have believed that the most crucial issue facing the entire country was prescription drugs for the elderly. Almost no other issue, including foreign policy (save for unending professions of support for Israel and militant opposition to Fidel Castro), was visible as both Bush and Gore sought votes from—or "pandered to"—Florida's citizens. Because of the misfortune that most of America's largest cities are in nonbattleground states, almost no presidential candidate in years has made a truly serious speech about the plight of these cities. Democrats can take the states containing New York, Chicago, Philadelphia, Boston, and Los Angeles for granted, while Republicans in turn have almost no incentive to devote themselves to consideration of their plight.

So one should concede that Al Gore's apparent popular vote victory—as with Nixon's far more narrow victory in 1960—may have been a simple artifact of the fact that there is no incentive for a candidate to try to maximize the national popular vote. Far better to spend scarce campaign resources attacking the battleground states than to elicit additional votes where, because of the Electoral College, they would simply be "wasted." A different system would produce a different turnout and a different distribution of votes. Perhaps Gore would have won, perhaps not, but at least we would have the satisfaction of knowing that all Americans participated in the election on an equal basis instead of the travesty created by the Electoral College.

Much of the previous chapter was devoted to the indefensible advantages given to low-population states. Here, too, these states exert special and equally indefensible power. Of course, there is a linkage because the source of that power is the bonus that each state gets for having two senators, in addition to however many representatives it has. Thus Wyoming, with 0.2 percent of the national population, has three times that weight in the Electoral College, as do Alaska and the District of Columbia.[17] California, on the other hand, with 12.2 percent of the national population, controls only 10.2 percent of the Electoral College votes. My home state of Texas, with 7.6 percent of the population, has only 6.3 percent of the electoral votes. Only five states—Arizona, Maryland, Massachusetts, Missouri, Wisconsin— enjoy parity between their percentage of the national population and their percentage in the Electoral College. As one would readily expect, every single state with 2.8 percent of the national population (North Carolina) or higher has less power in the Electoral College than pure proportionality would dictate.

Consider the fact that in the 2000 election Al Gore won New Mexico (five electoral votes) while losing Wyoming, Alaska, and North Dakota (nine electoral votes). According to the 2000 census figures, New Mexico had a total population of 1,823,821, while the total population of the three other states was 1,768,993. Thus, Bush gained almost twice the number of electoral votes by winning three states with a total population less than New Mexico's. One of the original consequences of the Electoral College was to give a bonus to the slave states, inasmuch as three-fifths of the numbers of their distinctly nonvoting and unrepresented slaves were nonetheless counted as part of the population to establish how many representatives (and, therefore, how many electoral votes) each state got. Thomas Jefferson, for example, would have lost the 1800 election to John Adams had he not been the beneficiary of the slave bonus.[18] We are now blessedly free of the awarding of bonuses to slaveholders. It is not at all clear, however, that the small-state bonus is any more defensible. It may be part of our political tradition, but then, so was slavery.

But wait, as the television pitchman might say, there's more. And, unlike the case with the products being pitched to us, more is not better. Consider that the disdain exhibited by the Electoral College system for popular majorities at the national level is mimicked within the state process of selection itself. Return once more, if one has the stomach for it, to the 2000 Florida election. Just as George W. Bush did not get a majority of votes within the nation at large, he even more certainly was not the choice of the majority of voters in Florida, even if we ignore the infamous "butterfly ballot" that counted almost certain Gore votes, more than enough to give him victory over Bush, as ones for Pat Buchanan. All one can say about Bush is that he received, according to the Florida election officials whose recount was temporarily shut down on December 9, 2000, by the U.S. Supreme Court— a decision made permanent three days later by the five conservative Republicans on the Supreme Court—approximately 600 more votes than did anyone else.[19] But Ralph Nader and Pat Buchanan were also on the Florida ballot, as were other small-party candidates, and they indisputably received far more votes than Bush's margin over Gore. None of this matters, of course, because the important thing, in language adopted from the English system of elections, is to be "first past the post." This makes good sense, no doubt, for the award of Olympic gold medals. It makes almost no sense in a system that professes to be truly democratic. Indeed, it should make Americans either ashamed (if they benefit) or angry (if they do not) from the particular operation, in any given year, of this system.

Yale law professor Akhil Reed Amar wrote in 1998 that the Electoral College was "A Constitutional Accident Waiting to Happen."[20] The accident to which Amar was referring was the selection by the Electoral College of the loser in the national vote. Writing in 1998, Amar could have had no idea that it would happen in 2000. He advocated the replacement of the Electoral College mechanism with a national election in which voters would cast what is called a *single transferable vote*, "with voters listing their second and third choices on the ballot, in effect combining the 'first heat' and 'runoff' elections into a single transaction." This has the virtue of producing someone who can plausibly be called the majority's choice, unlike the current system. His arguments were unanswerable in 1998. That is even more the case today.

Consider how deadlocks in the Electoral College are to be resolved. The answer, according to the Constitution, is that the president is to be chosen by the House of Representatives *on a one state, one vote basis*.[21] This provision is a national constitutional crisis just waiting to happen.

One reason for Americans' complacence, undoubtedly, is that only twice have there been Electoral College deadlocks that have gone to the House for resolution, in 1800 and 1824. But, as George Edwards demonstrates, "In seven elections, the shift of a very few votes would have deadlocked the electoral college and sent the election of the president into the House of Representatives."[22] Three of these elections are in the dim and distant past: 1836, 1856, and Abraham Lincoln's election of 1860, in which a shift of only 18,050 votes—less than 1 percent of the national total—in California, Oregon, Illinois, and Indiana would have certainly doomed Lincoln's prospects inasmuch as the deadlock would have been broken by the lame-duck, distinctly un-Republican House of Representatives. But consider that the four other elections are all post–World War II. A shift of 12,487 votes in California and Ohio—0.0003 percent of the national vote and less than 2 percent of the vote in the named states—would have deadlocked the 1948 Truman-Dewey race, given that Dixiecrat Strom Thurmond carried four states and won thirty-nine electoral votes. Indeed, Thurmond won in part because he appeared on the ballot in several states—Alabama, Louisiana, Mississippi, and South Carolina—as the Democratic nominee.[23] This underscores the fact that national parties are in some sense a legal fiction. It is the states themselves that control in substantial measure the process of electing national officials, including deciding who can gain access to the ballot. George Washington University law professor and *New Republic* legal affairs editor Jeffrey Rosen has identified what he calls "divided suffrage" as the "biggest constitutional mistake," derived from sections 2 and 4 of Article I and, rather surprisingly, section 2 of the Fourteenth Amendment, all of which have led to "a patchwork of inconsistent and parochial state restrictions" on ballot access and even the suffrage.[24]

In 1960, an even smaller shift, both in absolute numbers and by percentage—8,971 votes, 0.001 percent of the national total and only 0.134 percent of the total in Illinois and Missouri, the relevant states—would have required the House to choose between John Kennedy and Richard Nixon, inasmuch as Virginia senator Harry Byrd received fifteen electoral votes.[25] Fourteen of them were from so-called unpledged electors elected in Mississippi and Alabama. Where did the fifteenth

Byrd vote come from? The answer is Henry D. Irwin, a Republican elector from Oklahoma, who recognized that the Republicans themselves could not prevail over Kennedy in the Electoral College and who therefore "telegraphed all Republican electors" with the presumptive good news that "[s]ufficient conservative Democratic electors [are] available to deny [the] labor Socialist nominee," by whom he meant Kennedy, the presidency if they would shift their votes from Nixon to Byrd and throw the election into the House.[26] Had that occurred, Edwards writes, it is "very difficult to guess what would have happened" given that only twenty-three states, three less than a majority, were controlled by northern and border-state Democrats, whereas six were controlled by old-fashioned southern Democrats—this was, after all, before Lyndon Johnson and the Voting Rights Act of 1965 transformed southern politics—and seventeen were controlled by Republicans. The remaining four were equally split.[27] Given both the one state, one vote rule and the necessity to amass a majority of the states, truly anything could have happened, including political chaos and public disorder.

This episode underlines not only the potential mischief of Electoral College deadlocks, but also the fact that electors seemingly remain free, as a constitutional matter, to adhere to the original understanding of the college and to vote according to their own judgment rather than slavishly to follow the party line. There were many reports in the run-up to the 2000 election, when some polls suggested that it would be George W. Bush with the national plurality and Al Gore with a slender electoral vote majority, that Republicans were prepared to put great pressure on Democratic electors to switch their votes and recognize the alleged desire of the people for a Bush presidency. Needless to say, they did not have to test this strategy.

Richard Nixon had good reason to feel the victim of fate in the 1960 election. According to Edwards, he prevailed over Kennedy in the number of votes received, and he only narrowly lost the Electoral College battle. Fate was far kinder to him in 1968, when, with only 43.4 percent of the popular vote, he gained 301 electoral votes to Hubert Humphrey's 191 and George C. Wallace's 46 votes.[28] A shift of 53,034 votes in New Jersey, Missouri, and Montana (0.072 percent of the national total and 1.07 percent of the total vote in the three states) would have deadlocked the Electoral College.

Edwards includes the 1976 election in his list for a peculiar but by now not entirely surprising reason. One of the Washington state Republican electors pledged to Gerald Ford actually cast his vote for Ronald Reagan, apparently because Ford was insufficiently opposed to abortion.[29] Had only 5,559 voters in Ohio and 3,687 voters in Hawaii voted for Ford instead of Carter, and had Mike Padden, the Washington state elector, withheld his vote from Ford, then Ford would have had only 269 electoral votes to Carter's 268 and Reagan's 1. That would have been enough to send the choice to the House because the Constitution requires that a candidate get a *majority* of the electoral vote, which is 270 votes. (Another scenario discussed by Professor Edwards would have created a 269–269 tie between Ford and Carter.)

Or imagine that Ross Perot had run in 2000 instead of 1992 (when, as a third-party candidate, he gained an unprecedented 18.9 percent of the national total) and eked out a victory in even one state that went to George Bush. Then, that election would have gone to the House of Representatives.

Professor Edwards notes a wild-card contained even within the notion of one state, one vote. States do not exist as "real" entities; only the individual representatives do. So how would the decision as to the state's vote actually be made? One might think the answer is by majority vote of the state's representatives, though obvious problems are created if the delegation is split. (If a state does not agree on whom to vote for, it simply fails to cast a ballot in the House, though this could still work, in effect, to deny a candidate the absolute majority of states needed for election.) But what if, in a very close state, representatives from districts that voted for X even though the state at large voted for Y decided to honor the preferences of their constituents—who, after all, will be casting judgment on them in the next election—instead of remaining loyal to their political party? The opportunities for mischief are great. One can easily imagine the kinds of promises that would be made to potential switchers, given the stakes of the decision.

Any supporter of this aspect of the Electoral College system is all too similar to a heavy drinker who blithely speeds down the highway because, after all, he got home safely on other such occasions. That would be justly recognized as gross—indeed, criminal—negligence and wanton disregard for the risk to human life when the almost inevitable accident does take place. Americans should be equally indignant about the wanton recklessness buried within what may appear to be mere constitutional technicalities.

The Electoral College is especially important to this book for two reasons. The first is obvious. It is a good and sufficient reason for any citizen who cares about basic democratic values and even the preservation of political stability to support the referendum authorizing a new convention. It also illustrates, all too well, the extent to which the Constitution functions as an iron cage preventing necessary change. For the fact is that virtually no one defends the one state, one vote system described above. I expect vigorous argument against many of my critiques in this book, but not with regard to this one.

In an 1823 letter, James Madison wrote:

> The present rule of voting for President by the House of Representatives is so great a departure from the Republican principle of numerical equality, and even from the federal rule which qualifies the numerical by a State equality, and is so pregnant also with a mischievous tendency in practice, that an amendment of the Constitution on this point is justly called for by all its considerate and best friends.[30]

No one has ever put it better. Yet nothing has been done in the intervening 180 years to guard against this "mischievous tendency," even after the 1824 election the very next year exposed all of the problems: John Quincy Adams, who had received both fewer popular votes and fewer electoral votes than did his principal adversary, Andrew Jackson, nonetheless prevailed. The reason is that Henry Clay, who had come in fourth and therefore was not among the top three candidates who were available to the House for consideration, threw his support to Adams and, as a consequence, became secretary of state.

So why the stasis? One explanation is simply the difficulty of placing *any* issue on the modern legislative agenda. We saw an illustration
of this before with regard to the problem of the continuity in government after a catastrophic terrorist attack. Busy legislators prefer to think
about the most pressing problems and, concomitantly, ignore what are
only "hypothetical," even if easily predictable ones. (Every reader
should now immediately think of the Mississippi River and Lake Pont-
chartrain levees around New Orleans and the almost criminal disregard of the risks posed by "unlikely" major hurricanes.) But another,
less generous explanation may lie with the villains of the previous chapters, small states and their zeal to protect their illegitimate power within
the American political system.

National public opinion has long supported the abolition of the
entire Electoral College. The House of Representatives, for example,
in 1969 voted 338–70 for a constitutional amendment establishing
national direct election in which each and every citizen would have an
equal vote. "But in the Senate, southern and small state conservatives
ganged up to filibuster the proposition to death, because they believed
that reform might destroy [the] special influence the electoral college
gives their constituencies."[31] Fairness requires recognizing that "[t]en
years later, the Senate fell fifteen votes short of the needed two-thirds"
needed to propose a direct-vote amendment because "such liberals as
Bill Bradley of New Jersey, Daniel Patrick Moynihan of New York,
and Paul Sarbanes of Maryland moved into opposition after black and
Jewish organizations claimed that their supposed pivotal power in big
swing states would be threatened."[32] As Neil R. Pierce argues, not only
is there a tension between the claims that both small states and large
states are benefited by the Electoral College, but it is also the case that
such raw partisan considerations ought not dictate the maintenance
of what so clearly contradicts the notion that all citizens should play
an equal role in choosing our president.[33]

But, inasmuch as any formal change in the Electoral College,
whether it is the entire system or simply the modification of the potentially disastrous one state, one vote deadlock breaker, necessitates
a constitutional amendment, we appear to be locked in the iron cage
of Article V. Even if the Senate could be shamed into accepting the

desirability of an amendment, there would still be the task of persuading both legislative houses (or the unicameral legislature in Nebraska) in the fourteen states that benefit most from the senatorial bonus: Alaska, Delaware, Hawaii, Maine, Montana, Nebraska, New Hampshire, New Mexico, North Dakota, Rhode Island, South Dakota, Vermont, West Virginia, and Wyoming. And this list does not include the additional fourteen states whose percentage of the electoral vote is higher than their percentage of the national population.

Perhaps, though, one can escape the vise (and vice) of the Electoral College without having to pry open the bars of the Article V cage. Thus, an organization called the Campaign for a National Popular Vote has proposed that large states take advantage of two relatively obscure provisions of the Constitution. The first is Article II, section 1, which empowers each state to "appoint" its presidential electors in "such Manner as the Legislature thereof may direct."[34] The second is Article I, section 10, which authorizes Congress to consent to "any agreement or compact" by one state with another. (Interstate compacts are void in the absence of congressional consent.) Thus, the proposal is that large states compact with one another to appoint electors who will be directed to cast their votes for the person who wins the greatest number of votes in the overall national election. The compact would not come into effect until enough states (which could be as few as the eleven largest states) to constitute a majority of the electoral votes had agreed to the compact. Upon Congress agreeing to the compact, the United States would in effect move to a popularly elected presidency, and the perversities of the Electoral College would be effectively nullified.

This is not to say that significant problems would not remain with our election system. There is, for example, no good reason to name as president the person who is "first past the post" in the national count, inasmuch as that person could, as has been common, still not be, in any meaningful sense, the choice of the national majority. What would be best would be to adopt a runoff system that would assure that the winner indeed had received demonstrable majority support.[35] In any event, delegates to the forthcoming constitutional convention could address such issues.

WHEN DOES THE PRESIDENT BEGIN
TO GOVERN? OUR INDEFENSIBLY
BELATED INAUGURATION DAY

So, we have a president-elect, however dubious the process of election might be and regardless of whatever concerns we might have about the powers that he or she will possess on taking office. When will he or she actually begin service as our chief executive? If we were talking about Great Britain and its prime ministers, the answer would be, "the day after election." Consider the fact that when in July 1945 Clement Atlee won the first postwar election and therefore displaced Winston Churchill, Atlee promptly went to Potsdam, where a conference was in place among Harry Truman, Joseph Stalin, and Churchill, and took Churchill's place.

Our system is notably different. Putting 2000 to one side, we usually know on the evening of the first Tuesday in November who the next president will be, and on at least three occasions in the past thirty years, the winners (Carter, Reagan, and Clinton) were displacing incumbents (Ford, Carter, and George H. W. Bush). Yet it took another ten weeks, until January 20, for the displacement to become effective. In the interim, repudiated presidents continued to possess all of the powers of their office.

Or consider two earlier elections, in 1860 and 1932. Abraham Lincoln did not directly defeat James Buchanan, who had the wit not to run for reelection, but Lincoln's election was a thoroughgoing repudiation of everything for which the Buchanan administration stood (save for their shared belief that secession was unconstitutional). In 1932, Franklin Roosevelt most definitely did displace (and repudiate) the hapless incumbent, Herbert Hoover. Prior to the Twentieth Amendment, Inauguration Day was March 4, which meant that neither Lincoln nor Roosevelt took office for a full four months following their elections. In these two examples, one could well argue that the United States did not possess a functioning government during two of the greatest crises in its history, the secession winter and the depth of the Great Depression. The presidents who continued to hold office had been definitively rejected, and their elected successors were unable to exercise any authority to help resolve the crises that contributed to their elections.

Because of the Twentieth Amendment, FDR was the last president to be inaugurated on March 4. He took his 1937 oath of office on January 20. (This allows any reader the opportunity to win a bar bet, for FDR joined George Washington—inaugurated on April 30, 1789—as the only elected presidents living out their first terms who did not serve a "four-year term.") There is no doubt that the Twentieth Amendment made the Constitution better than it was, especially when we add, as noted in chapter 2, its movement of the date for the convening of the newly elected Congress from the following December back to the beginning of January immediately following the elections. But seventy years of experience following the Twentieth Amendment should lead us to question whether we are well served by even the ten-week hiatus between election and inauguration. Return to the Atlee-Churchill example. Prior to Roosevelt, presidents rarely if ever took part in international conferences. The most important exception was Woodrow Wilson's ill-fated participation in the Versailles Conference following the end of World War I, whose ultimate consequence, at least with regard to American politics, was the repudiation by the Senate of the Versailles Treaty and membership in the League of Nations. Today, however, presidents spend a substantial part of their terms in international gatherings and conferences. Even if they are not physically present, their delegates, whether the secretary of state or more junior officials, are nonetheless charged with representing the interests of the United States in international forums.

What if, as is almost invariably the case, there is genuine disagreement within the American public about what those interests are, and what if a major part of the election debate concerned the definition of those interests and how they should be protected in the international realm? Does it make any sense for a repudiated president or his delegates to represent the United States in delicate international negotiations? Clement Atlee had been chosen by the people of Great Britain as their champion, and it was only proper that he replaced Churchill as soon as possible. We, however, are stuck with knights who have been thrown off their horses, at least politically speaking, but who can continue to exercise formal legal power and, consequently, to make mischief for their successors. George H. W. Bush, for example, chose to send American troops to Somalia during the interregnum between his defeat by Bill Clinton and Clinton's inauguration in January. Bush may have had good reasons to do so, but it is also the case that Clinton was faced with an almost immediate crisis when the number of troops sent proved not to be enough to carry out the mission. It would have been far better had it been Clinton's decision in the first place instead of Bush's, who knew that whatever happened, he would not be the person held ultimately accountable.

Potsdam raised basic issues of war and peace. But consider the ever-present dilemmas presented by trying to maintain control over an ever more globalized economy. International financiers between November 1932 and March 1933 had no real idea what the policy of the United States would be in, say, April. It is all too easy to imagine similar problems today. Decisive action with regard to, say, international currency markets might be necessary, but an initial decision made in December would be subject to immediate overruling by the new president taking office in January.

Would anyone designing a constitution for the United States today—or designing a constitution for any other country in the world today—choose such a long period between the election and inauguration of a prime minister or president? The question almost answers itself, because we can look at every constitution drafted since World War II and discover that none has. This is yet one more feature of the Constitution that should reinforce the enthusiasm with which one in effect expresses a vote of "no confidence" in the current Constitution.

There is another consequence of the present system that is worth mentioning. The extended hiatus not only serves to create lame-duck presidents, who may have lost much of their nonlegal authority to govern; it also means that Americans during the political campaigns prior to elections have no real idea who will constitute their executive leadership. Presidents, after all, do not act alone. The Constitution recognizes that they will be appointing other "officers of the United

States," including cabinet officials who will actually have the day-to-day responsibility for managing the vast modern American government. Yet American voters when they cast their ballots have no idea who those officials will be. We are in effect electing a monarch, who will dispense his favors as he wishes.

In parliamentary systems, such as the British, there are "shadow governments" ready to take office. One usually casts a vote not only for a known prime minister–designate, but also for an equally known chancellor of the exchequer, foreign secretary, and the like. In the United States, on the other hand, we have the phenomenon of transition periods in which exhausted presidents-to-be make decisions with significant consequences as to who will occupy public office. Imagine that George Bush had not chosen Donald Rumsfeld as secretary of defense or John Ashcroft for attorney general, for starters. Perhaps we think that we don't have to know the identities of "minor" officials, but the post-Katrina fiasco involving the incompetence of the Federal Emergency Management Agency should dispel any such confidence. At the end of the day, one of the major powers possessed by presidents is to choose members of their administrations, and one of their major duties is to choose well. One might well believe that a serious political system would assure that voters possess significant information as to what a prospective administration will look like. Alas, that is not our own system.

One could amend the Constitution to provide for a more sensible Inauguration Day. This would, however, require functionally eliminating the Electoral College inasmuch as much of the delay is explicable only with regard to the need for that contraption to operate (including leaving time for the House to select a president should the Electoral College deadlock). So even this sensible change is held hostage by the states that benefit from the college.

PRESIDENTIAL POWERS

Having (finally) inaugurated a new president, it is time to address the all-important question of what powers he or she shall have.

The President as Commander in Chief and Savior of the Nation

Section 1, clause 1, begins as follows: "The executive Power shall be vested in a President of the United States of America." This short sentence contains an interpretive minefield. I elaborate it not in order to offer a resolution—as earlier indicated, this is not that kind of book— but, rather, to specify a dilemma that would be especially relevant to anyone charged with drafting a successor constitution to the one we have now. And the reader may well feel that the ambiguity presented by the sentence is sufficiently significant, given what is at stake, that it counts as yet one more reason to trigger the drafting of a constitution that better addresses the issues.

The interpretive problem is presented by the difference between the beginning of Article I—"All legislative Powers herein granted"— and the first three words of Article II: "The executive Power." Does this mean that there is something "preconstitutional" called "the executive power," which is automatically possessed by the president without any explicit grant by "We the People" in the text of the Constitution? And, if so, where do we find the definition of this very abstract notion and discover what the president is entitled to do under it? Devotees of presidential power are apt to proclaim that the quoted language is extremely important. They believe that presidents do indeed possess vast reservoirs of powers that can be invoked basically at their discretion.

One can have little doubt that many of the framers were familiar with John Locke's *Second Treatise on Government.* One of the most important arguments made by Locke concerns what he calls "prerogative," particularly of the executive. It is true that Locke viewed governments as instituted to protect individual rights and thus limited by this very purpose. But this notion of limitation did not translate, for Locke, into a government that must always act within the constraints of the established law. He articulated the notion of *prerogative*, defined by him as the "[p]ower to act according to discretion, for the publick [sic] good, without the prescription of the Law, and *sometimes even against it.*" When this power is "imployed [sic] for the benefit of the Community, and suitably to the trust and ends of the Government,"

it "never is questioned." Indeed, "the People . . . are far from examining *Prerogative*, whilst it is in any tolerable degree imploy'd for the use
it was meant; that is, for the good of the People, and not manifestly
against it."[36] Though Locke was writing against the background of the
English monarchy (whose powers he wished to limit), his theoretical
endorsement of prerogative is certainly not confined to monarchs.

One is hard-pressed to understand American constitutionalism
without including a place for the prerogative of leadership to ignore
the law on occasion. Many of those deemed to be our greatest presidents were more than willing to subordinate what they seem to have
viewed as constitutional technicalities to what they believed to be the
exigencies of the moment. The question is whether the exercise of
prerogative is a vital part of our constitutional tradition or, instead,
significantly threatens it.

Thomas Jefferson, for example, believed that the Louisiana Purchase, the most important single political and constitutional event
between the founding and the disintegration of the United States in
1861—to which the purchase mightily contributed—was unconstitutional.[37] Whether he was correct is irrelevant to this analysis, since it
is his belief that is the crucial issue. Yet he defended it by reference to
"the laws of necessity." Jefferson wrote in an 1810 letter, referring to
the purchase:

> A strict observance of the written law is doubtless one of the
> high duties of a good citizen, but it is not the highest. The laws
> of necessity, of self-preservation, of saving our country when
> in danger, are of higher obligation. To lose our country by a
> scrupulous adherence to the written law, would be to lose the
> law itself, with life, liberty, property and all those who are
> enjoying them with us; thus absurdly sacrificing the end to the
> means.[38]

Inevitably, one must confront Abraham Lincoln, at once the most
important and yet problematic of all American presidents.[39] Lincoln
was accused of acting unconstitutionally by unilaterally suspending the
writ of habeas corpus, the basic ability for someone under detention
to challenge its legitimacy, without prior congressional authorization.

Because the right to suspend habeas corpus, perhaps the most central of all individual rights against state oppression, was placed in Article I, dealing with the powers of Congress, it is certainly plausible to believe that the president could not suspend "the Great Writ" unilaterally. Although Lincoln claimed that he was *not* violating the Constitution, he also offered an example of what lawyers call "arguing in the alternative." Thus, he asked his critics if "all the laws, *but one*, [are] to go unexecuted, and the government itself go to pieces, lest that one be violated?"[40] He pushed the notion of presidential power to, and some would say beyond, its limit. And no one should believe that the issues raised by Lincoln and his critics are matters only of what may appear to be ancient history.

Both of these presidents, and others, could well resonate with James Madison's statement, in *Federalist*, No. 41, that "[i]t is in vain to oppose constitutional barriers to the impulse of self-preservation. It is worse than in vain; because it plants in the Constitution itself *necessary usurpations of power*, every precedent of which is a germ of unnecessary and multiplied repetitions."[41]

Some defenders of presidential power simply emphasize the opening of Article II. Others, like University of California law professor John Yoo, emphasize the designation, at the beginning of Article II, section 2, of the president as "Commander in Chief of the Army and Navy of the United States."[42] The most significant presentation of Yoo's argument was an August 1, 2002, memorandum that he helped to prepare when he served in the Office of Legal Counsel of the U.S. Department of Justice, involving the president's authority to order the torture of a suspected terrorist.[43] The United States had ratified the UN Convention Against Torture and Other Cruel, Inhuman or Degrading Treatment or Punishment, Article II of which explicitly states, "No exceptional circumstances whatsoever, whether a state of war or a threat of war, internal political instability or any other public emergency, may be invoked as a justification of torture." Article VI of the U.S. Constitution states that "all Treaties . . . which shall be made, under the Authority of the United States, shall be the supreme Law of the Land." Furthermore, section 3 of Article II requires that the president "shall take Care that the Laws be faithfully executed." And Congress had passed legislation firmly banning torture by American officials. None-theless, Yoo (and, therefore, the Department of Justice) informed then–White House counsel Alberto Gonzales that the Commander-in-Chief Clause rendered unconstitutional *any* limitation on the president's power to do what he thought necessary to prevail in any conflict in-volving the United States.

As it happens, the Office of Legal Counsel withdrew this memo-randum on December 30, 2004,[44] and Gonzales, during the hearings on his subsequent nomination as attorney general, stated that the dis-cussion of presidential power was irrelevant because President Bush would not ever countenance torture—a statement that is grossly mis-leading unless one adheres to an indefensibly narrow notion of tor-ture. More to the point, the Department of Justice, including Gonzales when testifying in his own confirmation hearing, did not actually re-pudiate the Yoo analysis of presidential power. Many of the arguments presented to justify the NSA intelligence gathering (or domestic spy-ing, depending on one's preferred nomenclature) rely on Yoo-like arguments, and one can be absolutely confident that they continue to express the basic understanding of the Bush administration (and, per-haps, those of other presidents).

University of Minnesota professor Michael Stokes Paulsen offers a somewhat different defense of basically untrammeled presidential power on the basis of another provision of Article II, the oath of office set out in section 1, clause 8: "I do solemnly swear (or affirm) that I will faithfully execute the Office of President of the United States, and will to the best of my Ability, preserve, protect and defend the Consti-tution of the United States." His article is tellingly entitled "The Con-stitution of Necessity."[45] So long, Paulsen argues, as presidents can plausibly be claiming to defend the overarching constitutional order, they are apparently authorized by the oath itself to disregard any par-ticular part of the Constitution if fidelity to it might, according to the president, threaten the survival of the order itself. Paulsen quotes Lin-coln: "I felt that measures, otherwise unconstitutional, might become lawful, by becoming indispensable to the preservation of the constitu-tion, through the preservation of the nation."[46] Paulsen fully recog-nizes that he is defending "dangerous principles,"[47] but, he concludes, "if I am mistaken in all this, so was President Lincoln."[48] An important part of his rhetorical argument, obviously, is that it is simply unthinkable that our sixteenth president, carved in stone on Mt. Rushmore, was "mistaken" in something that goes so deeply into the core of what it means to be a constitutionalist president.

Harvard political theorist Harvey Mansfield has recently written that "[t]o confirm the extra-legal character of the presidency, the Constitution has him take an oath not to execute the laws but to execute the *office* of president, which is larger. Thus," argues Mansfield, "it is wrong to accuse President Bush of acting illegally in the surveillance of possible enemies, as if that were a crime and legality is all that matters."[49] Such an emphasis on legal limits is "simplistic," according to this leading conservative philosopher. Instead, in what must be some of the most stunning sentences ever written by an American political theorist, he argues:

> [T]he rule of law is not enough to run a government. Any set of standing rules is liable to encounter an emergency requiring an exception from the rule or an improvised response when no rule exists. In Machiavelli's terms, ordinary power needs to be supplemented or corrected by the extraordinary power of a prince, using wise discretion. "Necessity knows no law" is a maxim everyone admits, and takes advantage of, when in need. Small-r republicans especially are reluctant to accept it because they see that wise discretion opens the door to unwise discretion. But there is no way to draw a line between the wise and the unwise without making a law (or something like it) and thus returning to the inflexibility of the rule of law. We need both the rule of law and the power to escape it—and that twofold need is just what the Constitution provides for.

I have mentioned the English philosopher John Locke as a possible source for such arguments, and Mansfield suggests that the Italian Machiavelli must also be attended to. But the most important twentieth-century proponent of "emergency power" was the brilliant German legal philosopher Carl Schmitt,[50] who was also the leading apologist for Hitler's coming to power on the shards of the Weimar

Constitution. Like Mansfield, he viewed as painfully naïve those who assert that one could or should genuinely limit the power of government even in times of emergencies. If, as many defenders of President Bush emphasize, "September 11 changed everything," then perhaps one of the things that it changed is a notion of a nonmonarchical (or non-Machiavellian) president. And, as already suggested, one can point to eminent predecessors of President Bush to validate such arguments.

At the very least, it should be clear that the present Constitution does not offer a clear understanding of the limits of presidential power, particularly during times of presidentially perceived emergencies. Indeed, as the examples of Yoo and Paulsen demonstrate (and many others could be added), it seems to offer an open invitation for those who would defend something close to presidential dictatorship. Emergency power is the single most important subject of constitutional law in the United States—and many other countries—at the present time. Suffice it for now to say that even if there may be occasions when "constitutional dictatorship" is warranted,[51] that does not automatically translate into the kind of presidentialism articulated by Yoo and Paulsen.

One might demand that Congress explicitly authorize in advance the president to go beyond the office's ordinarily understood powers.[52] There are, for better and for worse, dozens of statutes conferring emergency powers on the president.[53] As Professor Jules Lobel has noted, by the 1970s, 470 statutes passed by Congress delegated "power to the executive over virtually every facet of American life."[54] Although Congress during that decade attempted a mass repeal of such statutes and their replacement by more tethered delegations, there is no reason to believe that it has genuinely reined in executive power. The only circumstances under which we might actually expect Congress to be vigilant with regard to executive branch overreaching is when it is controlled by a different political party than that of the president. Otherwise, there is every reason to think that party loyalty will trump any kind of institutional vigilance. In any event, one meaning of the Bush administration's strong reliance on Article II itself—including the unwritten prerogative powers attached to the very notion of being the executive—is that whatever Congress attempts to do can then be dismissed as irrelevant. This is the position taken in Bush's signing memorandum concerning the McCain amendment.

Generally, I have been relatively dismissive in this book of the importance of ambiguous constitutional provisions, such as section 8 of Article I, dealing with the powers of Congress. I have emphasized that the best way to resolve such ambiguities is to elect compatible officials who will appoint (and confirm) equally compatible judges. The reader might legitimately expect me to be similarly dismissive of these problems posed by Article II and the Commander-in-Chief Clause, because they too derive from constitutional open-endedness rather than the kind of hard-wired cage that is the focus of this book.

Perhaps I should just quote Ralph Waldo Emerson's caution against seeking a "foolish consistency" and let it go at that. But the explanation for paying far closer attention to the power-conferring aspects of Article II than to the assignment of powers to Congress in Article I is that I am considerably less sanguine with regard to the claims of presidential authority being asserted under Article II. Among other things, we are learning once more that people—both Americans and others—die as the result of unilateral decision making by risk-taking (and perhaps painfully ignorant) presidents who manifest basic contempt for the view that they are under a duty to take Congress seriously as a partner in the decision-making process. The stakes seem to be higher with regard to imperial presidencies than with regard even to an overreaching Congress. The problem with Congress is an institutionalized gridlock that blocks the making of timely and effective public policy. The basic problem with the presidency is the possibility that the occupant of the White House is too unconstrained and can all too easily engage in dramatic exertions of power, especially in the realm of foreign policy.

We have seen in our own lifetimes, for example, how fundamentally irrelevant Congress's power "To declare War," set out in clause 11 of Article I, section 8, has become. It is a notorious truth that no war has been officially declared since December 8, 1941, which has obviously not prevented the Korean, Vietnam, and two Iraqi wars that killed hundreds of thousands of Americans and others. It is safe to say that no president, of either political party, feels significantly constrained by the Declare War Clause of Article I. President Clinton, for example, felt no such constraints with regard to his decision to send American troops to Haiti or the American Air Force to bomb Serbia, a clear act of war. And, it must be admitted, Congress has scarcely fought back against imperial presidentialism, not least because the president inevitably is a more commanding presence, in every sense, than any given legislator.

I invite you to ask yourself the following question: Would you support changing the oath of office to (something like): "I do solemnly swear (or affirm) that I will faithfully execute the Office of President of the United States, and will to the best of my Ability, *do whatever I believe necessary to defend the interests of the United States*"? If you do not support the replacement of the italicized passage for the present text, "*preserve, protect and defend the Constitution of the United States,*" is it because you believe the latter is meant to confine a conscientious president in a way that the new version does not? Or do you believe that the two are basically identical in meaning, even if not in words, so that "preserve, protect and defend the Constitution" does indeed authorize any contemporary president to emulate Jefferson and Lincoln by engaging in what would otherwise be unconstitutional actions because, after all, necessity requires them? This accepts the possibility that one can "preserve" the Constitution even while violating its prohibitions, just as one can amputate a limb in order to "preserve, protect and defend" the life of a patient. Machiavelli and his admirer Harvey Mansfield are extraordinarily able thinkers, and it is possible that they are correct. But we should be aware of the consequences of accepting their arguments, and we the people should have the opportunity to decide, in a new convention, what conception of the presidency is most congruent with our sense of republican government. Or, as Mansfield seems to be suggesting, we might decide that adherence to republican government is naïve and even dangerous in our modern world. If so, we should make a collective decision that we are modifying our most basic commitment and candidly announce to the world that "consent of the governed" and "the rule of law" are now subordinate to what Stuart Taylor labels "presidential autocracy."

Emergency power, especially in the present, is the most dramatic and fateful exercise of presidential power. It is, obviously, not the only way that the president exercises power, and many other powers are more explicitly authorized by the text of the Constitution. One of them has already been mentioned, his or her power as "Commander in Chief of the Army and Navy of the United States, and of the Militia of the several States, when called into the actual Service of the United States."

Presidents, of course, possess other powers as well. The primary powers of the president are set out in section 2, clause 2:

> He shall have Power, by and with the Advice and Consent of the Senate, to make Treaties, provided two thirds of the Senators present concur; and he shall nominate, and by and with the Advice and Consent of the Senate, shall appoint Ambassadors, other public Ministers and Consuls, Judges of the supreme Court, and all other Officers of the United States, whose Appointments are not herein otherwise provided for, and which shall be established by Law: but the Congress may by Law vest the Appointment of such inferior Officers, as they think proper, in the President alone, in the Courts of Law, or in the Heads of Departments.

Another important power, discussed in the previous chapter, is the power to veto congressional legislation.

It is worth noting the requirement that the ratification of treaties requires a vote of two-thirds of the Senate. It should be absolutely obvious, given the discussion in the previous chapter, that this in no way translates into a perhaps defensible, albeit still controversial, notion that two-thirds of "the American people" must concur, through their representatives, with a treaty that is, after all, then the law of the land. Instead, it is just one more assignment of a veto power to what may on occasion be the one-third-plus-one of the senators representing a tiny fraction of the American polity. Ironically, the best defense of the two-thirds rule is that it is the only way that one can guarantee, practically speaking, that representatives of the majority of the population do assent to the treaty.

An important response to the difficulty of senatorial ratification has been the nurturance of the president's power to enter into "executive agreements," which may need no congressional approval at all or may be presented to both Houses of Congress (not just the Senate) for *majority* approval.[55] This is, I believe, a more than defensible addition to the president's power to negotiate treaties inasmuch as its origin is best explained by reference to the indefensible power held by a minority of the Senate. However, it remains the case that some international agreements are still viewed as treaties, and the power assigned to the Senate continues to be of extreme importance with regard to the ability of the president to assure countries with which he is negotiating that any ensuing treaty will be ratified.

Clauses 1 and 2 basically exhaust the assignments of power to the president found in Article II. There may be political disagreements with the way such powers are exercised—as is the case for millions of Americans on both sides of the political divide with regard to judicial nominations—but it is difficult to take umbrage at these particular assignments of presidential power. One might, however, have reservations about the final sentence of clause 2: "The President shall have Power to fill up all Vacancies that may happen during the Recess of the Senate, by granting commissions which shall expire at the End of their next Session."

The power to make such recess appointments undoubtedly made a great deal of sense in 1787, when Congress met for quite short terms. It was therefore prudent to authorize the president to make such temporary appointments of officials who generally would require senatorial confirmation. In modern times, however, when the Senate meets for most of the year, recess appointments have become a device by which presidents can simply avoid the necessity of confronting senatorial disapproval of potential nominees. The most dramatic recent illustration of this was President Bush's recess appointment of John Bolton to be ambassador to the United Nations even though it was quite clear that he was not going to be confirmed by the Senate. Bolton was the "victim" of a Democratic filibuster, though one might recall that Democratic senators in fact received more overall votes

and represent more of the total population than do Republican senators. In any event, presidents of both parties have taken advantage of
this clause to do end runs around their political opponents in the Senate. The most serious problem may well be raised by making recess
appointments to the federal judiciary, inasmuch as the judges receiving such appointments are in effect auditioning for approval by the
Senate prior to the expiration of their terms. One can well believe that
this calls into question the degree of judicial independence they will
feel free to exercise should they fear antagonizing senators who will be
voting on their ability to transform the temporary recess appointment
into a permanent lifelong one. The recess appointment clause is a
perfect example of a highly sensible constitutional provision, at the time
of its writing, that has in the modern era become, with rare exceptions,
an anachronism and a potential vehicle for presidential abuse.

The Pardoning Power

A final presidential power is set out at the conclusion of section 2, clause
1, which begins with the commander-in-chief power. The last sentence
authorizes the president with the "Power to grant Reprieves and Pardons for Offences against the United States, except in Cases of Impeachment." Ordinarily, one might not spend any time at all on this
power. It is, after all, common that heads of state, whether monarchs
or presidents, have the power to dispense mercy on those who have
run afoul of the law. The firestorm that greeted President Clinton's
end-of-term pardon of Marc Rich, who had been convicted of securities manipulation and similar crimes, was directed at the possibility
that it was a quid pro quo for generous campaign contributions, though
some ungenerous persons suggested that the president might have had
a personal relationship with Rich's former wife, Denise. Though the
pardon scarcely seemed to have spoken well for Clinton's judgment—
like so much else in his presidency, alas—it hardly seemed to threaten
our republic in any serious sense.

But consider the Christmas pardons issued in 1992 by Clinton's
predecessor, George H. W. Bush, following his defeat in the presidential election that year. They had the consequence of stopping dead in

its tracks an ongoing investigation of the Iran-Contra episode and, more particularly, the possibility that then–Vice President Bush might have misled officials about his role in that scandal. He also pardoned former State Department official Elliott Abrams, who had been convicted of lying to Congress while testifying on Reagan administration policies in Nicaragua, apparently a praiseworthy act for presidential loyalists. And, just two weeks after a former aide to former Secretary of State Colin Powell denounced the "cabal" between Vice President Dick Cheney and Secretary of Defense Donald Rumsfeld, one read in the newspapers of President Bush's effusive praise of the indicted Lewis "Scooter" Libby, who had served as Cheney's chief of staff. One well-respected columnist for the *Washington Post* has alluded to rumors that Bush, who of course never has to face the electorate again, will "take care" of Libby if he continues to remain silent about other figures in the administration who participated in the outing of Valerie Plame as a CIA operative. "If Bush," writes E. J. Dionne, "truly wants the public to know all the facts in the leak case, as he has claimed in the past, he will announce now that he will not pardon Libby. That would let [the special prosecutor] finish his work unimpeded, and we would all have a chance, at last, to learn how and why this sad affair came to pass."[56]

As noted earlier, much of our Constitution—and critiques of the Constitution—can be explained by reference to what some might term paranoia, that is, the undue fear of oppression. As a matter of fact, some opponents of the original Constitution in 1787–1788 focused on the Pardon Clause and suggested that it would allow the president to plot with confederates to deprive us of our "Blessings of Liberty," secure in the knowledge that he could prevent their exposure to the full measure of the law should the plot be discovered. Thus, dissidents in the Pennsylvania ratification convention of 1787 wrote of their fears that the president, "having the power of pardoning . . . may screen from punishment the most treasonable attempts that may be made on the liberties of the people."[57] I confess that I tended to chuckle when I read such critiques a number of years ago. I am not certain any longer that the Pardon Clause is such a laughing matter. At the very least, it underscores the importance of having complete faith in the integrity of those who occupy the Oval Office.

ON MALFEASANCE AND MISFEASANCE: WHY CRIMINAL PRESIDENTS PRESENT LESS OF A THREAT THAN "MERELY" INCOMPETENT ONES

The final question posed in this chapter is very simple: What if we turn out to have been disastrously mistaken in our choice? To what degree are we, because of the Constitution, stuck with our mistakes? Let us, then, turn to the Impeachment Clause and its manifest inadequacy to the realities of contemporary politics.

Three separate clauses come together to cover the impeachment of a president or any other "civil officer" of the United States. The first two, in Article I, concern the role of Congress in the impeachment process. The last one, which concludes Article II, establishes the legal standard for an impeachable offense.

Thus Article I, section 2, clause 5, states: "The House of Representatives shall . . . have the sole Power of Impeachment." Section 3, clause 6, similarly assigns to the Senate "the sole Power to try all Impeachments. When sitting for that Purpose, they shall be on Oath or Affirmation. When the President of the United States is tried, the Chief Justice shall preside: And no Person shall be convicted without the Concurrence of two thirds of the Members present." Finally, Article II, section 4, applies the substantive standard that should guide first the House in impeaching, which may be analogized to indicting the president, and then the Senate in determining whether the evidence supports the charge: "The President, Vice President and all civil Officers of the United States, shall be removed from Office on Impeachment for, and Conviction of, Treason, Bribery, or other high Crimes and Misdemeanors."

The original proposal relative to impeachment, submitted to the Constitutional Convention on June 13, 1787, included the possibility of removal "on impeachment and conviction of malpractices or neglect of duty."[58] There was little discussion, not least because there was no agreement yet on how the president would be selected. (The June 13 proposal assumed that the president would be appointed for a single seven-year term by the Congress itself.) Our current Constitution had taken far more shape by September 8, nine days before the final passage of the draft by the convention on September 17. George Mason of Virginia moved that "or maladministration" be added to the list of impeachable offenses, though he withdrew his motion after Madison protested that "[s]o vague a term will be equivalent to a tenure during pleasure of the Senate." More dubiously, Gouverneur Morris expressed his confidence that an "election of every four years will prevent maladministration."[59] Thus, both the House and the Senate must be persuaded that a president has engaged in "Treason, Bribery, or other high Crimes and Misdemeanors" before they can legitimately act to remove him or her from office.

As one might imagine, there is an enormous literature on exactly what constitutes "high Crimes and Misdemeanors," much of it generated during the impeachment and subsequent trial of President Clinton in 1998–1999. Did, for example, perjury about a private matter (as distinguished from a matter directly relevant to the performance of public duties) constitute such an offense? Fortunately, such debates need not concern us, for they are basically irrelevant to the principal question of this concluding section. Why should the American people be stuck with a demonstrably incompetent president simply because, to adopt Richard Nixon's famous self-defense, he is not "a crook"?

Recall that, constitutionally speaking, it is grimly "better" that senators die than that they be disabled. Dead senators can be replaced immediately; merely disabled ones, unless the Constitution is amended, continue to hold their offices, however unable they may be to exercise their responsibilities. It should be obvious, incidentally, that "disabled" in this context has nothing to do with what might be termed "ordinary" disabilities involving mobility, deafness, blindness, or the like. I am referring to such things as comas or mental impairment. Similarly, we are better off, as a polity, if our president does turn out to be a crook (or worse), because then there is a constitutionally adequate, even if extremely clumsy and politically freighted, way of getting rid of him or her. If, on the other hand, he is "only" incompetent—alas, the use of scare quotes is completely apt—it appears, as a constitutional matter, that there is no alternative to allowing him to serve out his four-year term of office, with attendant possession of all powers granted by Article II.

Many contemporary defenders of a "strong presidency" are fond of quoting Hamilton and other proponents of an "energetic" chief executive as essential to confronting such modern challenges as terrorist threats and other perceived emergencies. Yet, as political theorist William Scheurman has aptly observed, "presidentialism arguably exacerbates the dilemmas of emergency government," when presidents claim extraordinary powers to meet national exigencies. Presidentialism's "relative inflexibility—e.g., the fact that presidential terms of office are fixed—probably makes it more difficult for the electorate to rid itself of an incompetent or unaccountable executive with a poor record of emergency management."[60] There is nothing academic in such an example. Even if one places the war in Iraq to one side, there is the utter failure of executive branch leadership in the aftermath of Hurricane Katrina. Scheurman aptly quotes an earlier political scientist, Herman Finer, who observed that "the whole potency of the presidency is founded on a gamble": The leadership presumably sought from a strong president "is based on the hazards of the nerves, brains, and character of a single man."[61]

The rigidity of the president's term of office is perhaps the most vivid contrast between the American system of government and the parliamentary systems that are far more common worldwide. Let us again return to Great Britain. When the Conservative party's members of Parliament in 1990 came to the conclusion that Margaret Thatcher, who was then the longest-serving prime minister in history, had turned into an electoral liability because she was pursuing patently unpopular (and, many thought, indefensible) policies, they unceremoniously dumped her. John Major literally moved into Ten Downing Street the next day and led the Tories to victory in the next general election in 1992. Three things are noteworthy about this. One is that the prime minister could so relatively easily lose her job. The second is that this did not in the least mean that the "government was brought down," triggering either a Labor takeover or even new elections. This was treated simply as a change in internal party leadership, even though the leader in question happened to be prime minister. Finally, there was no sense of crisis in Great Britain. It was simply the ordinary process of parliamentary government at work.

Such a transition is impossible in the United States. A noncriminal president is thought to have an unbreakable four-year lease on the White House. It should be amply clear, though, that noncriminality, however commendable, does not in the least guarantee that one is a wise, or even a competent, president. Why in the world should "We the People" not be able to break the lease and evict a manifestly unsuitable or incompetent president and replace him with someone presumably more able? As James L. Sundquist writes, "Criminal activity is only one circumstance that can render a president unable to lead and govern."[62]

One might be tempted to say that fixed terms are necessary to guarantee either good policies or even a suitable measure of political stability. Both assertions are demonstrably false. The only way to link the length of term to the quality of policy is to argue that it is important to encourage presidents to take certain decisions that have foreseeable short-run costs but, or so it is hoped, long-run benefits. Commentators have noted, for example, that presidents generally prefer business downturns in the first two years of their term, with consequent recovery in the second two years when, not at all coincidentally, they are running for reelection (unless stopped by the Twenty-second Amendment). Perhaps one should note that this also suggests that presidents will be loath to make risky, albeit beneficial, decisions in the second two years lest the public overreact to the costs they are suffering and underestimate the likelihood of future gains. The political stability rationale is even more demonstrably false inasmuch as peaceful, stable, democratic countries around the world, organized on a parliamentary basis, regularly undergo midterm—that is, before the legally mandated end of a parliamentary term—changes in leadership without disorder in the streets.

James Sundquist, in a chapter appropriately titled "Reconstituting a Failed Government," writes that the "United States . . . is in bondage to the calendar."[63] The reader may recall that this is part of a book devoted to the interplay between "constitutional reform and effective government." Not surprisingly, given Sundquist's language, he is rightly critical of our "bondage" and suggests a variety of alternatives. Even with regard to the impeachment of a criminal president, he notes that the process takes far too long a time and deprives the country of effective leadership during the time leading up to impeachment and trial and, quite likely, thereafter. Obviously, the principal question should be whether we believe that we are being well served by a president rather than whether he is a criminal or not.

Why did "maladministration" fail to be adopted at the Convention? The answer is probably that the framers feared that this would give too much power to Congress, which was fair enough as a judgment in 1787. The problem is that the framers had literally not the slightest conception of the role that the president of the United States would come to occupy not only within the boundaries of the country but also in the world at large. Article II does, to be sure, assign some formidable powers to the president. But the most important clause to most framers, as a practical matter, was the Take Care Clause, requiring faithful enforcement of the laws passed by Congress.

What might we do when presented with a "failed presidency" beyond comforting ourselves, if that is the right term, with the reminder that "in three years it will all be over (if we are still alive)"? Needless to say, I am tempted to offer contemporary examples. Republicans can dwell on Bill Clinton's presidency, which was surely a failure in some important respects. Democrats need no encouragement to list the various ways in which George W. Bush has proved himself to be an incompetent president. But consider two historical examples that are perhaps less provocative. By any conceivable measure, Andrew Johnson, Abraham Lincoln's successor, was a disastrous misfit as president. As it happens, he was impeached, though not convicted. Bruce Ackerman suggests, however, that he staved off conviction by basically agreeing to change some of his more disastrous policies involving Reconstruction.[64] Those defenders of Bill Clinton who evoked Andrew Johnson's impeachment as a caution against a similar response to their hero never once noted that bland acceptance of Johnson's use of presidential powers would, in effect, have doomed any prospect of serious Reconstruction. This would have meant, among other things, that the Fourteenth Amendment (and the Fifteenth as well, with its guarantee of the right to vote to African Americans) would never have been added to the Constitution. They should have been ashamed of themselves in effect endorsing Andrew Johnson's claim of a right to the presidency.

A second failed presidency was Herbert Hoover's. Hoover was a far better person (and even president) than Johnson was ever capable of being, but he "clearly failed to give the country the leadership it was demanding"[65] in the aftermath of the Crash of 1929 and subsequent collapse of the economy. People did what they could to change the leadership by bringing Democrats to within one vote of controlling the Senate and two votes of controlling the House in 1931. But Hoover remained in the White House. Moreover, an independent problem is that the newly empowered Democrats had no real incentive to try to work *with* Hoover to overcome our problems, because any truly bipartisan success might have redounded in his favor and bolstered his chances for reelection in 1932. What we had was a de facto divided government and a failed president, a toxic mixture for a country in crisis.

As Sundquist writes, "The United States government, and the state and city governments modeled after it, are virtually unique among all the world's organizations in possessing no true safeguard against executive failure."[66] Even if one regards impeachment as a safeguard against failure predicated on criminal misconduct, it provides no help at all if the failures are the result of sheer ineptitude.

I think I have shown that the limitations of what might be called the "impeachment system" constitute yet one more reason to vote no confidence in the current Constitution. It will be up to the subsequent convention to decide exactly what should replace the impeachment system, but I note three possibilities:

a. Congress, upon a declaration, by the vote of two-thirds of the entire Congress meeting in joint session (which will diminish somewhat the distortions attached to equal voting power in the Senate), that it has "no confidence" in the president, schedules a special election (in which the current president can run, as a way of testing whether Congress actually speaks for the people) to take place within a month to pick a successor to the discredited president.[67]

A principal objection may be the difficulty of actually scheduling an election in such a short period of time, and any longer period by definition subjects the country to ongoing leadership by a significantly delegitimized president.

b. Should a president be the subject of a two-thirds vote of no confidence by the Congress meeting in joint session, he or she must immediately resign, to be succeeded by the vice president. This approach is a perfect solution to what might be termed the "Clinton problem," which was the result of decidedly personal failings and not linked, for most Americans, to outrage at his general policy goals. Clinton would have been forced to resign, but Al Gore would have immediately taken the helm and continued what the country had amply demonstrated, in the 1996 election, were acceptable approaches to public policy. This approach would be far less appealing if the vote of no confidence were based on policy disagreements, for then it might be cold comfort if the vice president succeeded to office. (No critic of George W. Bush would be assuaged if Dick Cheney became president.)

c. Upon a vote of no confidence by two-thirds of the Congress in joint session, the members of the Congress who are of the same political party as the now-deposed president shall meet and, as soon as is reasonably possible, select someone to serve as president for the remainder of the term of office. This approach guards against the possibility that the vote of no confidence would in effect be a coup, whereby, in a divided government, an invigorated congressional majority could, by this means, attempt in effect to seize the presidency that it failed to win in the previous election.

It is not necessary in this book to decide which among these presents the best alternative or whether there are even better alternatives available. The point is that here is one more place in which the Constitution is broken, with potentially dire consequences, and we should have the wit and the will to try to fix it rather than continue whistling past the graveyard in the hope that nothing untoward will happen to us. Perhaps that is even a viable strategy when going past graveyards, since there are no ghosts or goblins who are poised, ready to attack us. That is not the case with regard to the possible consequences of continuing to remain blind to the constitutional goblins, which do constitute real threats.

There is one more cost of our constitutional inability to dismiss incompetent presidents. As psychologists who study what is called "cognitive dissonance" would predict, if we are presented with something that cannot be changed, there is a psychological tendency to turn what appears to be a necessity into a virtue. The president really isn't so incompetent, the emperor really is wearing clothes after all, even if they are hard to see. This tendency is reinforced by the fact that the U.S. president is not only chief executive, but also head of state, who upon his entrance into any public setting can hear the band strike up "Hail to the Chief." This is not republican government; it is, rather, more appropriate to a monarchy. And the president has taken on the overtones of a monarch because the very structures of the Constitution serve to infantilize "We the (adult) People."

AND WHAT ABOUT THE VICE PRESIDENT?

As tempting as it is to conclude this chapter with the last paragraph, I must run the risk of anticlimax by devoting at least a page to the *vice* president. The original assumption was that the person selected for that office would be the second-most-qualified person in the nation. That particular vision was yet another casualty of the rise of the party system that did in the entire cogency of the Electoral College (and much else besides). By 1800, almost no one could seriously argue that Aaron Burr was the second-most-qualified person behind Thomas Jefferson. The Jefferson-Burr ticket was the first example of a presidential candidate picking a running mate on considerations of geography or some other attribute having precious little to do with the genuine belief that he would be the best person in the country to take over should anything happen to the president. There have, of course, been occasional vice presidents and vice-presidential candidates of high caliber, especially in the post–World War II period. But even in modern times, there have been truly inexplicable choices, the most obvious example undoubtedly being J. Danforth Quayle, who for four years stood a heartbeat away from succeeding George H. W. Bush as president. More recently, even loyal Democrats like myself can wonder if John Edwards, for all of his real strengths, was really the appropriate choice to become president, should anything have happened to a President John Kerry, given that Edwards, as of 2004, was totally without training or experience in foreign or military affairs.

It may also be worth mentioning that, at the end of February 2006, Vice President Dick Cheney was, according to at least one respected poll, approved by only 18 percent of the American public. At the beginning of 2002, he was approved by 39 percent, though a full 49 percent "ha[d]n't heard enough" to have an opinion, which is itself an illuminating finding.[68] By 2006, 46 percent of the respondents had an "unfavorable" view of the vice president, though slightly more than a third (35 percent) continued to indicate that they did not know enough to have an opinion. In any event, should anything happen to George W. Bush, one can wonder if Vice President Cheney would have enough public support to provide effective leadership during the inevitable moment of national trauma. There is also the not insignificant possibility that Cheney will prove to have been involved in the White House machinations involving the disclosure of Valerie Plame's employment by the Central Intelligence Agency. Whatever one's politics, one can only hope that we do not have the opportunity to discover what would accompany a Cheney presidency in such circumstances.

For almost 200 years, there have been calls simply to eliminate the office of the vice president.[69] For two centuries, they have gone nowhere. But here, too, we see a potential accident waiting to happen if—and almost inevitably when—we once again experience a death in the White House and the succession of a person manifestly ill equipped—whether through lack of adequate experience or widespread popular disdain— to take on the monumental burdens and powers of the modern presidency. At the very least, no sensible person could see the office of the vice president as a reason to *support* the present Constitution, and most of us should realize that it is yet one more problem with which the delegates to the forthcoming convention will have to wrestle.

FOUR

LIFE TENURE FOR SUPREME COURT JUSTICES

AN IDEA WHOSE TIME HAS PASSED

In recent years, I have addressed the principal issue of this chapter—life tenure for Supreme Court justices—in my introductory courses in constitutional law when visiting the New York University Law School and then at my home institution, the University of Texas Law School. I have made very clear that I doubt the wisdom of life tenure, and I have noted that many admirable societies do without it. I then included in the final examination a question inviting an assessment of life tenure.

Many people cynically assume that students simply feed back to professors what they think professors would like to hear. Some, less cynically but perhaps more ominously, believe that professors are Svengalis able to shape the minds of impressionable students. What, then, is to be inferred from the fact that 104 of 108 NYU students and roughly the same proportion of UT students wrote that preservation of American liberties is dependent on life tenure of Supreme Court justices? One inference is that I succeeded in conveying my genuine belief that they should think for themselves and be completely indifferent to my own point of view. That would be very gratifying. Another inference is that I am simply wrong on the merits. But a final inference is that this overwhelming—and, to me, absolutely inexplicable—commitment to life tenure is evidence of what I described earlier as the "veneration" accorded to the Constitution and all of its aspects, however dubious they may be.

To be sure, only a fanatic would vote against the present Constitution solely because of life tenure for Supreme Court justices. Even if one believes it is deeply mistaken, even pernicious in some of its consequences, it scarcely is enough in itself to justify refusing to re-ratify the Constitution and convening a new convention. But it is a good and substantial reason to add to other such reasons, some of which (equal votes in the Senate, the Electoral College system) require no fanaticism at all to justify the calling of a new convention.

My primary concern in this chapter is *not* the power of the Court to declare legislation unconstitutional, as important as that power may be. Law professors continue to debate whether the Constitution actually assigns such power of "judicial review," especially with regard to *federal* legislation, to courts. Almost all analysts agree that Article VI of the Constitution authorizes judges to do so with regard to *state* legislation that conflicts with the Constitution. Still, almost everyone concedes that our operative political system includes the ability of courts to engage in similar review of national legislation. If one is opposed to judicial review, which is not a frivolous position,[1] then that is a good reason to vote against the Constitution and then beseech the delegates to the convention to follow the Dutch and Irish examples and explicitly prohibit the practice of judicial review. If one believes, on balance, that the country is better off with the practice, then one might advocate ending the debate, once and for all, by explicitly authorizing it.

My own view is mixed. I believe that Harvard Law School professor Mark Tushnet makes some powerful arguments that, overall, judicial review has not served the country well, even if particular decisions—and individuals will have different favorites in this regard—have done so. And certainly there are some admirable countries, the Netherlands, for example, that have maintained a polity that is congruent with the values of our Preamble without engaging in judicial review.[2] Moreover, I substantially agree with the arguments of University of Chicago political scientist and lawyer Gerald Rosenberg that courts have far less power to effect change than many people, on both the Right and Left, believe.[3] Even the fabled Warren Court, which for some is a beacon of constitutional possibility, for others a symbol of an "imperial judiciary," did not climb out on limbs as often as some of its admirers believe.[4] Usually, it was enforcing the constitutional vision of what was then the dominant liberal political coalition exemplified by the 1960 election of John F. Kennedy and, most certainly, the 1964 Democratic landslide victories for both the presidency and Congress. What the Warren Court did not foresee was how evanescent that landslide moment would be; it would be buried in the mud of Vietnam and a perception that liberals in general, and the Court in particular, were contributing to a terrifying decline in basic "law and order."[5] Still, at the moment of its height, the Warren Court ably represented the American majority in most of its rulings.

Similarly, even those unhappy with the current Supreme Court should recognize that it reflects electoral victories by the Republican party, especially its more conservative wing, more than a runaway conclave of judges disconnected from larger social and political movements. Conservative presidents, after all, have controlled the ability to nominate new justices—and the district and circuit judges on what the Constitution terms the "inferior" courts—for twenty-five of the past thirty-seven years (1969–2006). To be sure, Jimmy Carter, who served between 1977 and 1981, did not have the opportunity to appoint a single justice. This skewed the political distribution of the Supreme Court in an even more conservative direction than might otherwise have been the case.

Carter was unable to place anyone on the Supreme Court—and Bill Clinton got only two such opportunities in his eight years of office—because the United States, unlike most countries in the world today, has an indefensible system of life tenure for judges. This derives from the beginning of Article III, which concerns the judiciary: "The Judges, both of the supreme and inferior Courts, shall hold their Offices during good Behaviour." What, precisely, does "good behaviour" mean? I have argued elsewhere that the clause is scarcely self-evident in its meaning, which means, by definition, that it is open to good-faith differences in interpretation by well-trained lawyers.[6] I believe, for example, that one can legitimately interpret the Good Behavior Clause to mean that judges, *whatever their term of service*, cannot be removed from office for partisan political reasons that would, by definition, threaten the very idea of judicial independence. No judge can be fired because Congress concludes that he or she is too liberal or too conservative. So long as the judges' "behaviour" is within the range viewed as "good," that is, uncorrupted—which most certainly includes issuing controversial opinions that might antagonize part of the public —then they are protected against losing their positions. This interpretation easily rules out arguments by former House majority leader Tom DeLay that liberal judges should be impeached by Congress, just as would be the case, for example, if liberals unhappy with the ultraconservative opinions of Justice Clarence Thomas made similar suggestions.

However, it is the case that almost all lawyers and judges throughout our history have interpreted the Good Behavior Clause to mean life tenure. Candor requires me to concede that my own argument, however much I sincerely believe it, is very much a minority position. I therefore proceed on the assumption that my colleagues who disagree with me are "correct" (and not merely taking a different, and wrongheaded, position). In any event, life tenure, especially for Supreme Court justices, is an idea whose time has passed, and it offers a good reason for any concerned citizen, regardless of his or her substantive political commitments, to be dissatisfied with the Constitution.

One might believe that life tenure, if it is a problem at all, is equally problematic for *all* so-called Article III courts[7] that are established (the Supreme Court) or authorized (all "inferior courts") by the Constitution. The Good Behavior Clause applies across the board. Even though judges are now allowed to retire on a pension equal to their salary whenever their age (if over sixty-five) and length of service total eighty,[8] remarkably few do so.[9] "Since 1984, over 80 percent of all [eligible] federal judges have taken senior status," which allows them more flexibility over their workload but is altogether different from retirement.[10] One may get an idea of how long such judges continue to serve by discovering that more than 90 percent of district and circuit judges die within a year of moving to full retirement.[11] Knowledge of such statistics may also help to explain why judges are tempted to remain on the bench forever even though they are in effect working "for free."

I am not concerned about the life tenure of "inferior" judges, however, in part because I have seen no evidence that the country is disserved by it. When judges take senior status, they automatically create a vacancy that can be filled by the appointment of a new, younger judge, who can bring whatever new perspectives that the (relatively) young can bring. There are also informal ways of handling a senior judge who has demonstrated a diminished capacity for the work involved in judging. She will find herself no longer assigned any cases.

This is not true of the Supreme Court, however. With regard to that extraordinary—and extraordinarily peculiar—Court, life tenure is a sufficiently serious problem to offer an added justification for voting to call a new convention. I confess that one reason I was surprised to discover how many lower-court judges continue to serve even when they could retire on full pay is that service on district and circuit courts is genuinely difficult work. Judges are inundated by hundreds, even thousands, of cases to which they must devote at least some time. Many of these cases, moreover, are, even to dedicated lawyers, quite boring, whatever their importance to the particular litigants.

For better and, in some ways, distinctly for worse, what is true of judges on inferior courts is not true of the Supreme Court justices, who have the luxury of picking their own docket, which currently is somewhere between seventy-five and eighty-five cases a year. During the 2004 term of the Court, for example, which began in October 2004 and ended in June 2005, the Supreme Court issued "full opinions" in only seventy-nine cases. Because most of these cases (fifty-five) were non-unanimous, these seventy-nine cases generated a total of 203 opinions. Chief Justice Rehnquist, in failing health, wrote only nine opinions, seven of them majority opinions "for the Court" plus a concurrence and a dissent. The most prolific justice, Clarence Thomas, wrote thirty-four opinions (eight opinions for the Court; eleven concurrences, agreeing with the outcome but not necessarily the reasoning of the majority; and fifteen dissents). The other justices wrote between eighteen (O'Connor and Souter) and thirty (Stevens) opinions.[12] Given that each justice can call on the assistance of up to four law clerks to do the actual research and even the writing of the opinions—it is well known that most of the justices do not write their own opinions—this is scarcely a back-breaking workload.

Many of these cases raise extremely important issues of the day, including abortion, affirmative action, executive power during time of war, the relationship between church and state, or the ability to suppress hateful speech. It is readily understandable that the kinds of strong individuals who manage to get to the Court in the first place are attracted by the opportunity to affect public policies about which they have deep feelings. Supreme Court justices also have a significant degree of freedom in making their judgments. Seventh Circuit judge Richard Posner, perhaps the most distinguished—and certainly the most intellectually interesting—contemporary judge, recently argued in the pages of the *Harvard Law Review* that the law, with regard to cases that make it to the Supreme Court, is sufficiently unclear so that the justices basically have license to impose their own political preferences on the country.[13]

Definitive arguments against life tenure for Supreme Court justices can be found in a recent article by Northwestern Law School professors Steven Calabresi and James Lindgren.[14] It is worth pointing out that Calabresi is one of the founding fathers of the conservative Federalist Society, so the attack on life tenure is not a partisan one; political liberals like myself and conservatives like Calabresi are in strong agreement about the pernicious consequences of lifetime tenure. Calabresi and Lindgren demonstrate that "the real-world, practical meaning of life tenure has been expanding over time[:] justices have been staying on the Court to more advanced ages than in the past, and, as a result, vacancies have been occurring less frequently than ever before."[15] Over the past century, for example, the period 1911–1940 saw nineteen justices on the Court, serving an average length of exactly sixteen years. The following thirty-year period of 1941–1970 included seventeen justices, including several who served unusually short terms because of death or moving to other positions of service, which no doubt accounts for the average length of service dropping to 12.2 years. Between 1971 and 2005, however, only twelve justices served an average of 26.1 years, a full half decade more than the 1821–1860 cohort of eleven justices.[16] For example, Chief Justice William Rehnquist, who died at the age of eighty while still on the Court in 2005, had been appointed in 1971. (Some ungenerous persons suggested that he was consciously trying to break William O. Douglas's record of thirty-five years.) Seventy-five-year-old Sandra Day O'Connor submitted her resignation in the same year after "only" twenty-four years on the Court, though she continued to sit for a full six months beyond her ostensible resignation because of difficulties attached to appointing a successor. Justice John Paul Stevens, appointed in 1976, is embarking on his fourth decade of membership at the age of eighty-six.

Contemporary Supreme Court justices seem to treat life tenure as a literal boon of the office, so that only serious illness or death will necessarily remove them from the bench.[17] And, as Emery professor of history and law David Garrow has demonstrated, even serious illness, especially if it affects "only" mental capacities, seems unavailing in all too many instances.[18] When Justice William O. Douglas persisted in remaining on the Court even after a debilitating stroke, his colleagues resolved basically not to count his vote in any case in which it would have been decisive, as in 5–4 opinions.[19]

Alas, Douglas is not the only recent justice who has "stayed too long at the fair." Chief Justice Rehnquist may have demonstrated personal valor during his final illness, but it is also the case that he demonstrated as well a degree of egoistic narcissism in putting his own all-too-human desire to retain his office ahead of the interests of the country. It is true that both the Americans with Disabilities Act and ordinary decency counsel that one generally should accommodate persons who need medical treatment for serious illnesses. Both Justices O'Connor and Ginsburg, for example, had bouts of cancer when they were in their sixties, and no one, properly, suggested that they should resign. But it is also true that one should expect the truly elderly and ill to have some perspective about their condition if they occupy important public positions. Even if Rehnquist had a constitutional right to stay on the Court, he should not have done so. For what it is worth, the same issues, and the same cautionary notes, can arise with tenured professors, who share with federal judges—and almost no one else—a right to literal life tenure. Both the Supreme Court and many universities may be harmed by the willingness of certain individuals to stand on their legal rights and ignore the interests of the institutions in which they ostensibly serve.

The possibility of diminished capacity, however real and important, is not the only, or perhaps even the main, reason to find life tenure pernicious. Lucas Powe offers "three interrelated problems with life tenure" and the linked propensity of Supreme Court justices to remain in Washington far too long:

> Their formative adult experiences took place forty years earlier in a society often unrecognizable in the present. It is one thing to elect such individuals to govern.[20] It is another to have them govern because elected individuals approved of them twenty or thirty years earlier. Second, the political order that created their ascendancy (and for which they may have some fond feelings) may also be receding into history. Yet, like the Four Horsemen [of the 1930s, who tried to strangle the New Deal reforms of Franklin Roosevelt] or, alas, [William J.] Brennan or [Thurgood] Marshall, they try to live and serve until that old political order can somehow restore itself (and therefore replace them with younger lawyers of similar ideology). Third, as shown by the Reagan and [both] Bush Administrations, there are incentives for a current governing coalition to appoint youthful justices so that those appointees will have at least thirty probable years of service on the Court. This virtually guarantees that the first and second problems will crop up at some point.[21]

Washington and Lee professor of law Lewis H. LaRue is similarly critical, even as he readily concedes that there may have been good reasons for the generation of 1787 to support life tenure. This only underscores the fact that one need not disrespect the framers; one need only say that empirical evidence has served to belie some of their central presuppositions. Those who framed the Constitution "had to proceed upon assumptions, and it is not strange that some of these assumptions should turn out to be false."[22] We have seen similar language earlier in this book, relating to ways that subsequent developments in American history have belied the rationales for the creation of some of our institutions.

What were these assumptions with regard to the judiciary? To answer this question, LaRue turns to one of the foundational texts of American constitutional history, the *Federalist*, No. 78, authored by Alexander Hamilton, who defended "the permanency of the judicial office" as a way of avoiding "an arbitrary discretion in the courts." Hamilton thought it

> indispensable that [judges] should be bound down by strict rules and precedents which serve to define and point out their duty in every particular case that comes before them; and it will be readily conceived from the variety of controversies which grow out of the folly and wickedness of mankind that the record of these precedents must unavoidably swell to a very considerable bulk and must demand long and laborious study to acquire a competent knowledge of them. Hence it is that there can be but few men [*sic*] in the society who will have sufficient skill in the laws to qualify them for the status of judges. And making the proper deductions for the ordinary depravity of human nature, the number must be still smaller of those who unite the requisite integrity with the requisite knowledge.[23]

The problem, as LaRue demonstrates, is that almost no one today, regardless of his or her particular political viewpoint, shares the assumptions embedded in Hamilton's argument. Relatively few of those thought to be among our greatest Supreme Court justices had, for example, demonstrated at the time of their appointment a "long and laborious study" of the precedents that would ostensibly bind them. This was certainly not the case with Chief Justice Earl Warren, for example, nor was it the case with, say, Lewis Powell, whose extensive practice as a corporate lawyer in Richmond, Virginia, and as president of the American Bar Association scarcely required immersion in the materials that he would confront as a justice of the Supreme Court.

And, if truth be known, as LaRue argues, "none of us believes that our judges are 'bound by strict rules and precedents which serve to define and point out their duty in every particular case that comes before them.'" There are simply too many 5–4 decisions that demonstrate the relative meaninglessness of any such assertion.

Chief Justice Rehnquist himself, when dedicating a new library at Washington and Lee in Justice Powell's honor, had no difficulty in acknowledging that it matters who is appointed to the Court.[24] The late chief justice would have been the first to agree that judges are not impersonal machines who simply apply algorithms to resolve the cases that arrive. If that were the case, then the obvious divisions on the Supreme Court would be truly inexplicable. As Yale law professor Jack Balkin and I have written elsewhere, each judge possesses a "high politics" that consists of sometimes quite varying visions of how best to instantiate the goals set out in the Preamble,[25] and the great political struggles with which we are now familiar regarding judicial appointments are precisely struggles over which of these political visions shall prevail. There is nothing wrong with this. It is simply the way that our political system works. Rehnquist, for example, was committed to a high politics that emphasized states' rights, executive power, and harsh treatment of convicted criminals, especially those sentenced to death. This is widely thought to be true as well of his successor, John Roberts, and Samuel Alito, who has replaced Sandra Day O'Connor. There can be almost no doubt that Al Gore, if he had been given the opportunity, would have nominated equally capable justices with quite different high politics.

Justice Antonin Scalia spoke exactly to this aspect of our political system in a vitriolic dissent to a majority opinion that ruled unconstitutional certain patronage practices in Illinois because, according to the majority, they illegitimately took political party affiliation into account in dispensing certain government jobs.[26] Generally, the state must offer jobs or dismiss persons from jobs they hold with a "blindness" toward the politics of the persons involved. In exceptional circumstances, the state could attempt to demonstrate that "party affiliation is an 'appropriate requirement,'" but the majority left little doubt that the state could rarely meet this burden. "It is hard," wrote Scalia, to say precisely (or even generally) what that exception means, but if there is any category of jobs for whose performance party affiliation is not an appropriate requirement, it is the job of being a judge, where partisanship is not only unneeded but positively undesirable. It is, however, rare that a federal administration of one party will appoint a judge from another party. And it has always been rare. [Scalia here cites the famous 1803 case of *Marbury v. Madison*, in which John Marshall, a Federalist appointed by the lame-duck president, John Adams, and confirmed by a lame-duck Federalist Congress, ruled that James Madison, Jefferson's secretary of state, was behaving illegally in refusing to deliver a commission of appointment to William Marbury, another Federalist, who had been appointed justice of the peace in the District of Columbia.[27]] Thus, the new principle that the Court today announces will be enforced by a corps of judges (the Members of this Court included) who overwhelmingly owe their office to its violation. Something must be wrong here, and I suggest it is the Court.[28]

Scalia is entirely correct in his observation about the actual relevance of party affiliation to one's being appointed to the Supreme Court. It is futile to try to eliminate the relevance of party affiliation entirely; any proposed cure would be worse than the disease. To eliminate politics entirely would require reconceiving the very way we think about law and judging. We would have to adopt European notions of "professional judges" who enter the judiciary, at a suitably low level, at a young age and then are promoted to higher positions as they demonstrate their aptitude for judging. Along this path, American political scientist Dennis Mueller has advocated "professional appointment by existing judges, noting that the judiciary has internal incentives for competent [and, implicitly, nonpartisan] selection."[29] I am more than a bit dubious about placing in the hands of sitting judges such power to engage in what I believe would be the self-perpetuation of their own high politics—and, in some instances, "low politics" as well. In any event, it would obviously require yet one more transformation of our own Constitution inasmuch as the document clearly assigns the nomination power to the president and the confirmation power to the Senate. Our task is to tame some of the excesses produced by, rather than to eliminate entirely, the partisan selection of Supreme Court justices. One way of doing this is to reject life tenure and instead limit the terms of the justices so selected.

LaRue offers the following "assumptions that match our day," whatever Alexander Hamilton (or John Marshall) might have believed:

1. [W]e have a strong and independent judiciary;

2. our judges have the power to change the law, both common law and constitutional law;

3. our judges will exercise their power to change the law based upon their judgments about justice and utility;

4. this power to change the law is not unlimited, since there are political, institutional, and moral restraints that all judges feel;

5. this power has been used in the past sometimes for the good, sometimes for the bad;

6. we ought to accept and preserve this power, but we should also limit it.[30]

Thus, he correctly concludes, life tenure, which might have made eminently good sense given Hamiltonian assumptions, no longer makes sense in the world we actually inhabit.

Even the briefest look at other constitutions in the American states or around the world demonstrates that there is not the slightest need to grant life tenure in order to guarantee an independent judiciary that will enforce legal norms. Most of the post–World War II constitutions, for example, have ten- to fourteen-year term limits for service on the "constitutional courts," which have been assigned the specific duty of enforcing constitutional norms against potential infringement by other institutions in the political order. Almost no one believes that this lack of life tenure casts doubt on the integrity of these courts. And, as University of Illinois law professor Tom Ginsburg informs us, "Although one might think that lifetime appointments are always longer than designated terms, this is not the case because *virtually all other systems with 'lifetime' appointments provide for a mandatory retirement age of sixty-five to seventy years of age.*[31] Ginsburg also notes that, in some political systems, appointments come relatively late in life. In Japan, for example, judges are appointed at a sufficiently old age so that, given the mandatory retirement age of seventy, the average term of service is approximately six years.[32] Even if one properly believes that this is too short a term of office, it is obviously the case that one need not adopt both a younger age of appointment and then endless tenure as the solution. In any event, the United States may be unique among political systems in the entire world in defining "life tenure" as really and truly "for life," which means, as noted above, average lengths of service approaching four times that of Japanese judges.

It is also worth mentioning that most European and many other countries have chosen to establish special constitutional courts with the *exclusive* power to interpret the constitution. In contrast, the American political system allows, with irrelevant exceptions, each and every court in both the state and federal systems to engage in judicial review. Whether our way or the way chosen by almost all of the rest of the world is better will surely be a topic for discussion at the constitutional convention should a majority of voters cast their votes appropriately in our referendum.

Professor LaRue believes that "a Supreme Court justice should serve on that court for only ten or fifteen years, and then move down to a lower court." He selects that length because he believes, as an empirical proposition, that "most Supreme Court justices do their best work during the period of their fifth to tenth years." It takes roughly five years to become fully comfortable with their job. By the tenth year, though, "almost all judges start defending what they did in their early career[s]."[33] They have found their groove, for good or for ill, and increasingly become completely predictable with regard to the major issues that come before them. If, as Socrates suggested, the unexamined life is not worth living, there are few instances in our judicial history where such examination seems to take place after roughly a decade.

Professor Powe is somewhat more generous. Like many others who have examined the problems attached to life tenure, he suggests that members of the Supreme Court be appointed to single, nonrenewable terms of eighteen years. The major reason to pick eighteen-year terms is because eighteen is evenly divisible by nine, which has become the accepted number of members of the Court. The written Constitution may not require it; over our history, the official membership of the Court has varied between five and ten. But it seems clear, especially since the fiasco of Franklin Roosevelt's attempt to "pack the Court" by increasing the membership to fifteen, that the unwritten Constitution recognizes nine as the "correct" number. In any event, if there were nine slots, each of which carried an eighteen-year term, then each president would be guaranteed two appointments in each four-year term of office, and no one president would be able to appoint a majority of the Court.

Eighteen year terms would not resolve the problem posed by judicial debility, though one suspects that most instances of such debility have occurred in older judges who have served more than eighteen years, such as Douglas and Rehnquist. In any event, should a judge leave the bench earlier than the allotted eighteen years, a successor justice could be appointed to fill out the eighteen-year term. Perhaps former justices could be recalled for such limited service.

Changing to fixed terms might also help to diminish some of the *sturm und drang* attached to contemporary judicial nominations. As Ward Farnsworth, who actually supports life tenure, has noted, one incentive for presidents to pick young nominees—consider that Rehnquist's successor, Chief Justice John Roberts, was only fifty at the time of his appointment—is not only so that they will serve long into the future but also, in effect, to "lock up" the Court. That is, if the strategy is successful, immediate successor presidents of the opposite party may well be deprived of the opportunity to make any appointments at all. Thus, Jimmy Carter was the first president in more than a century—since Andrew Johnson—to make no appointments at all, and Bill Clinton, in his eight years in the White House, was able to appoint only two justices. (Richard Nixon, on the other hand, was able to appoint four justices in his first three years in office.)

This brings up a final problem attached to life tenure, which is the ability of judges to time their resignations to accord with their own political loyalties. It is difficult to believe, for example, that Republican justice Potter Stewart, appointed by President Eisenhower in 1958, did not consciously wait until after the 1980 election to submit his resignation on July 3, 1981, immediately following the end of the 1980 term of the Supreme Court. Perhaps he would have resigned had Carter won reelection, but he was surely gratified to give Ronald Reagan the opportunity to appoint his successor. It is similarly difficult to think that Byron White, who retired in 1993, the first year of Clinton's term in office, wasn't equally waiting to see if the 1992 elections would make it possible for a Democrat to appoint his successor inasmuch as White had been appointed by John F. Kennedy. It is also patently obvious that Earl Warren, who loathed Richard Nixon, submitted his resignation in the summer of 1968 in order to make sure that Nixon would not have the opportunity to appoint the next chief justice. As it happened, Warren's strategy failed when Johnson unwisely attempted to promote his close friend Associate Justice Abe Fortas to the position. A filibuster by some Republicans and southern conservative Democrats derailed that nomination, so that Nixon was able, upon election, to name Warren Burger to succeed Warren.[34] Some commentators have suggested that William O. Douglas's disgraceful unwillingness to leave the bench following his debilitating stroke after a full third of a century on the Court is explained not only by his general distaste for the prospect that a Republican would follow him, but also by his personal animosity toward President Gerald Ford, who as House minority leader had suggested impeaching Douglas in 1970.

There is no way, nor should there be a way, to prevent politics from playing an important role at the nomination and confirmation stages, at least so long as we place nomination in the hands of politically sensitive presidents and confirmation in the hands of equally attuned senators. From almost day one of our republic, presidents have selected nominees who are believed to have the appropriate high politics with regard to the major issues likely to come before the Court. Exhibit A in this regard was the appointment by John Adams of John Marshall as our fourth chief justice; Adams fully expected Marshall to do whatever he could to throw roadblocks in the way of the hated Thomas Jefferson. And there are also low politics considerations at times, such as the necessity to make good on campaign promises or on even narrower political deals. President Eisenhower, who later lamented his choice of Earl Warren as chief justice, was making good on a political commitment to Warren, as part of the politics of the Republican presidential nomination process, to name him to the next vacancy on the Court, which just happened to be the chief justiceship.[35]

Similarly, members of the Senate, who are assigned by the Constitution the power (and duty) to "advise and consent" to presidential nominees, are fully entitled to apply their own ideological criteria in assessing the fitness of nominees to serve on the federal judiciary. At the very least, it is impossible to complain that senators take such considerations into account when voting to confirm if one does not object to presidents applying such considerations in the nomination decision itself.

Even if one endorses, as I personally do, the more or less political selection of federal judges, which recognizes the ineradicable significance of the high political views of judges, that does not in the least suggest that we are not entitled to hope that justices will forget, as it were, their low political party identifications. This forgetfulness should obviously extend to the actual decision of cases, where one hopes that justices will not be taking potential electoral consequences for their preferred political party or, even worse, political candidates, into account when making decisions. (Suspicions about whether this was the case account for the continuing hostility of many, including myself, to the decision in *Bush v. Gore*. It was patently obvious that the chief beneficiary of the Court's remarkable intervention into the election was George W. Bush, the undoubted favorite of the five conservative Republicans who voted for that outcome.) But we are also entitled to assurances that justices will time their length of service with regard to other criteria than which political party will be able to fill their seats.

The most important such criterion is their basic ability to keep doing the job. It may, however, be expecting too much of human beings to be able to discipline themselves in such a manner. Certainly, the empirical evidence casts doubt on the proposition. Fixed terms are the only relatively sure way to limit politically timed resignations. In the absence of age limits, it may also be the only practical way to prevent judges from narcissistically remaining on the bench even after they have begun to lose a step (if not two or three) in the performance of their duties. As noted at the beginning of this chapter, I am not exercised by the fact that members of inferior federal courts also enjoy life tenure. However, were I forced to choose between limited eighteen-year appointments for *all* federal judges and maintaining the present practice of truly unlimited life tenure, I would have no hesitation in opting for the former.

FIVE

The Constitution as Creator of Second-Class Citizens

Americans take justified pride in the assertion by the Declaration of Independence that "all men [and today we would surely add women] are created equal" and by the linked notion that "there are no second-class citizens in America." It is often asserted that "every youngster in America can dream of growing up to be president," though, as we shall presently see, this is patently false. At the very least, we would like to think that the Constitution itself places no barriers on participation in the polity. Alas, that is not the case. Although what I will call the "second-class citizenship clauses" of the Constitution almost certainly do not justify in themselves supporting the forthcoming referendum, they could either tip the balance for those readers who remain uncertain or reassure those who have already decided to vote yes.

Of the seventeen formal amendments added to the Constitution since the Bill of Rights in 1791, a full five—almost one-third—involve guaranteeing the right to vote. The Fifteenth and Nineteenth amendments forbid states from denying the suffrage on the basis of race or gender, respectively. Why only states? The answer is simple: Each and

every election in the United States is run by the states or their subdi-
visions. The national government is elected entirely through state-run
processes, and each state, at least historically, had the right to determine who could vote on its own. Some states allowed African Americans to vote; most did not. Some states allowed women to vote; some
did not. The two amendments foreclosed states from continuing to
exercise their discretion with regard to race or gender. The Twenty-
fourth Amendment banned the use of poll taxes, by which states, all
of them southern, had made voting contingent on paying a fee. And
the Twenty-sixth Amendment lowered the national voting age to eighteen. Finally, the Twenty-third Amendment gave the District of Columbia three electoral votes in the Electoral College, which meant that
citizens in the District could now join other Americans in voting for
the president.

Given that the drafters of the Constitution basically left it to the
states to decide who could vote, the Constitution itself cannot accurately be described as having created the second-class citizenship by
which only white males, or then men but not women, could vote. This
is not true, however, of the discriminations that are the subject of this
chapter. They are, as with the allocation of voting power in the Senate
or the presidential veto power, hard-wired into the Constitution. But,
as we shall see, they are no more defensible than are these other attributes, whose defects we have already explored.

QUALIFICATIONS FOR THE HOUSE AND SENATE:
A BLOT ON DEMOCRATIC VALUES

One rarely thinks of the requirements for service in the House of Representatives or the Senate, though they present some interesting problems for anyone called on to judge the Constitution's conformity with
enlightened political values. "No Person shall be a Representative who
shall not have attained to the age of twenty-five Years, and been seven
Years a Citizen of the United States, and who shall not, when elected,
be an Inhabitant of that State in which he shall be chosen." The clause
relating to the Senate substitutes "thirty" for "twenty-five" and "nine"

for "seven." We see, therefore, that membership in the Congress is limited by *age, duration of citizenship,* and *place of habitation.*

Age

It is hard to deny the legitimacy of *some* kinds of age classification with regard to participating in the polity. After all, the Twenty-sixth Amendment, which stands for the proposition that one no longer has to be twenty-one in order to vote, still legitimizes denial of the ballot to seventeen-year-olds. And even if one wanted to argue that in today's world a sixteen-year-old should be allowed to vote, no one would take up the banner for a six-year-old to be able to do so. The question is not so much whether there can be *any* age qualification at all, but rather, whether we should exclude from public office those fellow citizens whom we accept as legitimate members of the voting public.

Yale professor Akhil Reed Amar has argued that age limits served an important purpose at the time of the founding, which was to put barriers in the way of political "dynasties," by which fathers could pass on their legislative seats to their sons. "Without a minimum-age rule," he writes, "voters and legislatures in each state might be tempted to send the state's favorite son, such as the governor's scion, to Congress as young as possible." After all, the aptly named William Pitt the younger took his seat in the English Parliament in 1781, at the ripe age of twenty-one, before becoming prime minister three years later.[1] It might be, as with much else about the 1787 Constitution, that the age limit was defensible on the grounds that Professor Amar so skillfully lays out. But there is no reason to feel attached to any such principle today, when American politics have, by and large, left well behind the politics of social deference that would have made gubernatorial scions plausible candidates.[2] I am inclined to agree with Professor John Seery that the explicit age limitations found in the Constitution are indefensible in our contemporary world.[3]

Still, there might be broad agreement that, on balance, we prefer as representatives or senators persons with more experience than the typical twenty-two-year-old is likely to have. There is still no good reason to constitutionalize such a view. A far more democratic solution is to rely on voters to decide about the tradeoffs, in any given election, between experience and the virtues that might be present in a young candidate. Most young candidates will undoubtedly be defeated. But consider our present situation, where a very controversial war, which by January 1, 2007, will have lasted longer than American participation in World War II, is being fought, as always, by large numbers of valiant young men and women facing death or lifelong disability. Would the American public not be potential beneficiaries of the presence as candidates—and voting members of the House or Senate—of twenty-two-year-old or twenty-eight-year-old veterans able to speak to the facts on the ground? Professor Seery notes that the Congress elected in 2004 is the oldest in our history, with the average age of representatives being fifty-five and that of senators being a full half decade older, at slightly more than sixty. No senator is under forty, while only ten members of the 435 members of the House were under thirty-five at the start of the 109th session in January 2005. Patrick McHenry of North Carolina was unique in being under thirty, and even he was twenty-nine when he took his oath of office. Might not the middle-aged members of Congress benefit from hearing the perspectives of, and having to engage in political bargaining with, young men and women whose lives were put at risk because of policies made far away by much older people, whose children, because of the realities of class in America, are notably unlikely to have volunteered to put themselves in harm's way?[4]

The president must be thirty-five, which is obviously even more disabling than the clauses relating to the age requirements for membership in the House and Senate. Matthew D. Michael has criticized this limitation in an essay, "The Presidential Age Requirement and Public Policy Agenda Setting."[5] The somewhat wonky title makes a major point: Presidential campaigns, among other things, are forums in which new proposals are often set out and the agendas for important public policy debates established. Among the major issues on the horizon are what Michael calls the "intergenerational transfer programs that will generate trillions of dollars of unsustainable future liabilities" to be paid for (or, just as much to the point, forgone) by today's young (where *young* is defined as anyone under thirty-five). Michael readily admits that a "Generation X candidate (say, age thirty) would likely not stand much of a chance of winning the presidency." But that is, in a fundamental sense, irrelevant if one's major interest is structuring the public agenda. A young candidate would, presumably, focus on such issues during the primary battles, luring many fellow youngsters to the polls. As, perhaps inevitably, the prospects of actually winning the nomination fade, he or she will still have established some genuine bargaining power with regard to endorsements and a seat at the platform table.

It is fatuous to rely on older candidates to emphasize issues of primary interest to the young, and not only because the American Association of Retired Persons is among the strongest of contemporary lobbying groups. It is a brute fact that the turnout rates for voters between eighteen and thirty are significantly lower than those for older groups.[6] Nor, as a practical matter, have the young mobilized behind certain issues in a way that has made them a distinctive presence in any election since 1976, when eighteen-year-olds first became eligible to vote. Perhaps this relative lassitude would remain even if citizens were presented with a serious twenty-eight-year-old willing to hit the campaign trail and ask pointed questions of his or her elders who blandly promise the sky to voters without explaining who is going to pay for the programs (and how). But we cannot find out because of this (yet one more) unjustifiable part of the Constitution.

Even if every voter under thirty-five is subject to at least one exclusion from public office, all of them are eligible to vote in the forthcoming referendum. Assuming that they have been persuaded by some of the earlier critiques of the Constitution, every self-respecting American voter under thirty-five has an additional incentive to send an important message by declaring nonsupport for a constitutional status quo that treats them as decidedly, if temporarily, second-class citizens.

Duration of Citizenship

Similarly, what is the defense of the seven- and nine-year citizenship requirements in a political system that professes to have no second-class citizens? (I shall have more to say below about the fact that presidents must be "natural born" citizens, which thus disqualifies from our highest office anyone born abroad as a noncitizen.) The Constitution in effect stigmatizes naturalized citizens by telling them that they are deemed unfit, in a Constitution ostensibly committed to the equal dignity of all citizens, to take part in governance for several years, and perhaps forever. At a less symbolic level, it is also true that a country that currently has almost 19 million resident aliens[7] might surely benefit from having in the House or Senate someone who very recently shared their status. If one disagrees with the desirability of such persons in official positions, then it would seem adequate to vote against them rather than to make such service unconstitutional. Recently naturalized citizens are in the same position as our eighteen- to twenty-four-year-old citizens: They can vote even if they are not eligible to occupy national office. As with the youngsters, recently naturalized citizens have no reason to endorse a Constitution that views them as only second-class citizens.

There is a special irony (or, for some, an outrage) linked to the years-of-citizenship requirement inasmuch as every naturalized citizen must demonstrate, prior to citizenship, "attachment" to the "principles of the Constitution."[8] One should certainly hope they are committed to the beautiful words and inspiring ideals of the Preamble. But do we really expect them to be attached to their own disability to represent their neighbors in Congress for many years? The easiest way to resolve this is simply, once more, to remember that we should never confuse the principles of the Constitution with the particular means set out below the Preamble. It is almost self-evident, for example, that no decent person should have felt truly attached to the provision of the original Constitution that barred any congressional prohibition of the international slave trade until 1808.[9] It is almost as clear that no woman naturalized before 1920, the date of the Nineteenth Amendment guaranteeing woman suffrage, should have felt the slightest attachment to the particular aspect of the Constitution that gave states carte blanche to restrict the electorate. One expresses the greatest fidelity to the deepest principles of the Constitution by relentlessly—at times, even unforgivingly—examining the extent to which the main body of the Constitution is indeed conducive to realizing the ends set forth and by being willing to change the Constitution whenever it is found wanting.

Residency and Localism

One could even raise questions about the requirement that members of Congress be inhabitants of the states they purport to represent. Even if one believes that this makes perfectly good sense, so that one would not herself vote for a "stranger," it is scarcely clear that the Constitution should actually prevent a state from selecting a distinguished "outsider" to represent it in Congress. As a matter of fact, this requirement is probably innocuous, practically speaking, given the extreme unlikelihood of a state's actually choosing a nonresident. Some would say, though, that both Robert Kennedy and Hillary Clinton were residents of New York only in a technical, legal sense when each was chosen to represent the Empire State in the Senate.

Nonetheless, the very casualness with which we accept the residency requirement exemplifies what is one of the most problematic features of the overall design of the Constitution. This is what might be termed its *bias toward localism* and, therefore, its bias against bringing to Washington persons who think in broad national terms. Former Speaker of the House "Tip" O'Neill famously declared that "all politics are local." One reason that this is especially true of American politics—one would never hear a similar utterance in most other political systems—is that *all* elected officials within the national government, including representatives, senators, and even the president, owe their elections to their appeal to specific localities. There is not a single individual in either the House or Senate who is liberated to think primarily of what might be termed the "common good." Every single incentive is to think of the "good of Kansas" or the "good of New York." And, if one is referring to members of the House of Representatives, it is the "good of the Second District of Kansas" or of the "Twenty-eighth District of New York," which may obviously differ from other districts even within the same state that are more rural or urban, more poverty-stricken or wealthier, and so on.

University of Maryland political scientist and law professor Mark Graber plausibly attributes the breakdown of American politics in the 1850s and the onset of a war that killed 2 percent of the American population to the overregionalism of American politics generated by the formalities of the Constitution.[10] There was nothing "natural" about the intense degree of regionalism of American politics in that era, even if it is obvious that the North and South had fundamentally different views about the propriety of slavery. Rather, the regional animosity manifested in Congress was constructed in significant ways by the formal, locality-based institutional structure set out in the Constitution itself. We will never know if a different system of representation would have forestalled the conflagration of 1861–1865. Perhaps one even would have welcomed the onset of war if the alternative was a transregional compromise, similar to those reached in 1820 and 1850, which further entrenched slavery. But the point, as Graber demonstrates, is that institutional design has consequences, and the spirit of compromise, whatever one might think of the results, that operated at an earlier period of American politics had simply disappeared in the 1850s as local electorates demanded a higher and higher degree of uncompromising intransigence from their representatives.

Contemporary American politics are nowhere near so regionally based today; even "red states" that voted Republican in the 2000 and 2004 presidential elections have Democratic senators and "blue states" that voted Democratic have Republican ones. This scarcely means, however, that members of the contemporary House and Senate can be trusted to sacrifice the interests of their local constituents for the good of the country in general, given the threat to reelection that might be posed by any such sacrifice (at least in the absence of a suitably national consciousness on the part of the constituents themselves).

One response to such arguments is to say that requiring the endless play of local and institutional interests against one another in order to achieve legislation *assures* that whatever passes will in fact serve the national interest. This argument mimics the defense of market forces offered by unabashed devotees of laissez-faire economics: *Whatever* triumphs in an unregulated market must necessarily serve the public, since the market is basically a perfect mechanism for picking and choosing among alternatives. Most of us, quite properly, are not such complete devotees. All of us have seen too many instances of abuses— economists call them "market imperfections"—that call for at least some degree of governmental regulation. Similarly, enthusiasts for the degree of localism that is present in both houses of Congress are almost willfully blind to the abuses attached to the disincentives, generated by the Constitution itself, for members of Congress to think in terms of broad national interests. What legislators will be so bold as to vote for programs that they themselves believe would benefit the nation in general if they impose significant costs on their own supporters back home (including, of course, contributors of campaign funds)? The United States may present a single national team at the Olympics, and Americans may chauvinistically shout "U-S-A" in support, but our national legislative institutions are far more like athletic conferences, where Ohioans care only about the fate of Buckeyes and Michiganders only about the Wolverines.

Those political scientists who engage in the formal analysis of properties of different institutional arrangements often work with the notion of the "prisoners' dilemma." The paradigm from which the name is taken describes a situation where two prisoners are being interrogated in adjoining rooms. Each is told the following: If he confesses and agrees to testify against the confederate in the other room, he will receive probation, which means no jail time at all. If he remains silent, and the confederate agrees to the same deal, then the confederate will walk while the prisoner will be sentenced to ten years in jail. The police admit that, if both remain silent, then each will serve only a two-year term on a lesser charge, because the testimony would be necessary to prove the commission of a felony. But what, the prisoner asks, if both confess? Then each will receive a six-year term, since each can be proven to have committed the felony. It is obvious that the best solution, from the perspective of the two prisoners as a group, is to remain silent, which generates a total jail term of only four years. Yet it is equally obvious that the best solution for the individual, unconcerned about the overall group advantage, is to confess, since that will *always* leave the individual better off. If the confederate, falsely believing that there is honor among thieves, staunchly remains silent, then the first prisoner can reduce his sentence from two years (if both remain silent) to zero (if he turns state's evidence). One need not have any sympathy with the criminal defendants who are the subject of prisoners' dilemma analyses. The basic structure of the dilemma has been generalized to a wide variety of circumstances, including, for example, the ability to produce sound national policies in the face of holdout states, which prefer to continue polluting or which refuse to apply certain welfare benefits to the poor (and therefore keep taxes low in an effort to lure industry from more generous and therefore higher-taxing states). All of them feature the same basic tension between the interest of a presumptively selfish individual—or congressional district or state—and the collective interests of the community. And even individuals in holdout states may very well be harmed if, for example, they are the poor who need the medical care or the adequate education denied them by budget-cutting state legislators.

To some extent, every American is the victim—one might even say the prisoner, in an iron cage—of the centripetal tendencies generated by the Constitution, even if we take comfort in knowing that our particular representative or senator is bringing home the bacon for some local interest while being indifferent as to who exactly is paying for the pork or what alternative uses there might be for the money involved. Should the forthcoming referendum demonstrate that a majority of Americans feel at least sufficient discontent with the present Constitution to authorize a new convention, the subsequent convention might well consider adding to the House of Representatives and Senate, assuming the retention of bicameralism, a number of new members elected on a nationwide basis. This would provide not only a more national focus but also, perhaps paradoxically, greater representation for individuals who belong to groups that, because they are distributed nationwide rather than concentrated in given localities, are unable to influence the political outcomes in strictly territorially based electoral districts.[11]

CAN ALL AMERICAN CITIZENS ASPIRE TO LIVE IN THE WHITE HOUSE?

Should America Really Say That No Immigrants Need Apply to Be President?

Article II, section 1, clause 5, states: "No person except a natural born Citizen . . . shall be eligible to the Office of President; neither shall any Person be eligible to that Office who shall have not attained to the

Age of thirty-five Years, and been fourteen Years as Resident within the United States." Each of these three qualifications presents problems. One of them, age, I have already discussed, and nothing further need be said. But consider the requirement that the president be a "natural born Citizen." Some professors like to play word games by asking if the clause would disqualify someone born in a cesarean operation or, in our modern world, through a process of in vitro fertilization. But these *are* mere games. It is close to self-evident that what this provision means, in our own time, is that no one who is not at birth a citizen of the United States is ever eligible thereafter to occupy our highest office. No such disability attends those who wish to serve in the Congress or the judiciary; the presidential disability stands alone.

Harvard law professor Randall Kennedy has discussed—and condemned—the clause in an essay suitably titled "A Natural Aristocracy."[12] Even if one takes into account age and citizenship qualifications, one can still say that each and every citizen of the United States can aspire to serve at the highest levels of government, although it might take a while to become eligible. Only with regard to naturalized citizens is the bar complete and permanent. It is irrelevant, as Kennedy notes, that they may have "invested their all, even risked their lives, on behalf of the nation." It is hard to disagree with him that "[t]his idolatry of mere place of birth seems to me an instance of rank superstition." It offers no evidence whatsoever "about a person's willed attachment to a country, a polity, a way of life." I share Kennedy's view that Henry Kissinger should not have become president of the United States, but that is most certainly *not* because he was born in Germany. Nor, incidentally, do I doubt for a moment that Kissinger has devoted his life to serving the interests of the United States as he sees them. My distaste for him is based entirely on policy disagreements. He is not one whit "less American" than I am because I was born in North Carolina.

"The natural-born citizen requirement," writes Kennedy, "embodies the presumption that some citizens of the United States are a bit more authentic, a bit more trustworthy, a bit more American than other citizens of the United States, namely, those who are naturalized. It establishes the most literal kind of 'natural aristocracy,'" altogether different, as he notes, "from Jefferson's own invocation of that notion" to describe those who by talent and merit are best fit to govern. Kennedy concedes that "the clause is of more symbolic than 'practical' importance." Yet symbolism counts, especially in a document meant to be venerated as well as obeyed. The symbolism of the Natural-Born Citizenship Clause is indefensible in a liberal democracy. It may be too late for gifted immigrants like Kissinger, Madeleine Albright (born in Czechoslovakia), or Ted Koppel (England) to consider running for our highest office. But consider Republican California governor Arnold Schwarzenegger (born in Austria) or the Democratic governor of Michigan, Jennifer Granholm (Canada). Whether either makes it to the White House should be the result of our collective choice at the ballot box instead of their being ruled out by a xenophobic text rooted in a fear of British or French domination of a vulnerable new nation.

Fortunately, millions of naturalized Americans are entitled to an equal vote in our national referendum, just as they can vote for, even if they cannot hope to become, president of the United States. This indefensible prohibition is a sound reason for them to resolve any doubts they might have about redrafting the Constitution.

Where Exactly Is the United States and How Does This Affect Who May Become President?

Surely the most esoteric qualification is the requirement that a president have "been fourteen Years as Resident within the United States." Perhaps I should confess that two colleagues and I once wrote an article that questioned whether George Washington was eligible to become president in 1789 inasmuch as the United States was not even "born" before 1776, the date of the Declaration of Independence, or even 1783, the date of the Treaty of Paris by which the existence of the brand-new country was formally recognized by the former colonial power, Great Britain.[13] This article was meant as a joke. But one can imagine modern circumstances where the language would have real bite and be no laughing matter.

Consider, for example, persons born in the United States but taken thereafter by their parents to a foreign country where, altogether plausibly in today's world, one or both of the parents had a job with a global corporation. Or, perhaps, the parent was an old-fashioned religious missionary or an active participant in Doctors Without Borders. You get the idea. The children return to the United States, say, at twenty-three, and twelve years later one of them decides to make a run for the White House. Would he or she be barred by the "fourteen Years as Resident" clause? I think the answer is clearly yes. One might well believe that such a candidate is exhibiting monumental *chutzpah*. But, as with the other qualifications, why should we constitutionalize such a bar instead of simply voting against the candidate? Are we not to be trusted to make such decisions for ourselves?

There are probably few persons who fit the suggested biography in the paragraph above. Unlike the young, or the immigrants, or other groups I have tried to mobilize as part of my pro-referendum coalition, this does not appear to be a promising group. There is, however, one group for whom the residency clause might actually make a difference, and that is Puerto Ricans.

It would take this book too far afield to consider fully the fascinating constitutional dimensions of Puerto Rico's transfer to the United States in the aftermath of the Spanish-American War of 1898 and its history as an American territory—or, as some would say, "colony"—thereafter.[14] Suffice it to say that, since 1917, persons born in Puerto Rico have enjoyed American citizenship, so they presumably suffer no bar under the Natural-Born Citizen Clause. Imagine, though, someone born and raised in Puerto Rico who comes to the mainland of the United States at the age of twenty-five and wishes to run for the presidency thirteen years later. Is *she* eligible? This requires us to address the seemingly odd question, "Where exactly is Puerto Rico?" The flippant answer, "in the Caribbean Sea," won't do, because, after all, Hawaii is in the mid-Pacific, far more distant from the mainland than is Puerto Rico. And there is no doubt that anyone born in Hawaii is eligible, however unlikely that might be, to become president of the United States even if he has never spent a day outside Oahu.

Note that the Qualifications Clause does not require that one be a citizen of a state as well as of the nation. All that is seemingly required is national citizenship, which Puerto Ricans have. And what would lead us to say that Puerto Rico is less "within the United States" than, say, the District of Columbia, which is also not a state even though it does have three electoral votes courtesy of the Twenty-third Amendment? Surely, someone who has never left the confines of the District of Columbia is eligible to become president.

There is one further twist that is even more directly relevant to the central conceit of this book, which is the forthcoming referendum on whether to retain the Constitution. Will Puerto Ricans be allowed to vote in the referendum? Is it not *their* Constitution as well as the Constitution of those of us who live in one of the fifty states plus the District of Columbia? Would it not be rank bigotry to deny our fellow citizens in San Juan a right to vote on the Constitution that has important consequences for their own lives, for good and for ill? But if they have the right to vote, it can only be because we do recognize them as inhabiting the "United States" in the same way that the District of Columbia is treated as part of the "United States." Statehood is not a prerequisite for being part of the United States. So, perhaps, Puerto Ricans do not have an incentive to disapprove of the Constitution, at least on this ground.

Eviction from the White House after Two Terms?

It may be difficult to view the president of the United States as a second-class citizen, but a second-term president, like the citizens discussed above, shares the disability of being unable to run for the presidency yet again. The Twenty-second Amendment, proposed in 1947, not at all coincidentally by the first Republican Congress following the death of Franklin Roosevelt, was ratified by the requisite thirty-six states (Hawaii and Alaska were not yet states) by 1951. Its relevant passage states:

> No person shall be elected to the office of the President more than twice, and no person who has held the office of President, or acted as President, for more than two years of a term to which some other person was elected President shall be elected to the office of the President more than once.

It is, then, a qualification for the presidency that one not already have served two terms—or, in the case of a vice president who succeeded to office in the first two years of a particular term, more than six years—as president. (Should the vice president succeed to office in the second two years of the term, then she would be eligible to run in the next two elections and thus serve a maximum of ten years in office.)

Some persons might suggest that the Twenty-second Amendment only codified what had been an unwritten part of the Constitution, which FDR violated: Presidents should serve only two terms. I must say that, as a result of visiting China in 1987 for a seminar on the bicentennial of our Constitution, I developed a deep admiration for George Washington that I had never before felt. His decision voluntarily to step down from the presidency after two terms was a remarkable gift to the entire nation. Leaders of national liberation movements, which Washington most certainly was, often develop a belief, encouraged by those around them, that they are indispensable and should serve forever. The two-term practice, whether or not it should be called a "rule," has been, overall, an important contributor to what is best in our constitutional system, including the peaceful transfer of power between otherwise hostile political parties. Washington truly deserves his memorial in the city named after him.

But, obviously, rules are also made to be broken, and one can still wonder whether the constitutionalization of the usually admirable practice is a benefit or a deficiency of the modern Constitution. Perhaps one can argue that FDR should not have run for a third term in 1940. Yet the German invasion of Poland had already occurred, not to speak of the Battle of Britain conducted by the Royal Air Force and the sudden fall of France in 1940. And, even if we acknowledge his weakened health, would it really have served the national interest to force him out of office in 1944 as the decisive battles (and negotiations attached to the looming end of the war) were occurring?

During my 1987 visit to China, two of the Chinese students, who otherwise tended to stay very much in the background, suddenly broke into a vigorous debate about the Twenty-second Amendment, which I confess I had not thought about much one way or the other prior to my visit. One praised it, because it does stand for the proposition that no leader is indispensable and that a vigorous democracy will always be able to generate new and capable leaders. My wife had seen Chairman

Mao's body, which is preserved in Tiananmen Square in Beijing, and it was absolutely clear to whom this student was referring in his critique of the cult of indispensability. He was answered by another student, who properly said that the amendment was paternalistic. The sovereign people were prevented, presumably for their own good, from deciding that a given leader had indeed done a fine job and should be retained in office. I have no idea whether he was unafraid of the rise of another Chairman Mao or was simply too young to remember his hold on the Chinese consciousness. In any event, these two students captured perfectly the theoretical tension captured in the amendment.

There are also practical issues generated by its operation. The most important is that it makes a newly reelected president an instant lame duck, for the one thing that everyone knew, on Inauguration Day in 1985, 1997, and 2005 is that the respective presidents—Reagan, Clinton, and Bush—would never again be running for the presidency. To some extent, of course, this might "liberate" them to make certain decisions precisely because they would be free of the particular kind of public accountability that comes through having to face the electorate and risk defeat. But it also means not only that a second-term president is more limited in the offers or threats he can deliver to political friends and adversaries, but also that the jousting for the next presidential election begins with the taking of the oath of office. Invariably, several senators believe, probably correctly, that they could be at least as competent as the current occupant of the White House. They therefore have every incentive to distance themselves from the incumbent if his popularity begins to wane, as is common in second terms.

It is impossible to argue that the Twenty-second Amendment itself offers sufficient reason to vote yea or nay on the Constitution. But, for any given voter, depending on how one evaluates the costs and benefits of the two-term limitation, it could provide a marginal reason, if one is still on the fence.

We saw earlier in this book how remarkably unequal the allocation of power is within the framework of government established by the Constitution. Californians might well think they are second-class citizens with regard to Wyomingites, given the seventy times greater weight that each voter in the latter state has when casting a vote for the Senate. Yet the Constitution does not inscribe this second-classness in quite the same way as is the case with the various Qualifications Clauses for national office. They are embarrassing anachronisms in a contemporary country devoted to the proposition that all citizens have equal status.

SIX

THE IMPERMEABLE ARTICLE V

Perhaps you now agree with me that there are significant defects in our constitutional system, with real consequences for the achievement of the kind of country that the Preamble sets forth as our collective aspiration. But you might well say that the drafters of the original Constitution knew that their handiwork was imperfect, as evidenced by their foresight in setting out a framework for amendment in Article V:

> The Congress, whenever two thirds of both houses shall deem it necessary, shall propose amendments to this Constitution, or, on the application of the legislatures of two thirds of the several states, shall call a convention for proposing amendments, which, in either case, shall be valid to all intents and purposes, as part of this Constitution, when ratified by the legislatures of three fourths of the several states, or by conventions in three fourths thereof, as the one or the other mode of ratification may be proposed by the Congress; . . . [although] no state, without its consent, shall be deprived of its equal suffrage in the Senate.

Almost literally the first thing that the First Congress did, upon assembling in New York in 1789, was to propose twelve amendments, of which ten were adopted[1] and are generally linked together as our Bill of Rights. So one can certainly say that the system worked and can continue to work to effect needed change.

That, sadly, is false, at least as an empirical matter. Article V constitutes what may be the most important bars of our constitutional iron cage precisely because it works to make practically impossible needed changes in our polity. As chapter 1 detailed, no other country—nor, for that matter, any of the fifty American states—makes it so difficult to amend its constitution. This is yet one more instance where Americans should ask themselves what the rest of the world (and American states) know that the framers, whatever their brilliance and dedication, did not. Perhaps they have taken more to heart John Marshall's injunction, in *McCulloch v. Maryland*, that we should always interpret the Constitution in a way that will allow adaptation to the "various *crises* of human affairs." Clever adaptive interpretation is not always possible, however, and Article V has made it next to impossible to achieve such adaptation where amendment is thought to be necessity.

"Next to impossible," of course, allows for the possibility of amendment, and I have, throughout this book, referred to a variety of amendments. So why, you might ask, does this not demonstrate that Article V is adequate? One response is that the most significant single amendment, the Fourteenth, was added only at the point of a gun, during the military occupation of the defeated Confederacy, which we call Reconstruction. The Fourteenth Amendment can hardly be viewed as an Article V amendment at all; we must, after all, assume that states have genuine freedom to accept or reject suggested changes and are not coerced to make only one possible choice. But Congress had made it absolutely clear that the elected representatives and senators of the former Confederate states would not be seated in the House or Senate unless and until each respective state ratified the Fourteenth Amendment. As a formal matter, Congress based its authority to exclude on Article I, section 5, clause 1: "Each House shall be the Judge of the Elections, Return and Qualifications of its own Members." You might wonder if this clause would genuinely justify, as a legal matter, a refusal by the current House of Representatives to seat any representative from a state that had declined to ratify a proposed amendment, say, to prohibit same-sex marriage. As it happens, I have no qualms about the methods used to procure the Fourteenth Amendment, but that is because I view it as an extension of the Civil War itself and believe that Congress was entitled, politically and morally, to do whatever it took to attempt to rectify the oppressive conditions in the South that had triggered the war in the first place. But this point is more appropriate to what might well be termed "emergency power"—perhaps we should call it an example of congressional "prerogative power"—than to what might be termed normal constitutional analysis.

The 1870 Fifteenth Amendment protecting, at least as a formal matter, the right of African-American males to vote—women would not be guaranteed the right to vote for another half century—was the last amendment for a full four decades. The Progressive era included quite a bit of amendment, of which the most illuminating, for the purpose of answering the question about the adequacy of Article V, is probably the Seventeenth Amendment, which ended the election of senators by state legislators and substituted popular election instead.

Doesn't the Seventeenth Amendment demonstrate that the Constitution offers a sufficient way to correct any problems it might have, that it is *not* an iron cage? The answer is no. Begin with the fact that it took many decades from the time that persons first became critical of legislatively appointed senators to the passage of the amendment. Indeed, the first calls to move to the popular election of senators occurred almost a century earlier, during the Jacksonian period.[2] Not surprisingly, given the truth behind Roche's dictum about the hesitancy of those who hold political power to cede it gracefully, senators delayed responding as long as they could to the appeals for amendment. After all, senators "were bound to see little to gain and much to risk through change."[3] Some of them very much owed their success to the kindness of state legislators—some of whom, in effect, had been bought by wealthy senators or their patrons—and might very well wonder if they would have the same success with the general electorate. Indeed, the House of Representatives, which for obvious reasons was less critical of popular elections, five times between 1894 and 1911 passed proposed constitutional amendments to require the popular election of their Senate counterparts. Only on the last occasion did the Senate finally allow the measure to come to a vote, and it did not attain the required two-thirds majority. (Perhaps this helps to explain the introduction on April 11, 1911, of a resolution by Representative Victor Berger of Wisconsin proposing the abolition of the Senate.)[4] By May 1912, the requisite votes were found, and three-quarters of the state legislatures assented in less than a year: On April 8, 1913, Connecticut became the thirty-sixth state to ratify the proposal.

One can hardly be confident that new perceptions of the public interest explained the Senate's action; by 1911, at least nineteen state legislatures had exercised their Article V prerogative of petitioning Congress to call a constitutional convention for the purpose of proposing such an amendment. The fear of such a convention was enough to generate the required two-thirds majority of the Senate to send the amendment on to the very quick ratification by the states. One might be surprised by the willingness of state legislators to give up their own power. The readiest explanation is that their constituents were letting them know, in no uncertain terms, that it was time for this power to go; indeed, many states had moved to de facto popular elections, where the state legislature in effect simply rubber-stamped the popular choice. Senators elected from such states presumably had little to fear from the Seventeenth Amendment. It was precisely the minority of senators from the minority of states that adhered to the "old ways" that could, because of Article V, block the proposal so long as they were at least one-third-plus-one of the Senate.

The Seventeenth Amendment at most proves that structural change is possible, if all of the stars are aligned correctly. It scarcely demonstrates that the Constitution allows needed changes when time may be of the essence. Perhaps it was worth waiting from 1894 until 1912 to gain the Senate's acquiescence. But one has to be extraordinarily risk- (or change-) averse to adopt this as a general principle. Moreover, the Seventeenth Amendment, however important it may be, was achieved more than ninety years ago. And it was part of a surge of constitutional amendments between 1913 and 1920 identified with the so-called Progressive era, ranging from the Sixteenth Amendment, which legitimized the federal income tax, to the Nineteenth Amendment, which guaranteed to women the right to vote at the end of the decade. Indeed, even the Eighteenth Amendment (1918), which prohibited the sale of alcohol, had, as Yale law professor Robert Post demonstrates, its "progressive" supporters inasmuch as it was viewed as conducive to creating a more disciplined workforce and saving families from the undoubted scourge of alcoholism.[5] One reason for this surge of constitutional amendment was a culture of what might be termed "constitutional irreverence," in which leading figures of the day, from pundits to professors to presidents, were more than willing to raise very basic questions about the adequacy of the Constitution.[6] I obviously believe that we in the early years of the twenty-first century are well advised to emulate our early twentieth-century predecessors in this regard.

It is also worth discussing one other theme of this book in the context of Article V. I have emphasized my reluctance to discuss clauses that are open to interpretation because such controversies can be settled by the operation of the ordinary political process. Some constitutional historians even speak of "revolutionary" changes in constitutional interpretation that have led to genuine transformations in the very nature of what might be called the American "regime." This is most often the case with regard to the changes triggered by Franklin Roosevelt's New Deal and its judicial legitimization in the years after 1937.[7] Jack Balkin and I have written an article, "Understanding the Constitutional Revolution,"[8] that offers an analysis of the transformation that may be under way as a result of the firm capture of the Supreme Court by conservative Republicans. I should note that many of our colleagues disagree that this can accurately be described as "revolutionary" in the special way that scholars of the Constitution use that term.[9] It may, however, turn out to be the case that the replacement of Sandra Day O'Connor, a relatively moderate Republican, by the far more conservative Samuel Alito—and the possible replacement of the now eighty-six-year-old John Paul Stevens by yet another conservative Republican picked by George W. Bush—will vindicate our perhaps premature argument.

In any event, adaptations by judicial interpretation are often met with outrage, whether that of conservatives angered by the post–New

Deal courts that upheld vigorous expansions of national powers and invalidated the abortion laws of most states in *Roe v. Wade*,[10] or of contemporary liberals who detest a number of recent decisions that limit congressional power to adequately protect religious minorities,[11] women who have been violently assaulted,[12] or disabled persons who have suffered discrimination by state agencies.[13] All such decisions, as already suggested, reflect the high politics of the judges, and many persons may justifiably believe that the best place for any such politics is the ordinary political marketplace and not the judiciary.

One can also detail the greatly increased power of presidents unilaterally to take the nation to war. Or the rise of the modern administrative state, which has essentially created what is sometimes referred to as a "fourth branch of government," especially with regard to so-called independent agencies whose members are not subject to being fired by dissatisfied presidents, and which has taken place without formal constitutional amendment. One might well offer such developments as evidence that the perceived necessity of change will triumph one way or another. If the Constitution is thought to be too inflexible in allowing formal change, then other, more informal methods will be developed. There is clearly something to this argument, but one must also recognize its limits.

If such informal methods were *always* available, then there would be little reason to be particularly upset—or to write this book. One might still object to the lack of transparency attached to the use of some of these informal methods. The degree of fundamental change is often covered up by being rationalized in incomprehensible legal jargon that requires inordinate faith in the lawyers and judges writing the opinions. If one believes that transparency is an important part of what Article IV of the Constitution identifies (but does not define) as a "Republican Form of Government," then the use of the judiciary as what many have called—some admiringly, some most definitely not—a "continuing constitutional convention" has real costs.

But the central thesis of this book is that there are limits to what even the most imaginative Congress, president, or Supreme Court can do to alleviate the deficiencies of the Constitution composed in 1787 and only infrequently formally amended thereafter. The Court is *not* going to declare—and would one really want it to do so?—that the imperative of equal protection of the law is denied by the patently unequal political power enjoyed by voters in small states as against those in large states. Nor did Congress declare that the Equal Rights Amendment, which, after all, gained the ratification of thirty-five states —more than two-thirds of the fifty states—with a significant majority of the national population, was now part of the formal Constitution because it is simply unacceptable, in a modern democratic country, that an amendment can be blocked by only thirteen of the states—and in at least one of those states, Illinois, the ERA had been assented to by one of the two legislative houses, but voted down in the other. Nor did President Clinton dare suggest that he would hand on his office to Vice President Al Gore inasmuch as Gore did, after all, prevail over George W. Bush in the popular vote. Readers should be able to offer almost endless similar examples of the extent to which formal structures limit possibilities of change.

Article V constitutes an iron cage with regard to changing some of the most important aspects of our political system. But almost as important is the way that it also constitutes an iron cage with regard to our imagination. Because it is so difficult to amend the Constitution— it seems almost utopian to suggest the possibility, with regard to anything that is truly important—citizens are encouraged to believe that change is almost never desirable, let alone necessary. The well-known Serenity Prayer asks for the wisdom to accept that which we cannot change. Or, to shift to the language of social psychology, we usually solve problems of cognitive dissonance—as when we want something that we know we cannot have—by deciding that what we want probably isn't that great anyway. Life is happier that way. Similarly, if we can't really change our Constitution, then we have every incentive in the world to believe that there are no real costs attached to the stasis and even to condemn those who suggest that this is a dangerous complacency. An important aim of this book is to challenge this complacency and to liberate us to think of alternatives.

But the question remains whether there is any way to escape the particular iron cage—with its almost kryptonite-like bars—of Article V. Are we ultimately trapped panthers in this cage, condemned to pace back and forth? A panther, however frustrated, presumably has no consciousness of its desperate plight. We do not share that advantage. But if we are indeed in the same position as the panther, we may see no alternative to endless pacing while we hope against hope that the worst—against which we are defenseless—does not happen to us. I will, in the final chapter, consider whether there may be any feasible way of breaking the bars and escaping the cage of Article V.

SEVEN

DISENCHANTMENT AND DESIRE

WHAT IS TO BE DONE?

I have now concluded my attempt to demonstrate why I believe that our Constitution is sufficiently defective to warrant significant revision and repair. I recount its truly grievous defects:

- The allocation of power in the Senate

- The almost certain presidential dictatorship that will follow any catastrophic attack on members of Congress

- Excessive presidential power

- The Electoral College

- The hiatus between the repudiation of a sitting president and the inauguration of a successor

- The inability to get rid of an incompetent president

- The functional impossibility of amending the Constitution with regard to anything truly significant

There are other defects that are very real, even if not so dangerous as those mentioned above:

- Life tenure for Supreme Court justices

- The creation of second-class citizens

Perhaps you still disagree with me about whether the Constitution is seriously defective, in which case this final chapter is largely irrelevant. Although I am disappointed that I did not persuade you, I am nonetheless extremely grateful that you read and considered my arguments. For those of you who share my concerns, however, the central question is, what now? How can we work together to begin fixing our Constitution?

WHAT IS TO BE DONE?

This is the title of a famous book by Lenin, both describing the czarist oppression and calling for political action to overcome it. I am certainly not a Leninist, and I do not believe that revolutionary action of the kind engaged in by George Washington and others who took up arms against an oppressive George III is called for. Still, Lenin's question always haunts anyone who is critical of the status quo. What, indeed, is to be done?

Fortunately, with regard to *some* of the problems that I have identified, I can advocate ordinary political action directed at members of the House and Senate. This is true of those constitutional defects that could be alleviated without challenging any strongly entrenched status quo. For example, there is no good reason that Congress should not propose (and the states quickly ratify) a corrective amendment with regard to the problem of the continuity of government following a catastrophic terrorist attack. The same may well be true about the various Qualifications Clauses discussed in chapter 5. Utah Republican senator Orrin Hatch introduced a proposed amendment that would have repealed the natural-born citizen limitation in Article II. Some persons referred to it as the "Arnold amendment" inasmuch as it seemed to be triggered by the desire of some Republicans to make the

Austrian-born governor of California eligible for the presidency. Like the continuity-in-government amendment introduced by Senator John Cornyn, it has also gone nowhere. One reason, perhaps, is that Governor Schwarzenegger's popularity has significantly faded; another may be that an almost terminally comatose Democratic party did not take up the cudgels itself for such an amendment. It would, after all, not only be the right thing to do in terms of democratic values, but it would also make eligible for the presidency or vice presidency one of the most attractive Democrats on the current horizon, the Canadian-born governor of Michigan, Jennifer Granholm. There is no doubt that the Constitution would be better with such amendments, but it should be obvious that they do not begin to touch on the most grievous problems of our Constitution. It may seem almost frivolous to suggest ordinary politics as the way to correct *these* defects. But can we imagine a plausible mode of "extraordinary politics"?

Daniel Lazare's conclusion to his often eloquent book *The Frozen Republic: How the Constitution Is Paralyzing Democracy*[1] exemplifies the difficulties facing advocates of substantial constitutional reform in the American context. He begins by telling a story, based on a threat by California to secede from the union, set in 2020, almost a full quarter century after the actual publication of his book in 1996. He then suggests that the correct (and likely?) response is what he terms a "democratic coup d'etat" by the House of Representatives. It basically declares itself to be the equivalent of the British Parliament, sweeping aside not only the Senate, but also the entire system of separation of powers that defines the present American system of government.[2] "[T]he rise of an all-powerful House would clear the way for precisely the sort of sweeping transformation that had previously been impossible."[3] (To be sure, the House's coup would be subject to a national referendum called within a month of its action.)

Lazare's notion is fantastic, and that is not meant as a compliment to what otherwise is a challenging and provocative book. By placing his story in the future, he in effect admits that nothing can be done at present. Moreover, his invocation of the House of Representatives, led by a charismatic, almost god-like Speaker, is the equivalent of the deus ex machina that emerges in (usually bad) drama, which clears up the disorder that has been presented to the audience. Furthermore, his almost Jacobin picture of an all-powerful House is scarcely the only, and certainly not the most attractive, alternative to what I readily concede *is* a frozen republic where "the Constitution is paralyzing democracy."

My own challenge, though, is whether I can do any better than Lazare and other critics of the Constitution whose conclusions often convey an overtone of futility with regard to the actual possibility of change. All of us have been taking on the role of Paul Revere. Instead of warning about the oncoming British, however, we are worried about further governmental paralysis or erosion in the most basic notions of American democracy and the hurdles facing the development of intelligent public policy across a plethora of important issues.

Revere could call on already mobilized Minutemen to confront the British. Our task—that is, the task of those of us who criticize the Constitution—is to *create* a movement that at the present does not exist. And one explanation for its nonexistence is precisely the belief that any political action will simply be futile because of the forbidding barriers to constitutional change constructed by Article V.

Perhaps the better—albeit even more depressing—analogy is not to Paul Revere but, rather, to patients informed by their doctors that they have Huntington's chorea or early-onset Alzheimer's disease. Both, of course, are absolutely disastrous pieces of news, and the first response is "So tell me, doctor, what can I do to stave off this catastrophe?" The reply, at least at present, is "Nothing. Your fate is in your genes (in the case of Huntington's chorea) or in some other basic biochemical structure (in the case of Alzheimer's), and we have no idea, at present, how to prevent the oncoming and predictable disaster in your life. If you have ever wanted to eat, drink, and be merry, now is the time!" If one does not simply commit suicide upon the diagnosis, then going off to Paris or buying the little red sports car that one always envisioned driving is a sensible response.

Similarly, if one is told that the Constitution contains within it virulent toxins *and* that there may be no effective cure, not least because one of the toxins is Article V itself, one may well feel limited in making an effective response. The first thing to do is to seek a second, and then a third, or even a fourth opinion until one finds someone—

perhaps a trained professional, perhaps not—who will offer a more comforting diagnosis. "Things aren't really so bad as the scaremongers suggest. If you change your diet or do more exercise, then you'll be all right." The second possibility, as already noted, is to enjoy life to the fullest until catastrophe occurs. After all, in the long run, we're all dead anyway. The third is to try one's damnedest to figure out effective ways to stave off the catastrophe. In the case particularly of Huntington's chorea, there seems to be no way to do that beyond contributing to institutions engaged in basic research on the disease. The same submission to fate may be necessary with regard to a giant asteroid that may be heading for earth, unbeknown to us, at this very instant.[4] Some have argued that this is true of global warming. But there is no reason to believe that the Constitution is "natural," beyond any human intervention and amelioration. The task is to try to determine how that can occur.

Given the central thesis of this book, it would be almost self-contradictory to say that the remedy to our most basic ills lies in ordinary politics. What the Constitution constitutes *is* what we regard as ordinary politics, which include exactly the factors, including a malapportioned Senate, the Electoral College, and Article V, that are the source of at least some of our problems. Even if large states start electing senators who promise to devote themselves to overcoming the disparity of power, it is wholly unclear how that might be attained. After all, one of the factors that gives small-state senators such effective power is their enhanced ability to offer what are perceived as good deals—requiring "only" voting for absurdities like bridges to nowhere—in a hundred-vote institution where they often hold the balance of power (and leadership positions).

New York or California will at times need, indeed beg for, the support of senators from Alaska or the Dakotas, and the process will continue to work as it has in the past. If New York refuses to do business with small-state senators, then surely competitors like Pennsylvania or Michigan will gladly step into New York's vacant chair. It is the obvious case that those seeking to construct majority coalitions will always be at the potential mercy of relatively small minorities who hold the balance of power in closely divided institutions. Robert Dahl famously observed that national politics is less a process of majority rule than of the gathering together of various minorities into more or less opportunistic majorities.[5] The Senate makes it strikingly more likely that small states will be especially privileged with regard to getting their way.

So, if you share my belief that aspects of the Constitution are a clear and present danger to the health of our republic—and of our own children and grandchildren—what constitute thinkable models and mixtures of both ordinary and extraordinary politics? When I embarked on this project, I imagined the possibility of a last chapter that would mimic the doctor in the paragraph above: "I'm sorry, but nothing can be done." To put it mildly, I am no longer satisfied with such a conclusion. Not only would readers justifiably find that immensely frustrating, but it is also true that in the course of actually writing this book I have become far more worried about the fate of our country. This has moved far from an academic project (in the pejorative sense) on my part. I now *feel* deeply, as well as *think* more concretely, that what most of us regard as our beloved Constitution is an abusive one in important respects. The first step is to recognize the abuse. The second is to do something about it.

I offer some highly tentative suggestions, but they are only a start. If you agree with my general diagnosis, I hope you will treat this conclusion as beginning an even more important conversation about what, as a practical matter, can be done. One suggestion, only half in jest, is that you recommend (and even give) this book to your friends. Although we must try to envision together how to begin a serious political movement, we must also remember the old adage that all journeys of a thousand miles must begin with the first step, which is to share one's concerns with friends. And if one discovers that one's friends develop the same gnawing fears that our Constitution may be as much a problem as a solution, then one naturally moves toward trying to spread the news even to strangers and, all important, to suggest concrete steps that might be taken. I certainly invite anyone taken with the analysis in this book to contact me at slevinson@law.utexas.edu. I anticipate setting up a Web site that can serve as a forum for discussion and imaginative suggestions.

Fortunately, one *can* begin with thoroughly conventional politics, even if, as I have already suggested, one can scarcely end there. One can mobilize to support such discrete amendments as those providing for the continuity of government in case of catastrophic attack or erasing the stigma of second-class citizenship from millions of our fellow Americans. If, as is likely, such efforts are unsuccessful because of the sheer press of other business on members of Congress, then we can collectively begin serious discussions with our friends and neighbors about the desirability of calling a new constitutional convention that would not be burdened with the obviously important tasks facing Congress and could, instead, devote all of its time, whether for six months, a year, or even two years, to full-scale consideration of the adequacy of the Constitution to our present realities.

Lazare imagines in his conclusion a coup by the House of Representatives. My own fantasies are far more limited: I desire at this point only a new constitutional convention that would feel itself legitimately empowered, and psychologically free, to do what the framers of 1787 did, which was to look at all existing constitutions as well as the lessons derived from their own experiences. In 1787, this meant looking primarily at ancient constitutions from Greece and more modern constitutionalist regimes in the Dutch republic and Switzerland. Moreover, the framers evoked the lessons of their resistance to what they regarded as British tyranny. Today, there is a wealth of experience that could be mined, as more than 150 countries have written constitutions and created polities that are, to one degree or another, actually structured by those constitutions. Moreover, we have had almost 220 years' experience in living under our Constitution.

What could be more American, fully in the spirit of the vision of the civic democracy that is at the heart of a "Republican Form of Government," than a nationwide petition campaign directed to members of Congress? Any such campaign must begin with the first small group in the first town or city, with the hope that the idea will catch on and move from group to group, city to city. Each signer would urge his or her representative or senator to vote to call a new constitutional convention empowered to assess the adequacy of the present Constitution to our contemporary needs. Article V itself provides for the possibility of a new convention on the petition of two-thirds of the states. There is no reason to interpret the Constitution as *requiring* such a petition before Congress could call a new convention. Instead, one should understand Article V as only setting out a procedure designed to *overcome the resistance* of Congress, rather than to *disempower* Congress.

But what if Congress resists these petitions and refuses to heed the call for a convention from what I am optimistically, but probably necessarily, assuming are millions of citizens? Then one moves on to the procedure set out in Article V and lobbies for state legislatures to send similar petitions to Congress, this time speaking on behalf of the state itself rather than the individual citizens who were part of the first petition drive. We are surely entitled to believe that Congress would adhere to the clear command of the Constitution and call a convention should two-thirds of the states agree.

The magic number of petitions necessary to call a convention is thirty-four, two-thirds of the fifty states. To be sure, one might doubt that the sixteen least populous states would have any incentive to support such a convention, especially if justified anger at the Senate and Electoral College were a primary motivation of calling one, but that leaves the other thirty-four. But a disciplined campaign by a majority of states (twenty-six) to call a new constitutional convention would surely create its own political dynamic, and we might hope that majority rule would prevail at least to the extent of leading Congress, at that point, voluntarily to call a convention even short of the magic number that would *require* Congress to do so.

I know from past discussions with many friends and students that even people who may even be sympathetic to the basic critique of the Constitution that I have offered will pull back in fear at the very idea of a new constitutional convention. And I strongly suspect that this fearfulness is today more likely present in persons who identify themselves as "liberals" than among "conservatives." Most liberals these days appear to be fully Madisonian in being close to terrified of the passions of their fellow citizens. They envision a runaway convention that would tear up the most admirable parts of the Constitution—of which there are many, though they are generally undiscussed in this book—were a convention given the authority to engage in the kind of wide-ranging discussion and redrafting that I suggest. Almost invariably, critics of the possibility of a convention focus on potential attacks on the rights-protective clauses of the Constitution, such as the First Amendment's protection of the freedom of speech and the press, or the protections offered by the Fourth, Fifth, and Sixth amendments to criminal defendants, or the protection against "cruel or unusual punishment" promised by the Eighth Amendment to those convicted of crimes.

I certainly believe that these rights-conferring provisions are important, though I also believe that they are all sufficiently ambiguous to be effectively interpretable however one wishes. More to the point, I continue to have a sufficient faith in the democratic ideal that I believe that most of the public, in a truly serious debate about the Constitution, could be persuaded to support the essential rights that are required for membership in a republican political order. If one does not have this degree of democratic faith, then it is very difficult to know why one would prate about the importance of democracy and encourage foreign countries, many of which lack the level of mass education and literacy of our own, to join us in the democratic experiment. It would be highly ironic if constitutional faith at bottom were synonymous with an utter lack of faith in the democratic potential of our fellow Americans.

Yet I know that there are millions of people who believe that the most important part of the Constitution consists of the rights-conferring passages and at the same time fear that their fellow citizens do not esteem them sufficiently to endorse them if they were ever given the practical possibility of doing so. Anyone with these views would presumably have recognized a kindred spirit in James Madison and shared his fear of the potentially dangerous ideas of Thomas Jefferson. And such fears are not based only on late eighteenth-century debates. I unhappily acknowledge that they are drawn from the experiences of the twentieth century and the potential for disaster in certain kinds of pseudodemocratic, demagogic politics from which the United States is certainly not immune.

It is this fear of the uncaged beast of American democracy—a view identified far more with the quasi-monarchical Hamilton than with the unabashedly democratic Jefferson—that helps to account for such arguments as those made by former Stanford Law School dean Kathleen Sullivan, who has attacked almost all proposals for constitutional amendment as exhibiting symptoms of the disease that she called "amendmentitis."[6] Still, even Professor Sullivan ultimately argues only that "we should keep in force a strong presumption against amending the Constitution," which may well be a thoroughly sensible presumption. And she writes, "That does not mean it should never be amended. The Constitution surely should be amended on occasion—for example, when changes consistent with its broad purposes are unlikely to be implemented by ordinary legislative means." My argument in this book is that our unamended Constitution has deep defects that serve as unacceptable barriers to fulfilling the "broad purposes" of our national project as set out in the Preamble. I readily agree with Sullivan that many recent proposals for new amendments are absurd or pernicious, including proposals to ban the burning of the American flag or to prohibit same-sex marriage. But it is a dreadful error for the opponents of such misguided proposals to denounce the idea of *any* amendment at all. Far better is to forthrightly attack *these* amendments while at the same time proposing other, far more desirable changes.

Support for the idea of a constitutional convention is not made any easier by the fact that those who drafted the Constitution in 1787 provided not the slightest clue of how a convention would actually be organized and what, if any, limits would be placed on its powers. Many questions attached to a convention mimic this book itself: How would delegates to the convention be chosen? Would each state have an equal number of delegates and/or an equal vote, by delegation, in the proceedings, as was the case in Philadelphia? Would the convention be limited merely to proposing amendments, which would then face almost certain doom if sent to the states for ratification via the procedures of Article V? Or, on the contrary, could the delegates to the new convention emulate their Philadelphia forebears by treating Article V as the latter did Article XIII of the Articles of Confederation? That article stupidly required unanimous consent by state legislatures of any amendments. This meant, by definition, that Rhode Island—which was almost always selected as the chief villain—could veto any change, at least if one felt bound by Article XIII. But the framers chose simply to ignore it, instead declaring, in Article VII of the Constitution, that ratification by the *conventions* (and not the legislatures) of *nine* (not all thirteen) states would be sufficient to bring the new government to life. (This explains why there were only eleven states in the union when George Washington took his oath of office on April 30, 1789; North Carolina and Rhode Island had not yet assented to the Constitution.)

I would personally endorse the suggestion of Yale Law School professor Akhil Reed Amar that a new convention could legitimately declare that its handiwork would be binding if ratified in a national referendum where each voter had equal power.[7] Amar's argument is that the strictures (and structures) of Article V are limits on the *agents* of the people rather than on the general citizenry itself (or ourselves). We could well be suspicious of the tendencies of our agents, even if we elect them to office, to attempt to aggrandize their own power. It is therefore rational to place a variety of chains around them with regard to the exercise of power, including the power to amend the Constitution. But, says Amar, these arguments do not apply when the sleeping giant, "We the People," reawakens and asserts the sovereignty announced in the Preamble to "ordain and establish" a constitution. The actual carrying out of Amar's visionary argument would be a transformative moment in American politics. But, then, so was Philadelphia, and, as Amar's colleague Bruce Ackerman has argued, so were the actions of the Reconstruction Congress between 1865 and 1868 that gave us the Fourteenth Amendment.

At this moment, all of these questions about the shape of a convention appear to be academic in the pejorative sense. No one, after all, sees a new convention on the immediate horizon. If, however, there were actually a national political movement seriously focused on gaining congressional assent to calling such a national conclave, I have no doubt that serious discussion of its operating procedures would take place. This would be especially true if the route to such a convention were petitions by thirty-four state legislatures, which Congress would be forced to heed unless it wished to trigger a genuine constitutional crisis. Congress would in effect be forced to set out the rules for the operation of a convention that would in turn have to satisfy what by now would be an aroused public. And I do not think that an aroused populace would tolerate, say, a filibustering minority blocking the passage of widely acceptable structuring rules for a convention.

MAKE THE REFERENDUM REAL

All of these suggestions focus on what might be termed ordinary political action, even if they envision a mass political movement directed at changing our system in important respects. Perhaps, though, you are not persuaded that organizing petition campaigns is likely to be any more effective than writing a letter to the editor or, for that matter, throwing a message in a bottle into the ocean or wishing upon a twinkling star. You may be right. So let me try one final idea: Make the referendum real, even in the absence of ordinary political authorization.

This book has been built around the conceit that we will have the opportunity—whether because of constitutional or statutory necessity is irrelevant—to offer our views on the adequacy of our Constitution. That is obviously not the case. To this extent, the book is only a thought experiment. But is there any reason that people convinced by the basic arguments of this book could not themselves transform the experiment from thought to action?

If the idea of organizing a national referendum on one's own, even with the aid of thousands of collaborators, is too daunting, a feasible alternative is suggested by the seminal work of Stanford professor James Fishkin, perhaps the most creative political theorist of our time. He has basically invented a new form of politics that he terms "deliberative polling."[8] This requires that scientifically selected random samples of people be brought together to deliberate for a period of several days about an important political issue. They trade ideas among themselves and listen to talks by a number of experts from across the relevant political spectrum. Lest one believe that this is merely an academic conceit, one should know that Fishkin has held such assemblies in the United States, Australia, Bulgaria, Great Britain, China, and many other countries, about a wide variety of issues, ranging from local decisions by public utilities to whether Australia should continue to recognize Her Majesty, the queen, instead of following the United States into a republican government that does without hereditary monarchs. What Fishkin and his colleagues have demonstrated—and I have personally observed in the first such deliberative poll carried out in Austin, Texas, in the run-up to the 1996 presidential election—is that people from remarkably disparate backgrounds will actually treat one another with respect and listen carefully to systematic presentations by non-demagogic speakers.

Observation of what goes on in such gatherings helps to overcome the corrosive skepticism about the possibility of what is sometimes called "deliberative democracy" and is really, I believe, what the Constitution means by a "republican form of government." Fishkin's ideas are based in part on the use of "citizen juries" in ancient Greek democracies, a concept that has much to teach us even today.[9] In any event, it would be wonderful to find out how a group of our fellow citizens would assess the Constitution after listening to a genuine debate about its present-day adequacy and what reforms they might be able to agree upon.

Such deliberative polls can be quite expensive as one thinks of the costs of bringing citizens from Maine and Hawaii to some location where they can spend several weeks together in serious reflection. But the expense probably would not come close to financing a single campaign for the U.S. Senate in a large state, let alone a serious run for the presidency. Imagine that even a million Americans in a country approaching 300 million residents are persuaded by the basic arguments of this book and wish to do something about it. If each were to donate five dollars to a "Make It Real" fund, that would, I am confident, be enough to finance a deliberative poll. And, were it to take place as the result of a serious mass movement and organized by someone with Fishkin's proven skills and impartiality, I am also confident that the American media would give it serious attention.

If such a deliberative poll were held, and if the representative Americans attending it agreed that something needed to be done beyond simply reaffirming the adequacy of the Constitution as it is, then the next stage could be the organization of a nationwide referendum, again conducted by private persons and organizations of the highest repute. One could imagine suitable campaigning ("Vote Yes!" "Reaffirm the Good

Old Constitution!"), voting booths, and independent vote counters to tabulate and announce the results, whatever they may be.

If only a few of you are persuaded by this book, or if the deliberative poll rejects its arguments, then the proposal for a national referendum is basically foolish. It would be perceived as the work of cranks, the subject of nasty jokes by Jay Leno and dismissive editorials across the country. But if a critical mass does indeed agree that our Constitution is seriously defective, then a campaign would have the potential to capture national attention and forge a new consciousness. At the very least, if the idea of a referendum took hold, one could well imagine that national polling organizations might begin asking questions relating to it. And if they asked enough people in enough states, and if a respectable percentage even close to a majority indicated that they took the possibility seriously, that in itself would become a very powerful political fact. Thomas Jefferson would yet live. Who knows where the spirit of critical reflection might lead? Perhaps it would contribute to the reinvigoration of the American experiment in government by the people and the construction of a constitution better fitted to meet the demands of our twenty-first-century society.

CODA

THE WISDOM OF WOODROW WILSON

This book opened with an extended quotation from Thomas Jefferson cautioning us not to treat the Constitution as the equivalent of the Ark of the Covenant. It is fitting to conclude with the words of another political philosopher/president:[1]

> The charm of our constitutional ideal has now been long enough wound up to enable sober men who do not believe in political witchcraft to judge what it has accomplished, and is likely still to accomplish, without further winding. The Constitution is not honored by blind worship. The more open-eyed we become, as a nation, to its defects, and the prompter we grow in applying with the unhesitating courage of conviction all thoroughly-tested or well-considered expedients necessary to make self-government among us a straightforward thing . . . , the nearer will we approach to the sound sense and practical genius of the great and honorable statesmen of 1787. And the first step towards emancipation from the timidity and false pride which have led us to seek to thrive despite the defects of our national system rather than seem to deny its perfection is a fearless criticism of that system. When we shall have examined all its parts without sentiment, and gauged all its functions by the standards of practical common sense, we shall have established anew our right to the claim of political sagacity; and it will remain only to act intelligently upon what our opened eyes have seen in order to prove again the justice of our claim to political genius.

APPENDIX

THE CONSTITUTION OF THE UNITED STATES

We the People of the United States, in Order to form a more perfect Union, establish Justice, insure domestic Tranquility, provide for the common defence, promote the general Welfare, and secure the Blessings of Liberty to ourselves and our Posterity, do ordain and establish this Constitution for the United States of America.

ARTICLE I

SECTION 1: All legislative Powers herein granted shall be vested in a Congress of the United States, which shall consist of a Senate and House of Representatives.

SECTION 2: The House of Representatives shall be composed of Members chosen every second Year by the People of the several States, and the Electors in each State shall have the Qualifications requisite for Electors of the most numerous Branch of the State Legislature.

No Person shall be a Representative who shall not have attained to the Age of twenty five Years, and been seven Years a Citizen of the United States, and who shall not, when elected, be an Inhabitant of that State in which he shall be chosen.

Representatives and direct Taxes shall be apportioned among the several States which may be included within this Union, according to their respective Numbers, which shall be determined by adding to the whole Number of free Persons, including those bound to Service for a Term of Years, and excluding Indians not taxed, three fifths of all other Persons.

The actual Enumeration shall be made within three Years after the first Meeting of the Congress of the United States, and within every subsequent Term of ten Years, in such Manner as they shall by Law direct. The Number of Representatives shall not exceed one for every thirty Thousand, but each State shall have at Least one Representative; and until such enumeration shall be made, the State of New Hampshire shall be entitled to chuse three, Massachusetts eight, Rhode Island and Providence Plantations one, Connecticut five, New York six, New Jersey four, Pennsylvania eight, Delaware one, Maryland six, Virginia ten, North Carolina five, South Carolina five and Georgia three.

When vacancies happen in the Representation from any State, the Executive Authority thereof shall issue Writs of Election to fill such Vacancies.

The House of Representatives shall chuse their Speaker and other Officers; and shall have the sole Power of Impeachment.

SECTION 3: The Senate of the United States shall be composed of two Senators from each State, chosen by the Legislature thereof, for six Years; and each Senator shall have one Vote.

Immediately after they shall be assembled in Consequence of the first Election, they shall be divided as equally as may be into three Classes. The Seats of the Senators of the first Class shall be vacated at the Expiration of the second Year, of the second Class at the Expiration of the fourth Year, and of the third Class at the Expiration of the sixth Year, so that one third may be chosen every second Year; and if Vacancies happen by Resignation, or otherwise, during the Recess of the Legislature of any State, the Executive thereof may make temporary Appointments until the next Meeting of the Legislature, which shall then fill such Vacancies.

No person shall be a Senator who shall not have attained to the Age of thirty Years, and been nine Years a Citizen of the United States, and who shall not, when elected, be an Inhabitant of that State for which he shall be chosen.

The Vice President of the United States shall be President of the Senate, but shall have no Vote, unless they be equally divided.

The Senate shall chuse their other Officers, and also a President pro tempore, in the absence of the Vice President, or when he shall exercise the Office of President of the United States.

The Senate shall have the sole Power to try all Impeachments. When sitting for that Purpose, they shall be on Oath or Affirmation. When the President of the United States is tried, the Chief Justice shall preside: And no Person shall be convicted without the Concurrence of two thirds of the Members present.

Judgment in Cases of Impeachment shall not extend further than to removal from Office, and disqualification to hold and enjoy any Office of honor, Trust or Profit under the United States: but the Party convicted shall nevertheless be liable and subject to Indictment, Trial, Judgment and Punishment, according to Law.

SECTION 4: The Times, Places and Manner of holding Elections for Senators and Representatives, shall be prescribed in each State by the Legislature thereof; but the Congress may at any time by Law make or alter such Regulations, except as to the Place of Chusing Senators.

The Congress shall assemble at least once in every Year, and such Meeting shall be on the first Monday in December, unless they shall by Law appoint a different Day.

SECTION 5: Each House shall be the Judge of the Elections, Returns and Qualifications of its own Members, and a Majority of each shall constitute a Quorum to do Business; but a smaller number may adjourn from day to day, and may be authorized to compel the Attendance of absent Members, in such Manner, and under such Penalties as each House may provide.

Each House may determine the Rules of its Proceedings, punish its Members for disorderly Behavior, and, with the Concurrence of two-thirds, expel a Member.

Each House shall keep a Journal of its Proceedings, and from time to time publish the same, excepting such Parts as may in their Judgment require Secrecy; and the Yeas and Nays of the Members of either House on any question shall, at the Desire of one fifth of those Present, be entered on the Journal.

Neither House, during the Session of Congress, shall, without the Consent of the other, adjourn for more than three days, nor to any other Place than that in which the two Houses shall be sitting.

SECTION 6: The Senators and Representatives shall receive a Compensation for their Services, to be ascertained by Law, and paid out of the Treasury of the United States. They shall in all Cases, except Treason, Felony and Breach of the Peace, be privileged from Arrest during their Attendance at the Session of their respective Houses, and in going to and returning from the same; and for any Speech or Debate in either House, they shall not be questioned in any other Place.

No Senator or Representative shall, during the Time for which he was elected, be appointed to any civil Office under the Authority of the United States which shall have been created, or the Emoluments whereof shall have been increased during such time; and no Person holding any Office under the United States, shall be a Member of either House during his Continuance in Office.

SECTION 7: All bills for raising Revenue shall originate in the House of Representatives; but the Senate may propose or concur with Amendments as on other Bills.

Every Bill which shall have passed the House of Representatives and the Senate, shall, before it become a Law, be presented to the President of the United States; If he approve he shall sign it, but if not he shall return it, with his Objections to that House in which it shall have originated, who shall enter the Objections at large on their Journal, and proceed to reconsider it. If after such Reconsideration two thirds of that House shall agree to pass the Bill, it shall be sent, together with the Objections, to the other House, by which it shall likewise be reconsidered, and if approved by two thirds of that House, it shall become a Law. But in all such Cases the Votes of both Houses shall be determined by Yeas and Nays, and the Names of the Persons voting for and against the Bill shall be entered on the Journal of each House respectively. If any Bill shall not be returned by the President within ten Days (Sundays excepted) after it shall have been presented to him, the Same shall be a Law, in like Manner as if he had signed it, unless the Congress by their Adjournment prevent its Return, in which Case it shall not be a Law.

Every Order, Resolution, or Vote to which the Concurrence of the Senate and House of Representatives may be necessary (except on a question of Adjournment) shall be presented to the President of the United States; and before the Same shall take Effect, shall be approved by him, or being disapproved by him, shall be repassed by two thirds of the Senate and House of Representatives, according to the Rules and Limitations prescribed in the Case of a Bill.

SECTION 8: The Congress shall have Power

To lay and collect Taxes, Duties, Imposts and Excises, to pay the Debts and provide for the common Defence and general Welfare of the United States; but all Duties, Imposts and Excises shall be uniform throughout the United States;

To borrow money on the credit of the United States;

To regulate Commerce with foreign Nations, and among the several States, and with the Indian Tribes;

To establish an uniform Rule of Naturalization, and uniform Laws on the subject of Bankruptcies throughout the United States;

To coin Money, regulate the Value thereof, and of foreign Coin, and fix the Standard of Weights and Measures;

To provide for the Punishment of counterfeiting the Securities and current Coin of the United States;

To establish Post Offices and Post Roads;

To promote the Progress of Science and useful Arts, by securing for limited Times to Authors and Inventors the exclusive Right to their respective Writings and Discoveries;

To constitute Tribunals inferior to the supreme Court;

To define and punish Piracies and Felonies committed on the high Seas, and Offenses against the Law of Nations;

To declare War, grant Letters of Marque and Reprisal, and make Rules concerning Captures on Land and Water;

To raise and support Armies, but no Appropriation of Money to that Use shall be for a longer Term than two Years;

To provide and maintain a Navy;

To make Rules for the Government and Regulation of the land and naval Forces;

To provide for calling forth the Militia to execute the Laws of the Union, suppress Insurrections and repel Invasions;

To provide for organizing, arming, and disciplining the Militia, and for governing such Part of them as may be employed in the Service of the United States, reserving to the States respectively, the Appointment of the Officers, and the Authority of training the Militia according to the discipline prescribed by Congress;

To exercise exclusive Legislation in all Cases whatsoever, over such District (not exceeding ten Miles square) as may, by Cession of particular States, and the acceptance of Congress, become the Seat of the Government of the United States, and to exercise like Authority over all Places purchased by the Consent of the Legislature of the State in which the Same shall be, for the Erection of Forts, Magazines, Arsenals, dock-Yards, and other needful Buildings; And

To make all Laws which shall be necessary and proper for carrying into Execution the foregoing Powers, and all other Powers vested by this Constitution in the Government of the United States, or in any Department or Officer thereof.

SECTION 9: The Migration or Importation of such Persons as any of the States now existing shall think proper to admit, shall not be prohibited by the Congress prior to the Year one thousand eight hundred and eight, but a tax or duty may be imposed on such Importation, not exceeding ten dollars for each Person.

The privilege of the Writ of Habeas Corpus shall not be suspended, unless when in Cases of Rebellion or Invasion the public Safety may require it.

No Bill of Attainder or ex post facto Law shall be passed.

No capitation, or other direct, Tax shall be laid, unless in Proportion to the Census or Enumeration herein before directed to be taken.

No Tax or Duty shall be laid on Articles exported from any State.

No Preference shall be given by any Regulation of Commerce or Revenue to the Ports of one State over those of another: nor shall Vessels bound to, or from, one State, be obliged to enter, clear, or pay Duties in another.

No Money shall be drawn from the Treasury, but in Consequence of Appropriations made by Law; and a regular Statement and Account of the Receipts and Expenditures of all public Money shall be published from time to time.

No Title of Nobility shall be granted by the United States: And no Person holding any Office of Profit or Trust under them, shall, without the Consent of the Congress, accept of any present, Emolument, Office, or Title, of any kind whatever, from any King, Prince or foreign State.

SECTION 10: No State shall enter into any Treaty, Alliance, or Confederation; grant Letters of Marque and Reprisal; coin Money; emit Bills of Credit; make any Thing but gold and silver Coin a Tender in Payment of Debts; pass any Bill of Attainder, ex post facto Law, or Law impairing the Obligation of Contracts, or grant any Title of Nobility.

No State shall, without the Consent of the Congress, lay any Imposts or Duties on Imports or Exports, except what may be absolutely necessary for executing it's inspection Laws: and the net Produce of all Duties and Imposts, laid by any State on Imports or Exports, shall be for the Use of the Treasury of the United States; and all such Laws shall be subject to the Revision and Controul of the Congress.

No State shall, without the Consent of Congress, lay any duty of Tonnage, keep Troops, or Ships of War in time of Peace, enter into any Agreement or Compact with another State, or with a foreign Power, or engage in War, unless actually invaded, or in such imminent Danger as will not admit of delay.

ARTICLE II

SECTION 1: The executive Power shall be vested in a President of the United States of America. He shall hold his Office during the Term of four Years, and, together with the Vice President chosen for the same Term, be elected, as follows:

Each State shall appoint, in such Manner as the Legislature thereof may direct, a Number of Electors, equal to the whole Number of Senators and Representatives to which the State may be entitled in the Congress: but no

Senator or Representative, or Person holding an Office of Trust or Profit under the United States, shall be appointed an Elector.

The Electors shall meet in their respective States, and vote by Ballot for two persons, of whom one at least shall not be an Inhabitant of the same State with themselves. And they shall make a List of all the Persons voted for, and of the Number of Votes for each; which List they shall sign and certify, and transmit sealed to the Seat of the Government of the United States, directed to the President of the Senate. The President of the Senate shall, in the Presence of the Senate and House of Representatives, open all the Certificates, and the Votes shall then be counted. The Person having the greatest Number of Votes shall be the President, if such Number be a Majority of the whole Number of Electors appointed; and if there be more than one who have such Majority, and have an equal Number of Votes, then the House of Representatives shall immediately chuse by Ballot one of them for President; and if no Person have a Majority, then from the five highest on the List the said House shall in like Manner chuse the President. But in chusing the President, the Votes shall be taken by States, the Representation from each State having one Vote; a quorum for this Purpose shall consist of a Member or Members from two thirds of the States, and a Majority of all the States shall be necessary to a Choice. In every Case, after the Choice of the President, the Person having the greatest Number of Votes of the Electors shall be the Vice President. But if there should remain two or more who have equal Votes, the Senate shall chuse from them by Ballot the Vice President.

The Congress may determine the Time of chusing the Electors, and the Day on which they shall give their Votes; which Day shall be the same throughout the United States.

No person except a natural born Citizen, or a Citizen of the United States, at the time of the Adoption of this Constitution, shall be eligible to the Office of President; neither shall any Person be eligible to that Office who shall not have attained to the Age of thirty-five Years, and been fourteen Years a Resident within the United States.

In Case of the Removal of the President from Office, or of his Death, Resignation, or Inability to discharge the Powers and Duties of the said Office, the same shall devolve on the Vice President, and the Congress may by Law provide for the Case of Removal, Death, Resignation or Inability, both of the President and Vice President, declaring what Officer shall then act as President, and such Officer shall act accordingly, until the Disability be removed, or a President shall be elected.

The President shall, at stated Times, receive for his Services, a Compensation, which shall neither be increased nor diminished during the Period for which he shall have been elected, and he shall not receive within that Period any other Emolument from the United States, or any of them.

Before he enter on the Execution of his Office, he shall take the following Oath or Affirmation: "I do solemnly swear (or affirm) that I will faithfully execute the Office of President of the United States, and will to the best of my Ability, preserve, protect and defend the Constitution of the United States."

SECTION 2: The President shall be Commander in Chief of the Army and Navy of the United States, and of the Militia of the several States, when called into the actual Service of the United States; he may require the Opinion, in writing, of the principal Officer in each of the executive Departments, upon any subject relating to the Duties of their respective Offices, and he shall have Power to Grant Reprieves and Pardons for Offenses against the United States, except in Cases of Impeachment.

He shall have Power, by and with the Advice and Consent of the Senate, to make Treaties, provided two thirds of the Senators present concur; and he shall nominate, and by and with the Advice and Consent of the Senate, shall appoint Ambassadors, other public Ministers and Consuls, Judges of the supreme Court, and all other Officers of the United States, whose Appointments are not herein otherwise provided for, and which shall be established by Law: but the Congress may by Law vest the Appointment of such inferior Officers, as they think proper, in the President alone, in the Courts of Law, or in the Heads of Departments.

The President shall have Power to fill up all Vacancies that may happen during the Recess of the Senate, by granting Commissions which shall expire at the End of their next Session.

SECTION 3: He shall from time to time give to the Congress Information of the State of the Union, and recommend to their Consideration such Measures as he shall judge necessary and expedient; he may, on extraordinary Occasions, convene both Houses, or either of them, and in Case of Disagreement between them, with Respect to the Time of Adjournment, he may adjourn them to such Time as he shall think proper; he shall receive Ambassadors and other public Ministers; he shall take Care that the Laws be faithfully executed, and shall Commission all the Officers of the United States.

SECTION 4: The President, Vice President and all civil Officers of the United States, shall be removed from Office on Impeachment for, and Conviction of, Treason, Bribery, or other high Crimes and Misdemeanors.

ARTICLE III

SECTION 1: The judicial Power of the United States, shall be vested in one supreme Court, and in such inferior Courts as the Congress may from time to time ordain and establish. The Judges, both of the supreme and inferior Courts, shall hold their Offices during good Behavior, and shall, at stated Times, receive for their Services a Compensation which shall not be diminished during their Continuance in Office.

SECTION 2: The judicial Power shall extend to all Cases, in Law and Equity, arising under this Constitution, the Laws of the United States, and Treaties made, or which shall be made, under their Authority; to all Cases affecting Ambassadors, other public Ministers and Consuls; to all Cases of admiralty and maritime Jurisdiction; to Controversies to which the United States shall be a Party; to Controversies between two or more States; between a State and Citizens of another State; between Citizens of different States; between Citizens of the same State claiming Lands under Grants of different States, and between a State, or the Citizens thereof, and foreign States, Citizens or Subjects.

    In all Cases affecting Ambassadors, other public Ministers and Consuls, and those in which a State shall be Party, the supreme Court shall have original Jurisdiction. In all the other Cases before mentioned, the supreme Court shall have appellate Jurisdiction, both as to Law and Fact, with such Exceptions, and under such Regulations as the Congress shall make.

    The Trial of all Crimes, except in Cases of Impeachment, shall be by Jury; and such Trial shall be held in the State where the said Crimes shall have been committed; but when not committed within any State, the Trial shall be at such Place or Places as the Congress may by Law have directed.

SECTION 3: Treason against the United States, shall consist only in levying War against them, or in adhering to their Enemies, giving them Aid and Comfort. No Person shall be convicted of Treason unless on the Testimony of two Witnesses to the same overt Act, or on Confession in open Court.

    The Congress shall have power to declare the Punishment of Treason, but no Attainder of Treason shall work Corruption of Blood, or Forfeiture except during the Life of the Person attainted.

ARTICLE IV

SECTION 1: Full Faith and Credit shall be given in each State to the public Acts, Records, and judicial Proceedings of every other State. And the Congress may by general Laws prescribe the Manner in which such Acts, Records and Proceedings shall be proved, and the Effect thereof.

SECTION 2: The Citizens of each State shall be entitled to all Privileges and Immunities of Citizens in the several States.

A Person charged in any State with Treason, Felony, or other Crime, who shall flee from Justice, and be found in another State, shall on demand of the executive Authority of the State from which he fled, be delivered up, to be removed to the State having Jurisdiction of the Crime.

No Person held to Service or Labour in one State, under the Laws thereof, escaping into another, shall, in Consequence of any Law or Regulation therein, be discharged from such Service or Labour, But shall be delivered up on Claim of the Party to whom such Service or Labour may be due.

SECTION 3: New States may be admitted by the Congress into this Union; but no new States shall be formed or erected within the Jurisdiction of any other State; nor any State be formed by the Junction of two or more States, or parts of States, without the Consent of the Legislatures of the States concerned as well as of the Congress.

The Congress shall have Power to dispose of and make all needful Rules and Regulations respecting the Territory or other Property belonging to the United States; and nothing in this Constitution shall be so construed as to Prejudice any Claims of the United States, or of any particular State.

SECTION 4: The United States shall guarantee to every State in this Union a Republican Form of Government, and shall protect each of them against Invasion; and on Application of the Legislature, or of the Executive (when the Legislature cannot be convened) against domestic Violence.

ARTICLE V

The Congress, whenever two thirds of both Houses shall deem it necessary, shall propose Amendments to this Constitution, or, on the Application of the Legislatures of two thirds of the several States, shall call a Convention for proposing Amendments, which, in either Case, shall be valid to all Intents and Purposes, as part of this Constitution, when ratified by the Legislatures of three fourths of the several States, or by Conventions in three fourths thereof, as the one or the other Mode of Ratification may be proposed by the Congress; Provided that no Amendment which may be made prior to the Year One thousand eight hundred and eight shall in any Manner affect the first and fourth

Clauses in the Ninth Section of the first Article; and that no State, without its Consent, shall be deprived of its equal Suffrage in the Senate.

ARTICLE VI

All Debts contracted and Engagements entered into, before the Adoption of this Constitution, shall be as valid against the United States under this Constitution, as under the Confederation.

This Constitution, and the Laws of the United States which shall be made in Pursuance thereof; and all Treaties made, or which shall be made, under the Authority of the United States, shall be the supreme Law of the Land; and the Judges in every State shall be bound thereby, any Thing in the Constitution or Laws of any State to the Contrary notwithstanding.

The Senators and Representatives before mentioned, and the Members of the several State Legislatures, and all executive and judicial Officers, both of the United States and of the several States, shall be bound by Oath or Affirmation, to support this Constitution; but no religious Test shall ever be required as a Qualification to any Office or public Trust under the United States.

ARTICLE VII

The Ratification of the Conventions of nine States, shall be sufficient for the Establishment of this Constitution between the States so ratifying the Same.

Done in Convention by the Unanimous Consent of the States present the Seventeenth Day of September in the Year of our Lord one thousand seven hundred and Eighty seven and of the Independence of the United States of America the Twelfth.

AMENDMENTS

AMENDMENT I: Congress shall make no law respecting an establishment of religion, or prohibiting the free exercise thereof; or abridging the freedom of speech, or of the press; or the right of the people peaceably to assemble, and to petition the Government for a redress of grievances.

AMENDMENT II: A well regulated Militia, being necessary to the security of a free State, the right of the people to keep and bear Arms, shall not be infringed.

AMENDMENT III: No Soldier shall, in time of peace be quartered in any house, without the consent of the Owner, nor in time of war, but in a manner to be prescribed by law.

AMENDMENT IV: The right of the people to be secure in their persons, houses, papers, and effects, against unreasonable searches and seizures, shall not be violated, and no Warrants shall issue, but upon probable cause, supported by Oath or affirmation, and particularly describing the place to be searched, and the persons or things to be seized.

AMENDMENT V: No person shall be held to answer for a capital, or otherwise infamous crime, unless on a presentment or indictment of a Grand Jury, except in cases arising in the land or naval forces, or in the Militia, when in actual service in time of War or public danger; nor shall any person be subject for the same offense to be twice put in jeopardy of life or limb; nor shall be compelled in any criminal case to be a witness against himself, nor be deprived of life, liberty, or property, without due process of law; nor shall private property be taken for public use, without just compensation.

AMENDMENT VI: In all criminal prosecutions, the accused shall enjoy the right to a speedy and public trial, by an impartial jury of the State and district wherein the crime shall have been committed, which district shall have been previously ascertained by law, and to be informed of the nature and cause of the accusation; to be confronted with the witnesses against him; to have compulsory process for obtaining witnesses in his favor, and to have the Assistance of Counsel for his defence.

AMENDMENT VII: In Suits at common law, where the value in controversy shall exceed twenty dollars, the right of trial by jury shall be preserved, and no fact tried by a jury, shall be otherwise re-examined in any Court of the United States, than according to the rules of the common law.

AMENDMENT VIII: Excessive bail shall not be required, nor excessive fines imposed, nor cruel and unusual punishments inflicted.

AMENDMENT IX: The enumeration in the Constitution, of certain rights, shall not be construed to deny or disparage others retained by the people.

AMENDMENT X: The powers not delegated to the United States by the Constitution, nor prohibited by it to the States, are reserved to the States respectively, or to the people.

AMENDMENT XI: The Judicial power of the United States shall not be construed to extend to any suit in law or equity, commenced or prosecuted against one of the United States by Citizens of another State, or by Citizens or Subjects of any Foreign State.

AMENDMENT XII: The Electors shall meet in their respective states, and vote by ballot for President and Vice President, one of whom, at least, shall not be an inhabitant of the same state with themselves; they shall name in their ballots the person voted for as President, and in distinct ballots the person voted for as Vice President, and they shall make distinct lists of all persons voted for as President, and of all persons voted for as Vice President and of the number of votes for each, which lists they shall sign and certify, and transmit sealed to the seat of the government of the United States, directed to the President of the Senate;

The President of the Senate shall, in the presence of the Senate and House of Representatives, open all the certificates and the votes shall then be counted;

The person having the greatest Number of votes for President, shall be the President, if such number be a majority of the whole number of Electors appointed; and if no person have such majority, then from the persons having the highest numbers not exceeding three on the list of those voted for as President, the House of Representatives shall choose immediately, by ballot, the President. But in choosing the President, the votes shall be taken by states, the representation from each state having one vote; a quorum for this purpose shall consist of a member or members from two-thirds of the states, and a majority of all the states shall be necessary to a choice. And if the House of Representatives shall not choose a President whenever the right of choice shall devolve upon them, before the fourth day of March next following, then the Vice President shall act as President, as in the case of the death or other constitutional disability of the President.

The person having the greatest number of votes as Vice President, shall be the Vice President, if such number be a majority of the whole number of Electors appointed, and if no person have a majority, then from the two highest numbers on the list, the Senate shall choose the Vice President; a quorum for the purpose shall consist of two-thirds of the whole number of Senators, and a majority of the whole number shall be necessary to a choice. But no person constitutionally ineligible to the office of President shall be eligible to that of Vice President of the United States.

AMENDMENT XIII: 1. Neither slavery nor involuntary servitude, except as a punishment for crime whereof the party shall have been duly convicted, shall exist within the United States, or any place subject to their jurisdiction.

2. Congress shall have power to enforce this article by appropriate legislation.

AMENDMENT XIV: 1. All persons born or naturalized in the United States, and subject to the jurisdiction thereof, are citizens of the United States and of the State wherein they reside. No State shall make or enforce any law which shall abridge the privileges or immunities of citizens of the United States; nor shall any State deprive any person of life, liberty, or property, without due process of law; nor deny to any person within its jurisdiction the equal protection of the laws.

2. Representatives shall be apportioned among the several States according to their respective numbers, counting the whole number of persons in each State, excluding Indians not taxed. But when the right to vote at any election for the choice of electors for President and Vice President of the United States, Representatives in Congress, the Executive and Judicial officers of a State, or the members of the Legislature thereof, is denied to any of the male inhabitants of such State, being twenty-one years of age, and citizens of the United States, or in any way abridged, except for participation in rebellion, or other crime, the basis of representation therein shall be reduced in the proportion which the number of such male citizens shall bear to the whole number of male citizens twenty-one years of age in such State.

3. No person shall be a Senator or Representative in Congress, or elector of President and Vice President, or hold any office, civil or military, under the United States, or under any State, who, having previously taken an oath, as a member of Congress, or as an officer of the United States, or as a member of any State legislature, or as an executive or judicial officer of any State, to support the Constitution of the United States, shall have engaged in insurrection or rebellion against the same, or given aid or comfort to the enemies thereof. But Congress may by a vote of two-thirds of each House, remove such disability.

4. The validity of the public debt of the United States, authorized by law, including debts incurred for payment of pensions and bounties for services in suppressing insurrection or rebellion, shall not be questioned. But neither the United States nor any State shall assume or pay any debt or obligation incurred in aid of insurrection or rebellion against the United States, or any claim for the loss or emancipation of any slave; but all such debts, obligations and claims shall be held illegal and void.

5. The Congress shall have power to enforce, by appropriate legislation, the provisions of this article.

AMENDMENT XV: 1. The right of citizens of the United States to vote shall not be denied or abridged by the United States or by any State on account of race, color, or previous condition of servitude.

2. The Congress shall have power to enforce this article by appropriate legislation.

AMENDMENT XVI: The Congress shall have power to lay and collect taxes on incomes, from whatever source derived, without apportionment among the several States, and without regard to any census or enumeration.

AMENDMENT XVII: The Senate of the United States shall be composed of two Senators from each State, elected by the people thereof, for six years; and each Senator shall have one vote. The electors in each State shall have the qualifications requisite for electors of the most numerous branch of the State legislatures.

When vacancies happen in the representation of any State in the Senate, the executive authority of such State shall issue writs of election to fill such vacancies: Provided, That the legislature of any State may empower the executive thereof to make temporary appointments until the people fill the vacancies by election as the legislature may direct.

This amendment shall not be so construed as to affect the election or term of any Senator chosen before it becomes valid as part of the Constitution.

AMENDMENT XVIII: 1. After one year from the ratification of this article the manufacture, sale, or transportation of intoxicating liquors within, the importation thereof into, or the exportation thereof from the United States and all territory subject to the jurisdiction thereof for beverage purposes is hereby prohibited.

2. The Congress and the several States shall have concurrent power to enforce this article by appropriate legislation.

3. This article shall be inoperative unless it shall have been ratified as an amendment to the Constitution by the legislatures of the several States, as provided in the Constitution, within seven years from the date of the submission hereof to the States by the Congress.

AMENDMENT XIX: The right of citizens of the United States to vote shall not be denied or abridged by the United States or by any State on account of sex.

Congress shall have power to enforce this article by appropriate legislation.

AMENDMENT XX: 1. The terms of the President and Vice President shall end at noon on the 20th day of January, and the terms of Senators and Representatives at noon on the 3d day of January, of the years in which such terms would have ended if this article had not been ratified; and the terms of their successors shall then begin.

2. The Congress shall assemble at least once in every year, and such meeting shall begin at noon on the 3d day of January, unless they shall by law appoint a different day.

3. If, at the time fixed for the beginning of the term of the President, the President elect shall have died, the Vice President elect shall become President. If a President shall not have been chosen before the time fixed for the beginning of his term, or if the President elect shall have failed to qualify, then the Vice President elect shall act as President until a President shall have qualified; and the Congress may by law provide for the case wherein neither a President elect nor a Vice President elect shall have qualified, declaring who shall then act as President, or the manner in which one who is to act shall be selected, and such person shall act accordingly until a President or Vice President shall have qualified.

4. The Congress may by law provide for the case of the death of any of the persons from whom the House of Representatives may choose a President whenever the right of choice shall have devolved upon them, and for the case of the death of any of the persons from whom the Senate may choose a Vice President whenever the right of choice shall have devolved upon them.

5. Sections 1 and 2 shall take effect on the 15th day of October following the ratification of this article.

6. This article shall be inoperative unless it shall have been ratified as an amendment to the Constitution by the legislatures of three-fourths of the several States within seven years from the date of its submission.

AMENDMENT XXI: 1. The eighteenth article of amendment to the Constitution of the United States is hereby repealed.

2. The transportation or importation into any State, Territory, or possession of the United States for delivery or use therein of intoxicating liquors, in violation of the laws thereof, is hereby prohibited.

3. The article shall be inoperative unless it shall have been ratified as an amendment to the Constitution by conventions in the several States, as pro-

vided in the Constitution, within seven years from the date of the submission hereof to the States by the Congress.

AMENDMENT XXII: 1. No person shall be elected to the office of the President more than twice, and no person who has held the office of President, or acted as President, for more than two years of a term to which some other person was elected President shall be elected to the office of the President more than once. But this Article shall not apply to any person holding the office of President, when this Article was proposed by the Congress, and shall not prevent any person who may be holding the office of President, or acting as President, during the term within which this Article becomes operative from holding the office of President or acting as President during the remainder of such term.

2. This article shall be inoperative unless it shall have been ratified as an amendment to the Constitution by the legislatures of three-fourths of the several States within seven years from the date of its submission to the States by the Congress.

AMENDMENT XXIII: 1. The District constituting the seat of Government of the United States shall appoint in such manner as the Congress may direct: A number of electors of President and Vice President equal to the whole number of Senators and Representatives in Congress to which the District would be entitled if it were a State, but in no event more than the least populous State; they shall be in addition to those appointed by the States, but they shall be considered, for the purposes of the election of President and Vice President, to be electors appointed by a State; and they shall meet in the District and perform such duties as provided by the twelfth article of amendment.

2. The Congress shall have power to enforce this article by appropriate legislation.

AMENDMENT XXIV: 1. The right of citizens of the United States to vote in any primary or other election for President or Vice President, for electors for President or Vice President, or for Senator or Representative in Congress, shall not be denied or abridged by the United States or any State by reason of failure to pay any poll tax or other tax.

2. The Congress shall have power to enforce this article by appropriate legislation.

AMENDMENT XXV: 1. In case of the removal of the President from office or of his death or resignation, the Vice President shall become President.

2. Whenever there is a vacancy in the office of the Vice President, the President shall nominate a Vice President who shall take office upon confirmation by a majority vote of both Houses of Congress.

3. Whenever the President transmits to the President pro tempore of the Senate and the Speaker of the House of Representatives his written declaration that he is unable to discharge the powers and duties of his office, and until he transmits to them a written declaration to the contrary, such powers and duties shall be discharged by the Vice President as Acting President.

4. Whenever the Vice President and a majority of either the principal officers of the executive departments or of such other body as Congress may by law provide, transmit to the President pro tempore of the Senate and the Speaker of the House of Representatives their written declaration that the President is unable to discharge the powers and duties of his office, the Vice President shall immediately assume the powers and duties of the office as Acting President.

Thereafter, when the President transmits to the President pro tempore of the Senate and the Speaker of the House of Representatives his written declaration that no inability exists, he shall resume the powers and duties of his office unless the Vice President and a majority of either the principal officers of the executive department or of such other body as Congress may by law provide, transmit within four days to the President pro tempore of the Senate and the Speaker of the House of Representatives their written declaration that the President is unable to discharge the powers and duties of his office. Thereupon Congress shall decide the issue, assembling within forty eight hours for that purpose if not in session. If the Congress, within twenty one days after receipt of the latter written declaration, or, if Congress is not in session, within twenty one days after Congress is required to assemble, determines by two thirds vote of both Houses that the President is unable to discharge the powers and duties of his office, the Vice President shall continue to discharge the same as Acting President; otherwise, the President shall resume the powers and duties of his office.

AMENDMENT XXVI: 1. The right of citizens of the United States, who are eighteen years of age or older, to vote shall not be denied or abridged by the United States or by any State on account of age.

2. The Congress shall have power to enforce this article by appropriate legislation.

AMENDMENT XXVII: No law, varying the compensation for the services of the Senators and Representatives, shall take effect, until an election of Representatives shall have intervened.

NOTES

PRELUDE

1. Thomas Jefferson, "Letter to Samuel Kercheval," Monticello, July 12, 1816, in *The Portable Thomas Jefferson*, edited by Merrill D. Peterson (Penguin, 1979), pp. 1397–1402, also at http://lachlan.bluehaze.com .au/lit/jeff14.htm.

INTRODUCTION

1. Walter Merrill, *Against Wind and Tide: A Biography of William Lloyd Garrison* (Harvard University Press, 1963), p. 205.
2. Sanford Levinson, *Constitutional Faith* (Princeton University Press, 1988).
3. See Frederick Douglass, "The Constitution of the United States: Is It Pro-Slavery or Anti-Slavery," in *Life and Writings of Frederick Douglass*, vol. 2, edited by P. Foner (International Publishers, 1975), pp. 467–480.
4. See Lawrence v. Texas, 539 U.S. 558 (2003).
5. See http://www.cbsnews.com/htdocs/CBSNews_polls/poll_0418.pdf.
6. See David Leonhardt, "For Bush, the Economy Is a Glass Half Empty," *New York Times*, May 7, 2006, Section 4, pp. 1, 3.
7. Adam Nagourney and Megan Thee, "Bush's Public Approval at New Low Point," *New York Times*, May 9, 2006, p. 1.
8. Id.
9. See http://www.sciencedaily.com/upi/?feed=TopNews&article=UPI-1 -20060111-19144800-bc-us-pew.xml.
10. See http://www.quinnipiac.edu/x11385.xml?ReleaseID=738.
11. "The American Public's Assessment of the Rehnquist Court," 89 *Judicature* 168, 170 (November–December 2005).
12. Id. at 174.
13. Id. at 175.
14. Alexander Hamilton, *Federalist*, No. 31.

CHAPTER 1

1. John J. Dinan, *The American State Constitutional Tradition* (University Press of Kansas, 2006), p. 31.

2. See the New York State Constitution, available at http://www.senate .state.ny.us/lbdcinfo/senconstitution.html.

3. See Robert J. Martineau, "The Mandatory Referendum on Calling a State Constitutional Convention: Enforcing the People's Right to Reform Their Government," *Ohio Sate L.J.* 31 (Spring 1970): 421–455.

4. See Article I, section 9.

5. See Frederick Douglass, "The Constitution of the United States: Is It Pro-Slavery or Anti-Slavery?" excerpted in Paul Brest et al., *Processes of Constitutional Decisionmaking*, 5th ed. (Aspen Law and Business, 2006), pp. 255–257.

6. See, e.g., David Hendrickson, *Peace Pact: The Lost World of the American Founding* (University Press of Kansas, 2003). He notes that the framers were much influenced by their readings of ancient Greek and contemporary European history, both of which counseled that peace was basically impossible if multiple polities shared the same broad geographical territories. Akhil Reed Amar analyzes the "geostrategy" behind the pressure for the unification of the American states at 44–53 of *America's Constitution: A Biography* (Random House, 2005).

7. See Arver v. United States (Selective Draft Law Cases), 245 U.S. 366 (1918). As the Court wrote in a case two years earlier, the Thirteenth Amendment "was not intended to interdict enforcement of those duties which individuals owe to the State. . . . The great purpose in view was liberty under the protection of effective government, not the destruction of the latter by depriving it of essential powers." Butler v. Perry, 240 U.S. 328, 333 (1916).

8. Sanford Levinson, *Constitutional Faith* (Princeton University Press, 1988).

9. Letter to John Cartwright, Monticello, June 5, 1824, in *The Portable Jefferson*, edited by Merill Peterson (Viking, 1975), p. 580.

10. Letter to James Madison, Sept. 6, 1789, in id. at 449.

11. Letter to J. W. Eppes, June 24, 1813, in *Jefferson's Letters*, edited by Wilson Whitman (Hale, n.d.), p. 287.

12. Letter to W. F. Dumas, Sept. 19, 1787, in id. at 79.

13. "I long to hear that you have declared an independency. And, by the

way, in the new code of laws which I suppose it will be necessary for you to make, I desire you would remember the ladies and be more generous and favorable to them than your ancestors." Abigail Adams to John Adams, Mar. 31, 1776, at http://www.thelizlibrary.org/suffrage/abigail.htm.

14. The quotations in this paragraph are taken from Alexander Hamilton, James Madison, and John Jay, *The Federalist*, ed. Benjamin Fletcher Wright (Harvard University Press, 1961), pp. 348–349. The text of *Federalist*, No. 49, can be found at http://www.yale.edu/lawweb/avalon/federal/fed49.htm.

15. *The Federalist*, No. 49, pp. 349–350.

16. Id. at 351.

17. Max Farrand, ed., *The Records of the Federal Convention of 1787*, vol. 1 (Yale University Press, 1937), p. 299.

18. See, e.g., John R. Vile, *Rewriting the United States Constitution: An Examination of Proposals from Reconstruction to the Present* (Praeger, 1991).

19. Vile offers a useful précis of the book: id. at 30–32.

20. Quoted in id. at 30.

21. See Tugwell, *The Emerging Constitution* (Harper's Magazine Press, 1974). Tugwell is discussed in Vile, supra note 18, at 106–110.

22. See J. Allen Smith, *The Spirit of American Government* (1907; reprint, Harvard University Press, 1965).

23. Charles A. Beard, *An Economic Interpretation of the Constitution of the United States* (Macmillan, 1913).

24. Vernon Louis Parrington, *Main Currents in American Thought* (Classic Textbooks, 1927).

25. Oliver Wendell Holmes, "The Path of the Law," 10 *Harv. L. Rev.* 457 (1897), reprinted in *The Collected Works of Justice Holmes*, vol. 3, edited by Sheldon Novick (University of Chicago Press, 1995), p. 391.

26. See, e.g., Edward Purcell, *Crisis of Democratic Theory: Scientific Naturalism and the Problem of Value* (University of Kentucky Press, 1973).

27. Letter of George Washington to Bushrod Washington, Nov. 10, 1787, in *The Origins of the American Constitution: A Documentary History*, edited by Michael Kammen (Penguin, 1986), p. 83 (emphasis added).

28. See Sanford Levinson, "The Political Implications of Amending Clauses," 12 *Const. Comment.* 107–123 (1996), reprinted in somewhat different form in *Constitutional Culture, Democratic Rule*, edited by John

Ferejohn, Jack Rakove, and Jonathan Riley (Cambridge University Press, 2001), pp. 271–287.

29. Donald Lutz, "Toward a Formal Theory of Constitutional Amendment," in *Responding to Imperfection: The Theory and Practice of Constitutional Amendment,* edited by Sanford Levinson (Princeton University Press, 1995), pp. 237, 261. At the time of his writing, the Yugoslav Constitution held that dubious honor, but it no longer exists. One will never know if the ravages that plagued the South Balkans might have been lessened had the constitution not been so rigid.

30. Sanford Levinson, "How Many Times Has the United States Constitution Been Amended? (A) < 26; (B) 26; (C) 27; (D) > 27: Accounting for Constitutional Change," in id. at 13.

31. Stephen M. Griffin, "The Nominee Is . . . Article V," in *Constitutional Stupidities, Constitutional Tragedies,* edited by William Eskridge and Sanford Levinson (New York University Press, 1998), p. 14.

32. See Bruce Ackerman, *We the People: Foundations,* vol. 1 (Harvard University Press, 1991); *We the People: Transformations,* vol. 2 (Harvard University Press, 1996). See also Ackerman, "Higher Lawmaking," in Levinson, supra note 29, at 63.

33. See Sanford Levinson, "Constitutional Norms in a State of Permanent Emergency," 40 *U. Ga. L. Rev.* 699–750 (2006). Consider President Clinton's decision to wage war in Serbia. He cared little either about statutory authorization by Congress—refused by the House of Representatives in a 213–213 vote on April 28, 1999, after the bombing had been going on for a month—or about compliance with our treaty obligations under the UN Charter.

34. See Bruce Ackerman and David Golove, *Is NAFTA Constitutional?* (Harvard University Press, 1995).

CHAPTER 2

1. See Shailagh Murray, "Some in GOP Regretting Pork-Stuffed Highway Bill," *Washington Post,* Nov. 5, 2005, p. A1. There is an airport on the island to which the bridge will go, which apparently receives approximately ten commercial flights a day for the adjoining mainland town of Ketchikan (population approximately 8,000). That does not change the fact that the ferry service is year-round, and no one has come close to making a compelling cost-benefit justification of the bridge. If, for example, one assumes that these flights generate an

implausible 100,000 passengers/year for twenty years, that would still make the cost of the bridge at least $23 per passenger use over this period.

2. See "Mr. Stevens's Tirade," *Washington Post*, Oct. 23, 2005, p. B6, at http://www.washingtonpost.com/wp-dyn/content/article/2005/10/22/ AR2005102201040.html.

3. See Murray, supra note 1.

4. Available at http://www.brainyquote.com/quotes/authors/e/everett _dirksen.html.

5. Wesberry v. Sanders, 376 U.S. 1 (1964). The Court has failed to explain, in the four decades since *Wesberry* and in other cases relying on the slogan, what it actually means by "one person, one vote." Consider, for example, that the Court tolerates greater population inequality among districts at the state level than in the crafting of districts for the U.S. House of Representatives, plus there are obvious differences between the number of residents in any area and the number of (potential) voters, so that it matters what the denominator is when comparing two districts. See Sanford Levinson, "One Person, One Vote: A Mantra in Need of Meaning," 80 *U.N.C. L. Rev.* 269– 297 (2002).

6. "U.S. Congress Approval Rating at 36 Percent," *Science Daily*, at http: //www.washingtonpost.com/wp-dyn/content/article/2005/12/25/ AR2005122500173.html.

7. T. Alexander Aleinikoff and Samuel Issacharoff, "Race and Redistrict- ing: Drawing Constitutional Lines After Shaw v. Reno," 92 *Mich. L. Rev.* 588 (1993) (emphasis added).

8. See Alan Wolfe, *Does American Democracy Still Work?* (Yale University Press, 2006).

9. See Samuel C. Patterson and Anthony Mughan, *Senates: Bicameralism in the Contemporary World* (Ohio State University Press, 1999), p. 3; George Tsebelis and Jeannette Money, *Bicameralism* (Cambridge University Press, 1997), p. 1.

10. Patterson and Mughan, supra note 9, at 3–4.

11. Tsebelis and Money, supra note 9, at 129.

12. Werner J. Patzelt, "The Very Federal House: The German Bundesrat," in Patterson and Mughan, supra note 9, at 78.

13. Akhil Reed Amar, *America's Constitution: A Biography* (Random House, 2005), p. 66.

14. See id. at 413.

15. Id. at 36.

16. Arend Lijphart, *Patterns of Democracy: Government Forms and Performance in Thirty-Six Countries* (Yale University Press, 1999), p. 2.

17. E-mail from Mark Graber to Sanford Levinson, May 4, 2006.

18. Mark A. Graber, *Dred Scott and the Problem of Constitutional Evil* (Cambridge University Press, 2006).

19. Quoted in Alastair Macdonald, "Bombs, Protests as Iraq Election Mood Sours," at http://www.washingtonpost.com/wp-dyn/content/article/2005/12/25/AR2005122500173.html.

20. 377 U.S. 533 (1964).

21. Quoted in Frances E. Lee and Bruce I. Oppenheimer, *Sizing Up the Senate: The Unequal Consequences of Equal Representation* (University of Chicago Press, 1999), p. 224.

22. See Patzelt, supra note 12.

23. See John Uhr, "Generating Divided Government: The Australian Senate," in Patterson and Mughan, supra note 9, at 105–108.

24. A sprightly essay demonstrating (and lamenting) this point is Frederick Schauer, "The Constitution of Fear," in *Constitutional Stupidities, Constitutional Tragedies*, edited by William Eskridge and Sanford Levinson (New York University Press, 1988), pp. 84–89.

25. Roger D. Congleton, "On the Merits of Bicameral Legislatures: Policy Stability Within Partisan Politics" (unpublished manuscript, Dec. 13, 2002), at http://www.rdc1.net/forthcoming/BICAMEURO3.PD; see also Congleton, "On the Merits of Bicameral Legislatures: Policy Predictability Within Partisan Polities," 22 *Y.B. of New Pol. Econ.* 29–49 (2003), at http://www.rdc1.net/forthcoming/DCD%20(Chap%206,%20Bicameralism,%20Congleton).pdf.

26. Mitchel A. Sollenberger, "Congressional Overrides of Presidential Vetoes," Congressional Research Service Report for Congress, Apr. 7, 2004, p. 1. Available at http://rules.house.gov/archives/98-157.pdfat. I am grateful to Marty Ledermen for bringing to my attention the existence of this invaluable document.

27. See Jose Antonio Cheibub, "Presidentialism and Democratic Performance," in *The Architecture of Democracy: Constitutional Design, Conflict Management, and Democracy*, edited by Andrew Reynolds (Oxford University Press, 2002), p. 112.

28. See Constitution of South Africa, Article 79 (Assent to Bills), at http://www.info.gov.za/documents/constitution/1996/96cons4.htm#79.

29. The Sollenberger collection, supra note 26, includes only 1,484 vetoes. The larger number of 2,550 includes 1,066 pocket vetoes, which are surely an important part of the president's arsenal of power and which are not subject to congressional override inasmuch as Congress is not in session to do so. See Ken Herman, "'Yes, but' Helps Bush Avoid Using Veto," *Austin American-Statesman*, Feb. 20, 2006; e-mail from Herman to Sanford Levinson, Feb. 20, 2006.

30. Clinton Rossiter, *The American Presidency* (Harcourt Brace, 1956), p. 14.

31. Scott James, "The Evolution of the Presidency: Between the Promise and the Fear," in *Institutions of American Democracy: The Executive Branch*, edited by Joel D. Aberbach and Mark A. Peterson (Oxford University Press, 2005), pp. 10–11.

32. See Gerard N. Magliocca, "Veto! The Jacksonian Revolution in Constitutional Law," 78 *Neb. L. Rev.* 205 (1999), for a very interesting study of Andrew Jackson's path-breaking conception of the presidential veto power.

33. Michael Stokes Paulsen, "The Most Dangerous Branch: Executive Power to Say What the Law Is," 83 *Geo. L.J.* 217, 265 (1998).

34. See, e.g., Walter Dellinger, "Presidential Authority to Decline to Execute Unconstitutional Statutes," November 2, 1994, reprinted in *Processes of Constitutional Decisionmaking*, 5th ed., ed. Paul Brest et al. (Aspen Law and Business, 2006), pp. 79–81. Dellinger was assistant attorney general of the United States (and head of the Office of Legal Counsel), and his memorandum was written to Abner Mikva, counsel to President Bill Clinton.

35. Congress passed a law authorizing such line-item vetoes by the president in certain circumstances, but the Supreme Court held that it violated the Constitution. See Clinton v. City of New York, 524 U.S. 417 (1998). I think there were good grounds to oppose that grant of authority inasmuch as it further strengthened presidential power, but I am not convinced that Congress was prevented from making that choice, especially if one acknowledges that what Congress gave, it could later take away should it find that presidents abused the exercise of line-item vetoes.

36. A 2002 Library of Congress compilation of "Acts of Congress Held Unconstitutional in Whole or in Part by the Supreme Court of the United States" lists 158 cases invalidating federal legislation. See *The Constitution of the United States of America: Analysis and Interpretation* (Congressional Reference Service, Library of Congress, U.S. Government Printing Office, 2004), pp. 2117–2150. However, another widely respected compilation lists 162 such cases up to 2002. See Lee Epstein et al., *The Supreme Court Compendium: Data, Decisions, and Developments*, 3d ed. (Congressional Quarterly Press, 2003), pp. 163–166 (Table 2-15: Supreme Court Decisions Holding Acts of Congress Unconstitutional in Whole or in Part, 1789–2002). It is also the case that some decisions might invalidate more than one federal act if their principles are applied to acts that were not the subject of the specific litigation. Still, it is beyond argument that presidential vetoes have accounted for more "legislative fatalities" than have decisions of the Supreme Court, especially if we take into account the frequency of legislative concessions produced by the anticipation reactions of legislators to potential presidential vetoes.

37. See especially Jacob Hacker and Paul Pierson, *Off Center: The Republican Revolution and the Erosion of American Democracy* (Yale University Press, 2005); Alan Wolfe, *Does American Democracy Still Work?* (Yale University Press, 2006), for persuasive analyses that American democracy is not only eroded but in outright danger as a result of the political tactics of the contemporary Republican party, which currently controls both Congress and the White House.

38. See, e.g., Charlie Savage, "Bush Challenges Hundreds of Laws: President Cites Powers of His Office," *Boston Globe*, April 30, 2006, p. 1.

39. See Michael Kinsley, "Constitutional Cafeteria," *Washington Post*, May 5, 2006, p. A19. A far harsher view is expressed by the *New York Times*: "Veto? Who Needs a Veto?" May 5, 2006, p. A24.

40. Christopher S. Kelley, "Rethinking Presidential Power—the Unitary Executive and the George W. Bush Presidency," paper presented at the Annual Meeting of the Midwest Political Science Association, April 7–10, 2005, available at http://www.users.muohio.edu/kelleycs/paper.pdf.

41. See George C. Edwards III, *Why the Electoral College Is Bad for America* (Yale University Press, 2005), p. 45, which demonstrates that the best analysis of the 1960 vote suggests that Richard Nixon received ap-

proximately 48,000 more popular votes than did John F. Kennedy. This requires a close analysis of the Alabama vote, and many books, which have not engaged in such an analysis, state that Kennedy narrowly edged out Nixon in the popular vote. They are wrong.

42. See Richard Bernstein with Jerome Agel, *Amending America: If We Love the Constitution So Much, Why Do We Keep Trying to Change It?* (Crown, 1993), p. 122.

43. See, e.g., Ralph Rossum, *Federalism, the Supreme Court, and the Seventeenth Amendment: The Ironies of Constitutional Democracy* (Lexington Books, 2001).

44. See James Sundquist, *Constitutional Reform and Effective Government*, rev. ed. (Brookings Institution, 1992), pp. 162–164. Sundquist advocates an eight-year term, with half the Senate to be chosen during each presidential election. He also advocates changing the term of members of the House of Representatives to four years and eliminating the "midterm" election. See id at pp. 151–153.

45. See especially Daniel Lazare, *The Frozen Republic: How the Constitution Is Paralyzing Democracy* (Harcourt Brace, 1996); Robert Dahl, *How Democratic Is the American Constitution?* 2d ed. (Yale University Press, 2003). See also Lynn A. Baker and Samuel H. Dinkin, "The Senate: An Institution Whose Time Has Gone?" 13 *J.L. and Pol.* 21 (1997); Richard Rosenfeld, "What Democracy: The Case for Abolishing the United States Senate," *Harper's Magazine*, May 2004, pp. 35–44.

46. Dahl, supra note 45, at 50.

47. Id. at 48.

48. See George C. Edwards, *Why the Electoral College Is Bad for America* (Yale University Press, 2005), pp. 166–167.

49. The data are collected at http://www.fairvote.org/?page=707.

50. Baker and Dinkin, supra note 45, at 30.

51. Frances E. Lee and Bruce I. Oppenheimer, *Sizing Up the Senate: The Unequal Consequences of Equal Representation* (University of Chicago Press, 1999).

52. Id. at 155.

53. Id. at 69.

54. There are clearly exceptions to this generalization, as with Delaware's Joseph Biden, whose major committees are indeed the Judiciary and Foreign Relations committees, and Vermont's Patrick Leahy, the ranking Democrat on the Senate Judiciary Committee.

55. Lee and Oppenheimer, supra note 51, at 226.

56. Id. at 134.

57. Id. at 165.

58. Id. at 173.

59. See http://www.calinst.org/datapages/dhs/DHSGrants-2004-ODP.htm.

60. Lee and Oppenheimer, supra note 51, at 177.

61. The reason an amendment was necessary is that the Constitution specifies, in Article I, section 8, clause 17, that Congress shall "exercise exclusive Legislation in all Cases whatsoever, over such District (not exceeding ten Miles square) as may, by Cession of particular States, and the Acceptance by Congress, become the Seat of the Government of the United States."

62. See William N. Eskridge, Jr., "The One Senator, One Vote Clauses," in Eskridge and Levinson, supra note 24, at 35–39; Suzanna Sherry, "Our Unconstitutional Senate," in id. at 95–97.

63. See Table 4.6: Effect of Senate Apportionment on the Partisan Composition of the Senate, 1915–97, in Lee and Oppenheimer, supra note 51, at 119.

64. See http://www.fec.gov/pubrec/fe2000/senparty.htm.

65. "The Potential for Minority Rule in U.S. Congressional Elections," *Fair Vote: Voting and Democracy Research Center,* Feb. 2005, at http://www.fairvote.org/filibuster/?page=707. The authors also note the possibility, though as a matter of fact this is far more implausible, that successful coalition of fifty-one senators from both parties could represent states with approximately 10 percent of the national vote.

66. This fact alone raises serious questions about the ridiculous emphasis placed on the Iowa caucuses and the New Hampshire primary as the initial events in the formal presidential campaign season, a subject beyond the scope of this book but nonetheless a further illustration of the extent to which large states are significantly disabled in the American political system.

67. See especially Senator Daniel Patrick Moynihan's introduction to Herman B. Leonard and Jay H. Walder, eds., *The Federal Budget and the States: Fiscal Year 1999* (Taubman Center for State and Local Government, J.F.K. School of Government, Harvard University, and Office of Senator Moynihan).

68. Id. at 10.

69. To be sure, two small states, New Hampshire and Delaware, are also

revenue exporters, even as Pennsylvania is a slight importer, but the general pattern is that large urban states do far worse than smaller states; see id. at 1.

70. Id. at 11, quoting Lars-Erik Nelson, "Pat Moynihan's Starting Idea: Junk New Deal," (New York) *Daily News*, Dec. 10, 1999.

71. Leonard and Walder, supra note 67, at 223.

72. Id. at 224.

73. Id.

74. As it happens, large-state senators get considerably more media coverage than do small-state ones. See id. at 133–140. Lee and Oppenheimer note that not only are the national media uninterested in most small-state senators, but also, and perhaps more significant from the perspective of my argument, "the national media is of no interest to 'those senators who want little more than to serve their constituents' local needs,'" which, of course, disproportionately describes small-state senators. Id. at 134, quoting Stephen Hess, *The Ultimate Insiders: U.S. Senators in the National Media* (Brookings Institution, 1986), p. 7.

75. Lee and Oppenheimer, supra note 51, at 224.

76. For an extended argument in this regard, see Daryl Levinson and Richard Pildes, "Separation of Parties, Not Powers," 119 *Harv. L. Rev.* 2311 (2006).

77. See, e.g., Theodore J. Lowi, "Constitutional Merry-Go-Round: The First Time Tragedy, the Second Time Farce," in Eskridge and Levinson, supra note 24, at 189–202.

78. See James L. Sundquist, *Constitutional Reform and Effective Government*, rev. ed. (Brookings Institution, 1992).

79. This point is made very strongly in Cheibub, supra note 27, at 110–117.

80. See David Mayhew, *Divided We Govern: Party Control, Lawmaking, and Investigations, 1946–2002*, 2d ed. (Yale University Press, 2005).

81. James Madison, *Federalist*, No. 51, in *The Federalist*, ed. Benjamin Fletcher Wright (Harvard University Press, 1961), p. 356.

82. Daryl Levinson, "Empire-Building Government in Constitutional Law," *Harv. L. Rev.* 118 (2005): 915–972. See also Pildes and Levinson, supra n. 76.

83. Mayhew, supra note 80, at 223–226.

84. This sentence must be modified, though, to take account of the fact that several members of Congress have retained their positions as

inactive members of the armed forces, even though, obviously, the armed forces are part of the executive branch. This issue was raised before the Supreme Court, see Schlesinger v. Reservists to Stop the War, 418 U.S. 208 (1974), but the Court in effect refused to rule on it.

85. Sundquist, supra note 78, at 42.

86. Quoted in id.

87. Quoted in id. at 43.

88. Quoted in id.

89. Id.

90. Id. at 232.

91. Although University of Chicago law professor Philip Kurland and Dean Willard D. Lorensen of the West Virginia University College of Law argued that this solution was too clever by half and violated the clear language of the provision, I agree with then Duke University Law School professor William Van Alstyne, who testified that it was an acceptable way of evading what has become a pointless and even perhaps counterproductive part of the Constitution. See the testimony collected in Paul Brest, *Processes of Constitutional Decisionmaking*, 1st ed. (Little Brown, 1975), pp. 17–26.

92. Sundquist, supra note 78, at 173.

93. Id.

94. Article I, section 2, clause 5.

95. Continuity of Government Commission, *Preserving Our Institutions* (Washington, D.C., 2003), available at http://www .continuityofgovernment.org/pdfs/FirstReport.htm.

96. See "Ensuring the Continuity of the United States Government: A Proposed Constitutional Amendment to Guarantee a Functioning Congress," Hearings Before the Committee on the Judiciary, U.S. Senate, 108th Cong., Jan. 27, 2004, Serial No. J-108-54, p. 9.

97. Though the Senate *did* convene in order to confirm Lincoln's nominees for the cabinet. The House, however, was not in session.

98. Clinton Rossiter, *Constitutional Dictatorship* (Transaction, 2002), p. 224.

99. Georgio Agamben, *State of Exception* (University of Chicago Press, 2005), p. 20.

100. On the latter, see Bruce Ackerman, *The Case Against Lameduck Impeachment* (1999; reprint, Seven Stories Press, 2004).

101. See John Copeland Nagle, "A Twentieth Amendment Parable," 72 *N.Y.U. L. Rev.* 470 (1997). I discuss the problem of lame-duck sessions in "Presidential Elections and Constitutional Stupidities," in Eskridge and Levinson, supra note 24, at 66 n.4.

CHAPTER 3

1. Available at http://www.whitehouse.gov/news/releases/2005/12/20051230–8.html.

2. See Matthew H. Franck, "How Alito Helped Bush 20 Years Ago," *National Review Online*, Jan. 2, 2006, at http://bench.nationalreview.com/archives/085715.asp.

3. See Charlie Savage, "Bush Challenges Hundreds of Laws," *Boston Globe*, April 30, 2006, p. 1.

4. Stuart Taylor, Jr., "The Man Who Would Be King," *Atlantic Monthly*, Apr. 2006, pp. 25–26.

5. George C. Edwards, *Why the Electoral College Is Bad for America* (Yale University Press, 2005), p. 45. Edwards credits 491,527 votes to Virginia senator Harry Byrd (who received 15 electoral votes, as against 303 for Kennedy and 219 for Nixon).

6. Id. at 70.

7. Id. at 42.

8. The italicized language has been changed because of the Twentieth Amendment, to be discussed below.

9. Edwards, supra note 5, at 10–11. The first chapter of his book, "How the Electoral College Works," is an extremely accessible primer that well fits its title.

10. See Bruce Ackerman, *The Failure of the Founding Fathers: Jefferson, Marshall, and the Rise of Presidential Democracy* (Harvard University Press, 2005).

11. Sanford Levinson, "2 Texans, Not 1," *New York Times*, Aug. 3, 2000, p. A29; Jones v. Bush, 122 F. Supp. 2d 713 (N.D. Tex., 2000).

12. Yale University Press, 2005.

13. "Drop Out of the College," *New York Times*, Mar. 14, 2006, p. A 30. See also Hendrik Herzberg, "Count 'Em," *New Yorker*, Mar. 6, 2006, pp. 27–28.

14. See John R. Koza et al., *Every Vote Equal: A State-Based Plan for Electing the President by National Popular Vote* (National Popular Vote Press, 2006), pp. 8–9, at http://www.nationalpopularvote.com/npv.

15. Id. at 10–11.

16. Id. at 12.

17. See id. at 166: Appendix B: Comparisons of State Population and Electoral Votes.

18. See Garry Wills, *"Negro President": Jefferson and the Slave Power* (Houghton Mifflin, 2003).

19. This is not the proper occasion to examine the validity of this perception.

20. In William N. Eskridge, Jr., and Sanford Levinson, *Constitutional Stupidities, Constitutional Tragedies* (New York University Press, 1998), pp. 15–17.

21. Sanford Levinson, "Presidential Elections and Constitutional Stupidities," in id. at 61–66.

22. Edwards, supra note 5, at 61. The table setting out the seven elections is at 62.

23. Id. at 63.

24. Jeffrey Rosen, "Divided Suffrage," in Eskridge and Levinson, supra note 20, at 81–83.

25. See Edwards, supra note 5, at 64–67.

26. See id. at 22.

27. Id. at 66.

28. Id. at 67–71.

29. Id. at 23.

30. James Madison to George Hay, Aug. 23, 1823, quoted in Edwards, supra note 5, at 73.

31. Edwards, supra note 5, at xi.

32. Id.

33. Id.

34. See John R. Koza et al., *Every Vote Equal: A State-Based Plan for Electing the President by National Popular Vote* (National Popular Vote Press, 2006), at http://www.nationalpopularvote.com/npv.

35. On the design of such election systems, see Giovanni Sartori, *Constitutional Engineering*, 2d ed. (Columbia University Press, 1997), pp. 5–6, 61–69.

36. John Locke, *Two Treatises on Government: Second Treatise*, edited by

Peter Laslett (Cambridge University Press, 1963), ¶¶ 160–161 (first emphasis added).

37. See Sanford Levinson and Bartholomew Sparrow, eds., *The Louisiana Purchase and American Expansionism* (Rowman and Littlefield, 2005).

38. Letter to John Colvin, Sept. 20, 1810, quoted in Gerald Stourzh, *Alexander Hamilton and the Idea of a Republican Government* (Stanford University Press, 1970), p. 34.

39. The most recent study of Lincoln's constitutionalism is Daniel Farber, *Lincoln's Constitution* (University of Chicago Press, 2003). For my own views, see Sanford Levinson, "Was the Emancipation Proclamation Constitutional? Do/Should We Care What the Answer Is," 2001 *U. Ill. L. Rev.* 1135 (2001).

40. Andrew Delbanco, *The Portable Abraham Lincoln* (Viking, 1992), p. 216 (emphasis in original).

41. *Federalist*, No. 41 (emphasis added), at http://www.yale.edu/lawweb/avalon/federal/fed41.htm.

42. Yoo's arguments are spelled out in *The Powers of War and Peace: The Constitution and Foreign Affairs After 9/11* (University of Chicago Press, 2005).

43. The memorandum is reprinted in Karen J. Greeberg, ed., *The Torture Debate in America* (Cambridge University Press, 2005), pp. 317–360.

44. See id. at 361–376.

45. 79 *Notre Dame L. Rev.* 1257 (2004).

46. Id. at 1283 (quoting from letter of Apr. 4, 1864, from Lincoln to U.S. senator Albert G. Hodges).

47. Id. at 1296.

48. Id. at 1297.

49. Harvey Mansfield, "The Law and the President: In a National Emergency, Who You Gonna Call?" *Weekly Standard*, Jan. 16, 2006.

50. See especially Carl Schmitt, *Political Theology* (University of Chicago Press, 2005).

51. As argued in an important—and highly troubling—book by Clinton Rossiter, *Constitutional Dictatorship*, originally published in 1948 and republished in 2002 (Transaction Books), with a picture of the World Trade Center in flames on its cover.

52. See, e.g., Samuel Issacharoff and Richard Pildes, "Between Civil Libertarianism and Executive Unilateralism: An Institutional Process

Approach to Rights During Wartime," in *The Constitution in Time of War*, edited by Mark Tushnet (Duke University Press, 2005).

53. See, e.g., Kim Lane Scheppele, "North American Emergencies," 4 *ICON* 213 (2006).

54. Jules Lobel, "Comment: Emergency Power and the Decline of Liberalism," 98 *Yale L.J.* 1385, 1408 (1989).

55. See, e.g., Bruce Ackerman and David Golove, *Is NAFTA Constitutional?* (Harvard University Press, 1995). Harvard law professor Laurence Tribe has criticized this de facto demise of the Treaty Clause in "Taking Text and Structure Seriously: Reflections on Free-Form Method in Constitutional Interpretation," 108 *Harv. L. Rev.* 1221 (1995).

56. See E. J. Dionne, Jr., "What the 'Shield' Covered Up," *Washington Post*, Nov. 1, 2005, p. A25.

57. "The Address and Reasons of Dissent of the Minority of the Convention of Pennsylvania to Their Constituents," Dec. 12, 1787, at http://www.constitution.org/afp/pennmi00.htm.

58. Max Farrand, ed., *The Records of the Federal Convention of 1787*, vol. 1 (Yale University Press, 1937), p. 236.

59. Id. at vol. 2, 530.

60. William E. Scheurman, "Emergency Powers and the Rule of Law After 9/11," *J. Pol. Phil.* 14: 61–82 (Spring 2006).

61. Id., quoting Herman Finer, *The Presidency: Crisis and Regeneration* (University of Chicago Press, 1960), p. 23.

62. James L. Sundquist, *Constitutional Reform and Effective Government*, rev. ed. (Brookings Institution, 1992), p. 201.

63. Id. at 199.

64. See Bruce Ackerman, *We the People: Transformations*, vol. 2 (Harvard University Press, 1998), pp. 228–229.

65. Sundquist, supra note 62, at 201.

66. Id. at 202.

67. Sundquist discusses "Special Elections as the Remedy," in id. at 204–226.

68. CBS News Poll, Feb. 27, 2006, p. 5, at http://www.cbsnews.com/htdocs/pdf/poll_bush_022706.pdf (poll taken Feb. 22–26).

69. See, e.g., David Currie, *The Constitution in Congress: The Jeffersonians 1801–1829* (University of Chicago Press, 2001), p. 44, on Twelfth Amendment debates.

CHAPTER 4

1. See, e.g., Mark Tushnet, *Taking the Constitution Away from the Courts* (Princeton University Press, 1999).

2. It must be noted, though, that all European countries that are members of the European Union and the even larger number of countries, including, for example, Turkey or Russia, that have submitted themselves to the European Convention on Human Rights are now in effect subject to judicial review by the courts charged with enforcing the relevant treaties.

3. See Gerald Rosenberg, *The Hollow Hope* (University of Chicago Press, 1991).

4. See especially Lucas A. Powe, *The Warren Court and American Politics* (Harvard University Press, 2000).

5. See Michael W. Flamm, *Law and Order: Street Crime, Civil Unrest, and the Crisis of Liberalism in the 1960s* (Columbia University Press, 2005).

6. See Sanford Levinson, "Life Tenure and the Supreme Court: What Is to Be Done?" in *Reforming the Court: Term Limits for Supreme Court Justices*, edited by Paul Carrington and Roger C. Cramton (Carolina Academic Press, 2005), pp. 375–383.

7. The presence in the federal system of some so-called Article I courts, such as specialized bankruptcy or tax courts, need not detain us.

8. See 28 U.S.C. ¶ 371, 1984 Amendments (July 10, 1984).

9. See Albert Yoon, "As You Like It: Senior Federal Judges and the Political Economy of Judicial Tenure," 2 *J. Empirical Legal Stud.* 495 (2005).

10. Id. at 497. See also Table 7: How Judges End Active Status by Pension Regime (1919–2002), id. at 518.

11. Id. at 527, Table 10: Mortality Trends for Senior Judges.

12. See editors of the *Harvard Law Review*, "The Supreme Court, 2004 Term: The Statistics," 119 *Harv. L. Rev.* 415, 420, 423 (2005). Justices obviously do a great deal besides prepare opinions. This includes listening to approximately eighty hours of oral arguments (and reading the briefs in preparation for arguments) and deciding which among the approximately 7,500 petitions for review will be heard by the Court. See id. at 425.

13. See Richard Posner, "Foreword: A Political Court" 119 *Harv. L. Rev.* 31–102 (2005).

14. See Steven G. Calabresi and James Lindgren, "Term Limits for the

Supreme Court: Life Tenure Reconsidered," in Carrington and Cramton, supra note 6, at 15–98.

15. Id. at 22–23.

16. See id. at 23, Chart 1: Length of Tenure on Court by Period of Leaving the Supreme Court (measuring 103 terms consisting of 101 justices, 1789–October 2005).

17. Justice O'Connor's resignation was widely attributed to the serious illness of her husband rather than to her own desire to leave the Court.

18. See David J. Garrow, "Mental Decrepitude on the U.S. Supreme Court: The Historical Case for a 28th Amendment," 67 *U. Chi. L. Rev.* 995 (2000). See also David N. Atkinson, *Leaving the Bench: Supreme Court Justices at the End* (University Press of Kansas, 1999).

19. See Bruce Allen Murphy, *Wild Bill: The Legend and Life of William O. Douglas* (Random House, 2003), p. 487.

20. South Carolina, for example, reelected a patently senile Strom Thurmond to the Senate when he was ninety-four. He became the first centenarian member of the Senate.

21. Lucas A. Powe, Jr., "Old People and Good Behavior," in *Constitutional Stupidities, Constitutional Tragedies*, ed. William Eskridge and Sanford Levinson (New York University Press, 1988), p. 78.

22. Lewis H. LaRue, "Neither Force nor Will," in id. at 57–60. All quotations in the next paragraphs, except as otherwise indicated, are taken from these pages.

23. *Federalist*, No. 78, quoted in *The Federalist*, edited by Clinton Rossiter (New American Library, 1965), p. 465.

24. William H. Rehnquist, "Remarks on the Process of Judging," 49 *Wash. and Lee L. Rev.* 263 (1992).

25. Jack Balkin and Sanford Levinson, "Understanding the Constitutional Revolution," 87 *Va. L. Rev.* 1045–1109 (2001).

26. Rutan v. Republican Party of Illinois, 497 U.S. 62, 93 (1990).

27. Marshall also famously ruled that the Court did not have jurisdiction actually to order Madison to deliver the commission.

28. Rutan v. Republican Party of Illinois, supra note 26, at 92–93.

29. Tom Ginsburg, *Judicial Review in New Democracies: Constitutional Courts in Asian Cases* (Cambridge University Press, 2003), p. 43, citing (but not quoting) Dennis C. Mueller, "Fundamental Issues in Constitutional Reform: With Special References to Latin America and the United States," 10:2 *Const. Pol. Econ.* 119, 125 (1999).

30. LaRue, supra note 22, at 59.
31. Ginsburg, supra note 29, at 40 (emphasis added).
32. Id.
33. LaRue, supra note 22, at 60.
34. Lucas A. Powe, *The Warren Court and American Politics* (Harvard University Press, 2000), p. 467.
35. Id. at 24–25.

CHAPTER 5

1. Akhil Reed Amar, *America's Constitution: A Biography* (Random House, 2005), pp. 70–72.
2. To the extent that dynasties continue to be a part of American politics, such as with the Kennedy and Bush families nationally or the Daley and Chafee families in Illinois and Rhode Island, respectively, the age limits have scarcely proved to be a deterrence.
3. See John Seery, "Jesus for President: The Case for a Constitutional Amendment to Lower the Age Requirements for Elected Federal Office" (unpublished manuscript, 2005). I am very grateful to Professor Seery for sharing his very interesting manuscript with me.
4. See id., particularly chapter 3.
5. In William Eskridge and Sanford Levinson, eds., *Constitutional Stupidities, Constitutional Tragedies* (New York University Press, 1998), pp. 67–70. All quotations in this paragraph come from this article.
6. Thus 34.9 percent of citizens between 18 and 29 voted in the 1996 election, and only 42.3 percent voted in the far closer and more acrimonious 2000 election. However, 51.6 percent voted in the 2004 election. See the Center for Information and Research on Civil Learning and Engagement, "Youth Turnout Up Sharply in 2004," available at http://www.civicyouth.org/PopUps/Release_Turnout2004 .pdf. Still, this is considerably less than the "[s]ixty-four percent of U.S. citizens age 18 and over [who] voted in the 2004 presidential election, up from 60 percent in 2000." See U.S. Census Bureau News, "U.S. Voter Turnout Up in 2004, Census Bureau Reports," May 26, 2005, available at http://www.census.gov/Press-Release/www/releases/archives/voting/004986.html.
7. See http://www.censusscope.org: Table DP-2: Profile of Selected Social Characteristics: 2000.
8. See Sanford Levinson, *Constitutional Faith* (Princeton University Press, 1988), ch. 4, for a discussion of this problem.

9. See Article V.

10. See Mark Graber, *Dred Scott and the Problem of Constitutional Evil* (Cambridge University Press, 2006).

11. See Bruce Ackerman, "Beyond Carolene Products," 98 *Harv. L. Rev.* 713 (1985). This last example necessarily brings up the all-important topic of how best to design electoral systems, a topic whose full treatment is certainly beyond the scope of this book. Suffice it to say that I believe that there are many other countries that have better election systems than we do in the United States, led, I believe, by Germany.

12. In Eskridge and Levinson, supra note 5, at 54–56. All quotations in this and the following paragraph come from this article.

13. Jack M. Balkin, Sanford Levinson, and Jordan Steiker, "Taking Text and Structure *Really* Seriously: Constitutional Interpretation and the Crisis of Presidential Eligibility," 74 *Tex. L. Rev.* 237 (1995).

14. See Burke Marshall and Christina Duffy Burnett, *Foreign in a Domestic Sense: Puerto Rico, American Expansion and the Constitution* (Duke University Press, 2001).

CHAPTER 6

1. At least by 1791. Rather incredibly, the original Second Amendment, dealing with congressional salaries, was declared ratified 203 years later, when a spate of states ratified it in the 1970s and 1980s. See Sanford Levinson, "Authorizing Constitutional Text: On the Purported Twenty-Seventh Amendment," 11 *Const. Comment.* 101–113 (1994).

2. See the essay on the Seventeenth Amendment in John Vile, *Encyclopedia of Constitutional Amendments, 1789–1995* (ABC-CLIO, 1996), p. 272.

3. James L. Sundquist, *Constitutional Reform and Effective Government*, rev. ed. (Brookings Institution, 1992), p. 64.

4. See "Seventeenth Amendment," in John Vile, *Encyclopedia of Constitutional Amendments, Proposed Amendments, and Amending Issues, 1789–2000*, 2d ed. (Santa Barbara, Cal.: ABC-CLIO, 2003), p. 405.

5. See Robert Post, "Traditional Values and Positive Law: The Case of Prohibition in the Taft Court Era" (unpublished manuscript, 2005).

6. See, e.g., J. Allen Smith, *The Spirit of American Government* (1907; reprint, Harvard University Press, 1965). Teddy Roosevelt, in his

1912 Bull Moose campaign, was caustically critical of the power of the Supreme Court to block progressive legislation, and he proposed ways of clipping, even eliminating, the Court's power of judicial review. For examinations of other proposals during this period, see John R. Vile, *Rewriting the United States: An Examination of Proposals from Reconstruction to the Present* (Praeger, 1991), pp. 51–64.

7. See, e.g., William E. Leuchtenburg, *Supreme Court Reborn: The Constitutional Revolution in the Age of Roosevelt* (Oxford University Press, 1995); and Barry Cushman, *Rethinking the New Deal Court: The Structure of a Constitutional Revolution* (Oxford University Press, 1998), to name only two notable books elaborating this theme. Leuchtenburg and Cushman have profound disagreements about the actual date of the "revolution"—did it occur in 1937 or 1942?—but both agree that one occurred.

8. Jack Balkin and Sanford Levinson, "Understanding the Constitutional Revolution," 87 *Va. L. Rev.* 1045 (2001).

9. See, e.g., Lucas Powe, "The Not-So-Brave New Constitutional Order," 117 *Harv. L. Rev.* 647 (2003).

10. 410 U.S. 113 (1973).

11. See City of Boerne v. Flores, 521 U.S. 507 (1997).

12. See United States v. Morrison, 529 U.S. 598 (2000).

13. See Board of Trustees of the Univ. of Ala. v. Garrett, 531 U.S. 356 (2001).

CHAPTER 7

1. Daniel Lazare, *The Frozen Republic: How the Constitution Is Paralyzing Democracy* (Harcourt Brace, 1996).

2. Id. at 293.

3. Id. at 296.

4. See Richard Posner, *Catastrophe: Risk and Response* (Oxford University Press, 2004).

5. Robert Dahl, *Preface to Democratic Theory* (University of Chicago Press, 1956).

6. See Kathleen Sullivan, "Constitutional Amendmentitis," *American Prospect*, Sept. 21, 1995, at http://www.prospect.org/print/V6/23/sullivan-k.html.

7. See Akhil Reed Amar, "Popular Sovereignty and Constitutional Amendment," in *Responding to Imperfection: The Theory and Practice of*

Constitutional Amendment, edited by Sanford Levinson (Princeton University Press, 1995), pp. 89–115.

8. See, e.g., James Fishkin, *The Voice of the People: Public Opinion and Democracy* (Yale University Press, 1999); Fishkin, "Toward Deliberative Democracy: Experimenting with an Ideal," in *Citizen Competence and Democratic Institutions*, edited by Stephen L. Elkin and Karol Soltan (Pennsylvania State University Press, 1999). See also Ethan J. Leib, *Deliberative Democracy in America: A Proposal for a Popular Branch of Government* (Pennsylvania State University Press, 2004).

9. See especially Paul Woodruff, *First Democracy* (Oxford University Press, 2004), for an engaging and readily accessible defense of Athenian democracy as a potential model for our own time.

CODA

1. Woodrow Wilson, *Congressional Government: A Study in American Politics*, 15th ed. (1900; reprint, Transaction, 2002), pp. 332–333.

ACKNOWLEDGMENTS

As always, the most pleasant pages to write are those acknowledging the assistance of persons and institutions without which this book would either not have been written at all or would have been considerably worse. One institution certainly has justified priority: The Rockefeller Foundation, by inviting me to spend a month as a fellow at its center in Bellagio, not only provided me (and my wife, about whom more presently) an unforgettable opportunity to experience an almost Edenic life, given the beauty of the venue and the attentiveness of everyone who operates the center, but also made it possible for me actually to write this book. There are few acknowledgments more truly merited than this one. I also express my deepest thanks to three colleagues and friends who wrote persuasive letters of recommendation on behalf of my residency and project, George Fletcher, Barry Friedman, and Linda Mullenix.

Part of what is special about Bellagio is the range of people there. This book is directed at a lay audience, and I am immensely grateful for the helpful (and encouraging) feedback received from Dr. David Coster and Polly Pen, both nonlawyers who nonetheless threw themselves into reading the manuscript at its earliest stage. I also benefited and received encouragement from having the opportunity to present an outline of my project to the fellows, all of whom asked probing questions and offered helpful suggestions. It is especially fortunate that the group during my stay included Raul Pangalangan, the dean of the University of the Philippines Law School, not least because his country has, perhaps unwisely, borrowed more extensively from the U.S. Constitution than other countries that have written post–World War II constitutions.

I have often received helpful feedback from my wife, Cynthia, but never more so than in this case. She is a better writer than I am.

Moreover, as a nonlawyer, she is part of the target audience. She was willing to read multiple versions of every chapter and to offer many helpful suggestions (especially with regard to such writing tics of mine as the overuse of parenthetical phrases). I have no doubt that she has made the book more reader-friendly and better than would otherwise have been the case.

Another institution that deserves ample mention is the University of Texas Law School, to which I am endlessly grateful for the ways it has allowed me to flourish for what is now more than a quarter century. Although there are many colleagues who deserve to be mentioned, I must single out Scot Powe, a dedicatee whose friendship and general colleagueship have been an important part of my life at UT over this entire period. He read both the earliest and latest versions of this manuscript and saved me from some errors, at least of fact. I must also single out my friend and now, alas, former dean, William Powers, though the "alas" is mitigated by the knowledge and pleasure that he is now president of the University of Texas at Austin. He was a major reason that I came to UT in 1980 and that I will live out my career at UT. Other colleagues—Ernie Young, Mitch Berman, Lynn Baker, Larry Sager, and Charles Silver—offered me valuable feedback, including, in some cases, sharp criticism of my own criticisms of the Constitution. I should also single out one other University of Texas friend and colleague, Philip Bobbitt, who consistently expressed his dismay at my ideas as I set them out in many pleasant walks around Town Lake in Austin.

I have also been blessed by a number of important friendships with colleagues from institutions other than the University of Texas, though my relationships with two of them began there. Jack Balkin left Texas for Yale, but, fortunately, that has not hindered a close friendship and collaboration in the ensuing years. It was during a joint seminar on constitutional design that we offered at the Yale Law School that I fully realized how deservedly uninfluential the U.S. Constitution was among constitution drafters in the half century following World War II. (Conversations with another Yale friend, Bruce Ackerman, also brought home this point.) Another very special colleague is Mark Graber. His extraordinary book on the politics of slavery taught me the baleful importance of the Constitution's exclusive reliance on narrowly based local representation in the Congress, though the importance of Mark to my work goes far beyond this one citation. From commenting on my initial proposal to Oxford University Press to reading several different versions of the manuscript, he has proved himself to be the consummate friend and colleague. I am confident that he made the book far better than it would have been otherwise; perhaps it would have been still better had I accepted even more of his suggestions with regard to substantive points on which we disagree. He is an admirable adherent of the Madisonian tradition that I, who discovered my unexpectedly deep Jeffersonian roots in the course of writing this book, am attacking.

In some ways, the gestation of this book is a long walk that Bill Eskridge, John Ferejohn, and I took back to our hotel in New Orleans after a 1995 conference at Tulane University on constitutional design, when we started riffing on what were the "stupidest" parts of our own Constitution. That conversation ultimately led first to a symposium published in *Constitutional Commentary* and then a book, *Constitutional Stupidities, Constitutional Tragedies* (1998), both of them co-edited by Bill and myself. I am grateful not only to Bill and to the editors of *Constitutional Commentary*, but also to Linda Greenhouse, who wrote about the symposium in the *New York Times* and thus encouraged NYU Press to publish the book in 1998. I am also grateful to the Georgia State University School of Law, which in 2000 gave me an opportunity to deliver a lecture on "Why It's Smart to Think about Constitutional Stupidities." Later that year, following the *Bush v. Gore* debacle, the *Washington Post* gave me space to discuss the extent to which the Constitution generated the possibility of various train wrecks, in this case through the operation of the electoral college. Finally, Findlaw .com in 2003 printed a column in which I initially explained my refusal to "sign the Constitution" at the National Constitution Center.

The Internet serves to create a world of colleagueship even among people who have never met and who often sharply disagree with one another. I have been a long-time user—and sometime abuser—of a constitutional law listserv created by my friend Eugene Volokh of the UCLA Law School, and a law-and-politics discussion group moderated by another friend, Howard Gillman. One of the participants in the former is Danny J. Boggs, a member of the U.S. Court of Appeals for the Sixth Circuit, who provided me with valuable information about the makeup of the Senate that saved me from an embarrassing error.

I am deeply grateful to the following friends, several of them, very importantly, nonlawyers, who read the manuscript and offered valuable suggestions: Sam Bagenstos, Lief Carter, Betty Sue Flowers, Roberta Krakoff, Dana Lee, Rosemary Mahoney, Bill Marshall, Richard Rabinowitz, Miguel Schor, Louis Michael Seidman, Margo Shlanger, Ariel Waldman, and Alan Wolfe. And, as always, I appreciate beyond measure my two splendid daughters, Meira and Rachel, the first a political philosopher and middle-school social studies teacher, the other a lawyer, both of whom offered valuable perspectives in conversations about the themes of this book.

Finally, once again I happily praise Dedi Felman, who was sufficiently intrigued by a brief outline of this book to offer me a contract. Even more important is the consistent interest she has taken in every aspect of the project throughout its preparation. She is indeed a model editor—and friend.

INDEX